TAKE BACK
CONSERVATION

TAKE BACK
CONSERVATION

Dave Foreman

Second in the *For the Wild Things* series by
The Rewilding Institute and Raven's Eye Press

Raven's Eye Press
Durango, Colorado

Raven's Eye Press
Durango, Colorado
www.ravenseyepress.com

Foreman, Dave.
   Take Back Conservation/Dave Foreman
   p. cm.

1. Conservation
2. Conservation Movement
3. Wilderness
4. Wildlife
I. Title

ISBN: 978-0-9840056-3-5
LCCN: 2012948080

Cover & interior design by Lindsay J. Nyquist, *elle jay design*

Printed in the United States of America
1 3 5 7 9 10 8 6 4 2

"There are some who can live without wild things, and some who cannot. These essays are the delights and dilemmas of one who cannot."

From the Introduction to *A Sand County Almanac*
by Aldo Leopold, 1949

Dedication

Katie Lee

Actress, singer, songwriter, river runner,
and a true Hellcat for the Wild
And all the other Cannots with whom I have worked
to keep the wild things of Earth hale and hearty

OTHER BOOKS BY DAVE FOREMAN

Ecodefense: A Field Guide to Monkeywrenching
(editor with Bill Haywood)

The Big Outside
(with Howie Wolke)

Confessions of an Eco-Warrior

Defending the Earth
(with Murray Bookchin, edited by Steve Chase)

The Lobo Outback Funeral Home
(a novel)

The Sky Islands Wildlands Network Conservation Plan
(lead author and editor)

New Mexico Highlands Wildlands Network Vision
(lead author and editor)

Rewilding North America:
A Vision for Conservation in the 21st Century

Man Swarm and the Killing of Wildlife

TABLE OF CONTENTS
Annotated Chapter List

ACKNOWLEDGEMENTS

OFTEN ONE OF THE HARDEST CHORES in writing a book is the Acknowledgements. At least for me, I get help of sundry kinds from many folks. What makes writing my acknowledgements so danged hard is recalling everyone to thank. One is almost sure to leave someone out. However, I don't have this worry for *Take Back Conservation*. Don't get me wrong—lots of folks helped. But owing to the kind of book *Take Back Conservation* is—straight from the shoulder in saying who and what are undercutting and misleading true wilderness and wildlife conservation, setting out straightforward, unyielding thoughts about the hot marrow of American conservation and how we get that marrow back in its bones... well, it's best for those who helped me to stay unnamed.

Therefore, instead of a long tally of names, let me just say that many of the best conservationists in America prodded me to write *Take Back Conservation* and gave me their tales about what is wrong and their thoughts about what is needed to set things right. They have my heartfelt thanks both for their upstanding work on behalf of all Earthlings and for helping me with the book. Please be aware that although there are many orphan quotations in this book (those not fastened to someone), they are all true quotes and not made up by me.

Though many folks helped with *Take Back Conservation,* nameless and soon to be named below, I don't know—forsooth, I rather think not—that anyone would be of the same mind with everything I write herein, or always go along with my curmudgeonly snorts.

I can thank a few folks by name since their names are on the book in one way or another. This does not mean they should be blamed for what follows. Ken Wright with Raven's Eye Press and Lindsay Nyquist of *elle jay design* in Durango have again been good to work with on publishing *Take Back Conservation.* It's so good to work with folks who know and care about what they are doing. I'm happy to know we will keep working together on the three books left to do in the *For the Wild Things* series.

I write these Acknowledgements as the last little bit for the book while healing from neck surgery (anterior discectomy and fusion if you want the gore) in my window-side recliner watching chattering swarms of bushtits, goldfinches, hummingbirds, thrashers, scrub jays, ladder-backed woodpeckers, and others just outside. Free from the pain and numbness of a disc crunching my spinal cord, I understand a few things more sharply now. For one, I seem to have been living in this recliner chair for many months, but having wild things come calling keeps me alive and even happy, though I haven't been able to walk a mile in over a year. I also understand how lucky I am in my gimpy fettle to have such good, truehearted, skillful friends and fellow-workers as Susan Morgan, John Davis, and Christianne "Hawkeye" Hinks to keep The Rewilding Institute alive and to get *Take Back Conservation* done. It's hackneyed to say so, I know, but I could *not* have gotten this book done without them. I'll leave it here before I get sappy. Roxanne and Monica Pacheco work behind the scenes on bookkeeping and order fulfillment part-time.

Things would fall apart without them. They know how much I care for them.

Thanks, too, Nancy, for putting up with a beat-up, book-scribbling husband who seems to live twenty-four hours a day in a chair. My big, ol' gray tabby, Blue, just looked up at me and said he would like to thank *me*—now there's something queer!—for my being a posh couch with built-in, magic-fingers massage for him while writing the book.

I've dedicated *Take Back Conservation* to Katie Lee. Katie is one of the few living legends of the wilderness clan and the most outspoken, straightforward, and downright tough defender of the wild we have. I think of Katie as my wilderness aunt and she has backed me, coaxed me, heartened me, and whipped me into shape for staying tough and true and unyielding for what we love most of all. Wild Things. Drylands. River Canyons.

As an actress in Hollywood, Katie was a regular on *The Great Gildersleeve* and *Gunsmoke* and a cocktail lounge singer. But, as a true daughter of the West (born and raised in Tucson), she ran the Grand Canyon when the women who had done so could be easily named. In the 1950s, she floated Glen Canyon many times and wandered its side canyons. Along with Ken Sleight, she fought plans to dam the Glen with all the fire and fury she had. Since the fight over Glen Canyon Dam fifty and more years ago, she's written books, recorded music, and been a steadfast fighter for wild things.[1] My most liked gigs have been Katie and Dave shows. As I did with Dave Brower, I've learned much of my craft before a crowd by watching how Katie can take over a hall with her singing, tall tales, and charisma.

Nancy and I have a home overrun with wilderness and wildlife art, from African carvings to my photographs. Of all our shelf-perchers and

---

1   Please go to katydoodit.com and find out more about Katie. Buy a book. Buy a music album. Or three or four. Also learn a little more about the Greatest Old Broad for Wilderness there ever was.

wall-hangers, the one I like best is a black-and-white full-backside nude of Katie on rounded slickrock in Glen Canyon from sometime in the 1950s. Wild Thing, I call it.

So, Katie, here's to you around our sandy beach campfire. If I've been tough fighting for wilderness and wildeors, at least a little bit of why is that I haven't wanted to let you down—by not being a true Westerner, a true eco-warrior, a true child of the wild in your eyes. You are the Sweetheart of the Wilderness. This book's for you.

Dave Foreman
At Home Where the Wild Things Come to Call
October 2012

Quick, Quirky Word Hoard

Below are the meanings for some words, phrases, and technical terms the reader may not at first understand.

Cannot – One who, like Aldo Leopold, cannot live without wild things; a conservationist

Club – organization, group with volunteer activists (see Team)

Deor – animal, beast (see Wildeor)

Earthling – any living being on Earth

Good(s) – value(s)

Good – good-in-itself in Ethics

Grassroots – those for whom conservation is a calling; not only a job for hire

Grassroots Conservation – nonprofit conservation clubs; not government agencies

Inborn – inherent, intrinsic

Kind – species of animal, plant, etc.

LAND (AND/OR SEA) – environment

MAN, MEN – when capitalized, humans; uncapitalized, male humans

NETWORK – a political, etc. movement

SHELTER (v) – protect, save

SHIELD (v) – protect, save

TEAM – group that is all staff without active members (see Club)

TREE OF LIFE – Nature, biodiversity (see Wild Things)

WARD (v) – guard, defend

WIGHT – an individual

WILDEOR – wild animal, untamed, undomesticated (see Deor)

WILDERFOLK – wilderness and wildlife conservationists (see Cannot)

WILDERNESS – self-willed land, sea

WILD HAVEN – protected area, such as a National Park, Wilderness Area, Biosphere Reserve…

WILDLIFE – undomesticated animals, plants, and other life kinds

WILDLOVERS – wilderness and wildlife conservationists (see Cannot)

WILD NEIGHBORHOOD – ecosystem, natural community, land community

WILD THING – wildlife; also ecological processes, landscapes, geological features, weather, and so on that is free of Man's will

WILD THINGS – Nature, biodiversity (see Tree of Life)

WORT - plant

PREFACE

Five Little Birds and Their Lessons

AFTER FALLING AND HURTING MY LOWER BACK and neck at the beginning of the new century, I had to give up my greatest love—backpacking. My fitness to hike comes and goes; I haven't walked more than a mile in a year. Most of my time now is spent working on a laptop in my living room recliner beside a bay window. Just outside, Nancy and I have a birdbath (heated in winter) and a bevy of bird feeders. Here, the wild things come and endlessly enthrall our gray tabby Blue and me. I've tallied sixty-four species in and over our yard. I cannot overstate how thoroughly I need and love these birds—they are the wild things without which I would not want to live.

Thanks to my living room birding blind, I've gotten to know some birds and who they are rather well. They have taught me much, five birds most of all, and I think that they can teach my fellow Cannots much, too. (A *Cannot* is one like Aldo Leopold, who wrote that there were some who can live without wild things, and others like him who *cannot*.)

You will see that these birds are not those often held up as beacons of strength or wisdom such as eagles or owls. Nor are they bright flashes of many-hued loveliness such as orioles and hummingbirds. But in their behavior and mood they are anything but drab. As I have gotten to know them better, their true grit fairly blazes. They are indeed beacons of strength, wisdom, and other goodness.

So, let's meet them and hear their tweets of wisdom.

Western Scrub Jay—Vision

The Corvid family—jays, crows, and ravens—are the smartest birds and Western Scrub Jays might be the smartest of all. That is why a Western Scrub Jay is on the cover of this book entitled *Take Back Conservation*. The recall of these jays is staggering. A Scrub Jay knows where it has hidden upward of a thousand nuts. It goes beyond sheer recall, however. Research shows they have a so-called "theory of mind," which means they understand that other beings also think—that there are minds other than one's own. Such studies have found that when a Scrub Jay hides a nut, but knows another jay is watching, it will go back later and put the nut in another hiding spot when the other jay isn't watching. I put out peanuts for the four jays in my yard and have watched them do this trick. They not only have to watch to see if one of the other three jays sees where they hide a peanut, they also have to watch for Curve-billed Thrashers, who gladly scarf up jay-hidden goodies. There are thousands of peanuts hidden all over my yard, some in the most outlandish spots. I wonder what my neighbors think when they find a peanut stashed in a lawn chair? I swear if you fell asleep in a hammock you might wake up with a peanut shoved up a nostril.

Scrub Jays are smart, strategic, farsighted, and visionary. We can learn much from them. A blend of paths to keep wild things is good, but all of them—from that of the Sierra Club to that of the Sea Shepherd Conservation Society—need to be steered by thoughtful strategy. Key gains in wilderness and wildlife keeping have come from great visions.

The 1980 Alaska National Interest Lands Conservation Act gave us more than 100-million acres of National Parks, National Wildlife Refuges, Wilderness Areas, and Wild Rivers. Thousands of Cannots from all over the United States put in many hours of work on the bill, building backing for it from all kinds of folks and then lobbying their members of Congress. Behind all that hard, slogging grassroots work, though, was the daring and wonderful vision that began with a handful of women and men who knew well the wilderness of Alaska. Likewise, bringing back wolves to Yellowstone National Park came from much grunt work both in federal agencies and wildlife clubs. Before the work, though, was the foresight and boldness of a few who saw the need to bring wolves back to the wilderness from which they had been killed out seventy years earlier.

One vision, of which I've been proud to be a player, is that of The Wildlands Project (now called Wildlands Network). When we began in 1992, we called for networks of National Parks, Wilderness Areas, state parks, and such brought together by wildlife-movement linkages— or Wildways. We also called for putting back big, wild hunters, such as wolves and big cats, owing to the scientific research showing that without top carnivores ecosystems crumble. This vision, which came to be called Rewilding, was shunned and put down at first, even among many conservation biologists. But now it is the wonted path on all continents, among government agencies, scientists, and grassroots conservationists alike. True, it is not always carried out or carried out well, but the vision only a few of us had twenty years ago has taken hold.

Let us be, then, like Western Scrub Jays. Think. Plan ahead. Have a vision.

BUSHTIT—GRASSROOTS

Bushtits are tiny, drab, and gray, but lively, lovable, and winsome in a way that fairly leaps out. They fly through our neighborhood in a throng of a score or so, swarming into a piñon tree and cleaning it of bugs and caterpillars, then—zoom—without a blatant leader, they are off in a straggling, chattering rush to another tree. They are not seedeaters but pack predators. Were they raven-size, Bushtits would be the fright of Earth.

I have had wonderful run-ins with wildeors from Leopards to wolves in sprawling, deep wilderness over the world. In the summer of 2010, I narrowly dodged being gored and trampled by a cranky bull Musk Ox on the banks of the Noatak River above the Arctic Circle. But maybe my merriest wildlife meeting was that same summer in my yard. I was watering a little patch of Rocky Mountain Penstemons and went to scoot the sprinkler to a dry spot. As I lifted the hose with the sprinkler head drizzling down, I glimpsed a sudden flash of gray from a nearby New Mexico Locust. I looked down and there was a Bushtit boldly perched on my toenail and gleefully showering under the sprinkler. It fluffed and fluttered and flapped its wings for half a minute then flew off. I was blown into wild-bliss for what was left of the day.

As I wrote, Bushtits have no out-and-out leader. For all I know, some (grandma and grandpa?) may show leadership now and then thanks to knowledge, age, or wisdom, but overall their might is in the flock. They teach the strength of grassroots work. Historian Stephen Fox sees two traditions in conservation: Amateur and Professional (to wit: John Muir/Sierra Club and Gifford Pinchot/Forest Service). These pathways are not split by whether one is paid or not to do conservation work, nor do they have anything to do with how good one is. The cleavage is in feeling, with amateurs working for wild things out of love and professionals working to manage land and resources because it's their job. Some of us who have worked for conservation outfits all our lives are yet amateurs—such as Bruce Hamilton, the associate executive director of the Sierra Club. And there are those who have worked all their lives for a government agency who are also in the amateur pathway—such as Dave Parsons, who was the U.S. Fish and Wildlife Service team leader for Mexican Wolf reintroduction.

And—alack—too many heads and staffers of nonprofit conservation outfits are in the professional camp these days. It's not whether you have a buttoned-down job or not, it's why you do it. Cannots are truly amateurs.

Just as Cannots need to hew to the amateur pathway, conservation outfits should think of themselves as clubs or teams of like-minded folks, not as institutions or corporations, though they might be legally set up as such. And for those blessed to be paid by a conservation outfit, wild things should come before one's career, job, or the organization for which one works.

As folk conservationists in the Cannot Club, let us be a flock of Bushtits.

Curve-billed Thrasher—Toughness

I almost snapped my brain working to think of any Earthling I love more than Curve-billed Thrashers. Their orange eyes and the madcap way they run about on the ground, leaping through the cat doorways in our wooden gates, notwithstanding, they have a loftiness and steadfastness about them that cows me. It cows the other birds in our neighborhood, too. Though jays, robins, and doves outweigh them, thrashers are the boss birds. They own our yard. I put both peanuts and mealworms in one small tray feeder outside my bay window in the winter. I watch it while drinking my first cup of coffee and petting my lap-cat Blue. There might be four brassy jays swooping in and out with peanuts to grab and hide, but when a Curve-billed Thrasher settles in to smack up mealworms, the Scrub Jays sit back and wait.

Curve-billed Thrashers are tough and won't be shoved aside. We need to learn that better. Sometimes I get a feeling that conservationists are almost sheepish asking for what we want. We should never be shy or afraid. We in the Cannot Club are on the most righteous calling in the world—to care for other Earthlings, to let them live their lives in their wild neighborhoods, and not to be elbowed off our blue-green ball of rock and water by Man's greed and shortsightedness.

In the United States, we Cannots have come up with the best tools in the world for keeping other Earthlings hale and hearty. They are National Parks, the National Wilderness Preservation System, and the Endangered Species Act. We should never back off from holding these up as marks of American greatness just as we do with the Bill of Rights. We should never shy away from our best tools for shielding Earth's wild things; we shouldn't switch them or water them down for new fads or political/cultural nudging. We need to stand up for what is right with the same pluck and steadfastness as that of the Curve-billed Thrasher.

Ladder-backed Woodpecker—Doggedness

I once watched a Ladder-backed Woodpecker in our yard drill into a tree trunk for thirty minutes until she got what she was after. These little woodpeckers work harder than any bird I know. They are dogged. When they hear or otherwise know a beetle or grub is under bark or in the wood of a branch, they keep pecking away at it. If one drill hole doesn't reach their prey, they hammer away at their target from another. They don't just dumbly keep pounding their heads against a trunk; they stop and cock their heads to see or hear if they are on the right track. They shift if they need to, but they doggedly keep at it.

It should be the same for us. If one path doesn't work, try another, but never back away from warding wilderness and wildeors. It took Howard Zahniser eight years to get Congress to pass the Wilderness Act. Polly Dyer, now in her nineties, is still working after sixty years to get more Wilderness Areas and National Parks in the North Cascade Mountains in Washington. Next to Polly, I'm a whippersnapper—I've worked on getting some Wilderness Areas for only forty years and haven't given up. We lovers of wild things win against mightier foes time and again thanks to sticking to it.

Owing somewhat to the world of speedy computers on which we now lean for nearly everything, many conservationists want things to happen quickly, and I see it all the time with some foundations backing wilderness clubs. They have no forbearance; no inkling that it can take years to work a Wilderness Area bill through Congress. They hound the clubs they fund for new Wilderness Areas every two years. Some funders don't seem to fathom how long it takes to build a winning team for a Wilderness, how long it takes to sidetrack the hometown foes. Badgering from some funders leads even the best to cut quick, iffy deals to get any Wilderness bill—or a step-down to a National Monument—okayed to make the foundations happy. This peevishness, this lack of knowledge about the need for long-haul, dogged work is a tide I see in conservation that undercuts meaningful gains and plays into the hands of members of Congress who don't want hard fights and into the hands of landscalpers who are learning that to slow down a Wilderness Area bill for a few years will often lead funders and conservation outfits to waver.

Had this been so in the 1950s, I don't know if Howard Zahniser would have been given the eight years it took to get a good Wilderness Act passed and signed by the President.

The best conservationists are like Ladder-backed Woodpeckers. We never, never give up.

Mountain Chickadee—Own Sake

I've never heard anything happier and merrier than *chick-a-dee-dee-dee.* When these snazzy little gray birds with the sharp black stripe through their eyes show up and tell all the world—*chick-a-dee-dee-dee—We are here! And we are chickadees!*—I can't help but smile and *chick-a-dee-dee-dee* back at them.

Mountain Chickadees have a good time. Why? Because they live for themselves and for the day. They don't see themselves as a mirthful show for me; they don't see themselves as any kind of good or help for Man or any other being. No, they are chickadees and that is all they need to be to answer for their lives and what they do.

And so, the Mountain Chickadees popping into and out of our winter neighborhood carry the most worthwhile teaching of all for us. They know they are good-in-themselves and do not think Man has anything to say about it. We do not need to weave knotty, tangled ethical theories on how wild things might have inborn worth. All we need to do is listen. Chickadees tell us so. Chickadees laugh at our outlandish gall that only we—the upright ape—can give something worth.

Chick-a-dee-dee-dee!

It means that wild things are good for their own sakes.

And when we sing back:

Chick-a-dee-dee-dee!

It means we have the wisdom, the generosity of spirit, the greatness of heart to smile, nod our heads, and let beings be.

Chick-a-dee-dee-dee!

Dave Foreman
October 2012

(Note: This is taken from my talk at the 2010 Western Wilderness Conference in Berkeley. I dedicated the talk to Polly Dyer who was there.)

Introduction

Why Wilderness and Wildlife Lovers Need to Take Back the Conservation Network Now

These are the times that try men's souls: The summer soldier and the sunshine patriot will, in this crisis, shrink from the service of his country; but he that stands it NOW, deserves the love and thanks of man and woman.

—Tom Paine, December 23, 1776[1]

IN MY FORTY YEARS AS A CONSERVATIONIST, I have never beheld such a bleak and dreary lay of the land as I see today. Three whacks to my ribs bring me woe: the sinking health and wholeness of wild Earth; the strength and hotheartedness of the Nature Haters; and, within the conservation band, backing down, weakness, and even being taken over by the foes of wildness. None of this gives we who love wild things leave to shrug our shoulders and give up, however. The bleakness before us is all the more call to stand tall for the inborn good of wild things and to not wince in the good fight. Conservationists also need to understand

---

1   Thomas Paine, "The Crisis; Number One," December 23, 1776, in Sidney Hook, ed., *The Essential Thomas Paine* (The New American Library, New York, 1969), 75.

all the cogs and wheels of our plight, so we might find ways to do better. Hence this little book.

SINKING HEALTH OF WILD THINGS

In 2004, I wrote a book, *Rewilding North America*, the first third of which looked deeply into the Seven Ecological Wounds driving the Sixth Great Extinction—The Big Thing in the World Today. All over Earth, straightforward killing of wildlife, landscalping, fragmentation of wildlands, loss of ecological and evolutionary processes, takeover by exotic species and diseases, biocide pollution, and global weirding from greenhouse gases are worsening—and shoving more and more Earthlings ever nearer the dark pit of extinction.[2] We seven-billion too-clever apes alone have done the bloody deed. Duke University ecologist Stuart Pimm has shown with careful step-by-step reckoning how Man is now taking 42 percent of Earth's Net Primary Productivity (NPP).[3] As we add half again or more as many mouths in the next few score of years, how much NPP will we be gobbling up?[4] How much will be left for the other ten or more million kinds of Earthlings with which we share our lovely, enthralling world? As the heretofore-unthinkable doom of wholesale climate upset and ocean acidification

---

2   *Rewilding North America* shows in great depth that we have been warring on wild things for a long time. We are behind today's mass extinction. Moreover, in my book, *Man Swarm and the Killing of Wildlife* (2011), I look at how Man's overpopulation is the root of each of the Seven Wounds driving wholesale extinction. Therefore, in this book, I take Earth's bloody ecological plight as a given and don't run through it again. Dave Foreman, *Rewilding North America: A Vision for Conservation in the 21st Century* (Island Press, Washington, DC, 2004); Dave Foreman, *Man Swarm and the Killing of Wildlife* (Raven's Eye Press, Durango, CO, 2011).

3   NPP is the reckoning of the yearly sunlight hitting Earth and being changed into life-energy by photosynthesis.

4   Man's worldwide population will shoot up from today's seven billion to between ten and twelve billion in the lifetimes of those already in their twenties. Foreman, *Man Swarm.*

unfolds before us, extinctions will pile up as from a landslide of skulls. Notwithstanding good gains here and there, the overall state of wild things keeps crumbling—faster and faster. This is the hard truth, even though we are scolded not to be doom-and-gloomers. It is not doomsaying, my friends, to warn someone not to jump off a high cliff— or to stop someone from shoving another off that cliff.

MIGHT OF THE NATURE HATERS

In the United States, the federal government under George Bush Junior was the sworn foe and evil-undoer of conservation laws and work. His administration and the Republican-run Congress for much of his term worked for those who want to wring all the greenbacks they can out of the land and who flick away science as if it were a bothersome biting fly. Not only did the authoritarian right-wingers stop any big gains for shielding and rebuilding wild things, they wanted and still want to overthrow the twentieth century's ledger of conservation and environmental law, policy, and programs. They make no bones about wanting to go back to the unfettered, uncaring time of the robber barons and landscalpers in the late nineteenth century. Their overthrowal of the twentieth century is both philosophical and hands-on. The authoritarian right and the newcomer Tea Baggers want to shred science, biology foremost, and time travel back to before the Enlightenment, at least to before Darwin.[5]

While the United States is politically outstanding in this, elsewhere some of the seemingly most civilized nations on Earth, such as Canada, Norway, and Japan, are again waging nineteenth-century bloodbaths against wild things: frontier-forest mining, slaughter of nettlesome wildeors (such as seals, wolves, and bears), and commercial whaling,

---

5   The so-called Tea Party, or Tea Baggers as I call them, is not new at all. In my forthcoming book in the *For the Wild Things* series, *The Nature Haters*, I'll show how they are but the latest breakout of an old American clan of common-man populists. In Chapter 9 of this book, I'll lay out why I write "authoritarian right."

just for starters.[6] Japanese, European, Chinese, and North American businesses are looting the last wildlands and wildseas for fish, timber, pulp, wildlife, minerals, and oil, opening them up for further shattering of wild neighborhoods and for bushmeat hunting by folks in the hinterlands.

Although the authoritarian right/Tea Baggers lost their stranglehold in Congress in 2006 and the Presidency in 2008, they took back the House in 2010, and are backed by a strong and riled-up gang of tax-whiners and by a big lump of Americans who have made a worrisome dive into prescientific irrationality and now want to make all of us go along. The way nutty haters have risen up against Obama and the Democrats in Congress is almost as frightening as when Bush-Cheney ran things. Wait. Hold that thought. It may be more frightening. I'll look into this grim foreboding in more depth in *The Nature Haters*, another book in the *For the Wild Things* series.

President Obama and congressional Democrats are far from stouthearted in their feelings and care for wild things. You have to go back to Woodrow Wilson to find a Democratic President as little touched by wild things as Obama. Against the authoritarian right/Tea Bagger blitz on America's conservation bequest, the Democrats are meek, weak, and feckless. Wild things and those of us who love wild things have few true, skilled fighters on our side in national politics. Indeed, I can't think of another time when we conservationists have had so few strong friends in national government.

6   A key insight of Charles Darwin's is that all lifekinds can track their beginnings back to a shared forebear. Biologists today call this forebear the Last Common Ancestor or LCA. We—plants, animals, fungi, and microorganisms—are kin. Thus we all should share the name "Earthling." Some think "wildlife" means only mammals, but all untamed living things, plants and fungi, too, should be called wildlife. *Wildeor* is an earlier English word for wild animal. I'll write wildlife with a broad brush for all untamed life and wildeor only for wild animals. I'll also sometimes write the lovely old word for plants—*wort*. Such words make me feel as though my fingernails are full of damp dirt and my nose is down in the duff. To my ears, plants sound potted and animals brushed.

Backing Down and Weakness in the Conservation and Environmental Networks

Work to keep wilderness and wildeors and to clean up pollution have come up against inside undermining from the right and left that leads to backing off on policies and on bedrock beliefs. These calls to back down come from cheerleaders for sustainable development, resourcism, wilderness deconstruction, politically correct progressivism, and Man-first environmentalism—all of which, when they elbow their way into conservation, I name *enviro-resourcism*. It is this heart and bones weakening of conservation that is the meat and potatoes of *Take Back Conservation*.

Let me lay some groundwork here at the beginning:

(1) *Conservation* or *Nature conservation* or *wild conservation* is the network to keep and rebuild wilderness and wildlife (wild things for their own sakes; also land and sea shielding for aesthetic, "spiritual," recreational, and ecological/evolutionary goals).

(2) *Resourcism* or *resource conservation* is the resource-extraction mindset of "multiple-use/sustained yield" as done by the U.S. Forest Service and other agencies all over the world (natural resources for Man[7]).

(3) *Environmentalism* is the work to clean up and stop pollution for Man's health, quality of life, and to make cities livable (the "built environment" for Man). When environmentalists look at wild Earth, they can be either conservationists or resourcists. Those environmentalists with a resourcist mindset for wild things are the *enviro-resourcists*—the main target of this book.

---

7   I use *Man* or *Men* capitalized for the species *Homo sapiens*, *woman* for the female of the species, and *man* uncapitalized for the male. This is more in keeping with earlier English, which had another word for male *Homo sapiens*: *wer*, which lives on today as werewolf. Today's English is odd for a modern tongue not to have a straightforward word for our kind that is not also the gendered word for the male. To have to call ourselves by a Latin word, human, is cumbersome and abstract. I do not write Man in a sexist way but for the goodness of the English tongue.

Worldwide since the 1980s, conservation work to shield wildlife and wilderness by means of National Parks, game reserves, and other protected areas (*wild havens* as I name them) has been undermined as financial-aid agencies, foundations, and even some top international conservation groups have shifted to backing "community-based conservation" and so-called "sustainable development" instead of wild havens for wildlife. Dutch botanist Marius Jacobs warned the IUCN (now the World Conservation Union) against this path in 1983 but went unheeded. Although some kinds of sustainable development and community conservation can sometimes be sound within a bigger strategy that is first and foremost grounded in big wild havens with well-armed wildlife rangers, in truth they have elbowed wild things aside. They have also drawn off the Euros and dollars meant for nearby dirt tillers into fat consulting fees for the poverty establishment and for big stashes hidden in Swiss banks for the crooks running such countries. This establishment undercutting of wild conservation has been helped by the leftist beliefs of some anthropologists and social engineers against wild havens and for so-called "indigenous extractive reserves" and land redistribution for the hungry and downtrodden (*socioambientalistaism* as it is called in Latin America). "Conservation" is now seen by some as a poverty-alleviation tool, not as a way to keep wildlife and wildlands. Some academics have become deconstructors of Nature, saying that it doesn't exist outside of our minds, that we cook it up ourselves, and that therefore there is no need to keep it. Right-wing and business backers of resource extraction glom onto the far-fetched hatchlings of the wilderness deconstructionists' minds. I will go into all this in *True Wilderness: Where Man Is a Visitor* forthcoming in the *For the Wild Things* series.

Hammered from the left and right during the last twenty-five years, conservation and environmental outfits worldwide have stepped away from forthright calls for zero population growth, even though Man's overpopulation is behind all conservation and environmental plights. We hear a growing drumbeat that there is a dearth of births and that wealthy nations will be economically hurt with fewer young folks. Conservationists and environmentalists stand mostly still before this cornucopian nightmare. Likewise, conservationists and environmentalists overall shy away from acknowledging the truth and breadth of Man-driven mass extinction, even when they work on this or that Threatened or Endangered Species. And seldom does anyone acknowledge how bad tomorrow will be thanks to the greenhouse gases already in the atmosphere and how bloody hard it's going to be to do anything about it—*if anything can still be done about it*. If we don't even truthfully state our plight, and the toughness of it, how can we do anything about it?

We can also see a shift in the United States from conservation to resourcism among some leaders in the field. Once the foremost keeper of biological diversity (wild things in wild neighborhoods), The Nature Conservancy (TNC) has been steadily drifting over to resourcism. The once-great outfit now talks of "working timberlands and ranches," slippery, befogging words for logging and livestock grazing, and tells their staffers not to talk about Endangered Species.[8] Right behind TNC are Conservation International (CI), World Wildlife Fund (WWF), and the Wildlife Conservation Society (WCS).[9] When once-mighty stalwarts for wild things like TNC, CI, WWF, and WCS bring corporate bigwigs onto their boards so as to wring big bucks out of them, is it any wonder that they begin to do the bidding of those who rack up wealth by industrializing the last wild spots and homes for wildeors?

I am deeply worried about the strengthening hand with which enviro-resourcists now steer the conservation network. Enviro-resourcists are mostly progressive-movement professionals who believe that conservation should be about Man, not Nature. They are

8   Memo to TNC and Trust for Public Land from Public Opinion Strategies, June 1, 2004.
9   Johann Hari, "The Wrong Kind of Green," *The Nation*, March 4, 2010. This article is an outstanding look at what is wrong with the conservation gathering and backs up much of my stand in this book.

found among staff and board members of grantmakers, consulting and training firms that help conservation clubs with "organizational effectiveness," media consultants watering down the words and beliefs of conservationists, new leaders and staffers for conservation clubs who are driven by selfishness for "career" headway and who lack a gut feeling for wild things, and among anthropologists and other social scientists working for "poverty alleviation." With a crowbar of greenbacks and organizational sway, enviro-resourcists gain their way into big national conservation clubs, then into local grassroots wilderness and wildlife clubs, sliding them over into enviro-resourcism in these ways:

(1) Downplay wild-things-for-their-own-sakes beliefs, and instead say we should show that keeping some wildlife and wildlands is good economically.

(2) Nudge aside wild havens, such as Wilderness Areas and National Parks, for "sustainable development," "ecosystem management," "working" ranches, and "extractive reserves."

(3) "Retire Cassandra" by downplaying straight talk and trotting out smiley-face Pollyannaism, foremost on overpopulation and mass extinction.

(4) Work out deals with other "stakeholders," even anti-conservationists, that are "win-win."

(5) Get "measurable results," such as the designation of new wild havens, even if they are an overall loss of wildness, and then crow about the unbridled win—Canadians seem awfully good at this.

(6) Lift the health of the organization over its mission, and remake conservation clubs into fundraising machines and corporate-framed institutions.

(7) Tout techno-fixes as the answers for all of our woes.

Not all enviro-resourcists hawk all of these paths, which are not a seamless whole. Many truly believe they are helping conservation with their new, more "sophisticated" ways (which also help their own careers). Funding institutions such as the World Bank, corporations, and United Nations' agencies help such enviro-resourcists worldwide.

"The Environmentalist Stereotype," which is somewhat true, sees environmentalism and therefore conservation as leftist or progressive, tying conservation to gun control, gay rights, vegetarianism, political correctness, and so on. In the United States, the overwhelming linkage of environmentalism with progressivism and the Democratic Party is key for why it lacks trust with some Americans. We need to show that conservation does not *have* to be linked to these progressive social causes (even if many conservationists are progressives and Democrats), and to make moderates and thoughtful conservatives welcome. Nor does conservation need to take on the rubbery backbone of the Democrats.

I also worry about today's conservationists, foremost the youngsters. To be blunt, many of the staffers and workers with conservation clubs, though they may love wild things and work hard, are weak on our lore and have not read the key books of conservation. Oftentimes, they don't understand the issues and policies on which they work as well as they should; I have heard and read unlearned blather and outright mistakes from some that leave me blushing. There is a lack of intellectual curiosity in our crowd today.

Young outdoorsfolks, who once would have been backpackers and cross-country skiers, now seek swift thrills on mountain bikes and snowboards and are thus cut off from knowing true wilderness. Love of wilderness gained from one's own knowledge is key for keeping roadless areas wild and free of wheels. Moreover, I don't see kids outside playing in little wild spots; they're inside, plugged in to a virtual reality, or watchfully shepherded by Rottweiler mommies from skinning their knees or finding healthy and hearty loneliness outside.

TAKE BACK THE CONSERVATION NETWORK

I am warning about and lambasting trends. My grumbling doesn't target the whole wilderness and wildlife web. There are true wilderness lovers in all conservation outfits, as well as in land- and wildlife-managing agencies. I underscore this: I am talking about *some* not *all* folks and outfits. However, what I do knock is true, and overall I am not happy with how the conservation ship sails today. (I shared my take on this plight in 2002 in an email to friends, and wrote an early manuscript of this whole book in 2005, which my then-publisher thought was too hot, hence the *For the Wild Things* series with Raven's Eye). Things have gotten worse since then. Of those I do gripe about, I may be a little rough but I truly do not mean to be mean. Indeed, often in the pages ahead, I do not give the names of those I flay. Nor do I say enviro-resourcists are bad men and women; I think most are well meaning—some, however, are not. And some who I flay I name. I'm friendly with some in the enviro-resourcist crowd and we work together on some things. Please keep these clarifications in mind as you read the book. Were I to spread them throughout the book, it would become such a greasy sheet your eyes would slide right off the leaf. Writing about the plight of conservation is the first step in finding a way for wildlovers to bring the conservation network back to its roots, which I believe we must do for halting the scalping of wild things. In the last two chapters of *Take Back Conservation*, I lay out the following steps in depth to take back the conservation network:

ORGANIZATIONAL STEPS
- Know how conservation and environmentalism are unlike, and conservation and resourcism. Understand enviro-resourcism.
- Overcome the "Environmentalist Stereotype," which tars all environmentalists and conservationists as being left-wing, politically correct, vegetarian, gun-control Democrats.
- Reach out to the political mainstream, such as thoughtful Republicans in the U.S.
- Reach out more to wilderness recreationists and naturalists and lead them to become wilderness and wildlife shielders.

- Thoughtfully target conservation funding to build a mighty network for the long haul and to end the warping harm money sometimes does to the conservation network.
- Foster strong thinking and ongoing learning within the wilderness and wildlife network.
- Deal with the threats of overprofessionalism, corporatism, and institutionalization in our clubs.

GOODS, POLICIES, AND WORK STEPS

- Rebuild natural history as craft and science, and bring it back as the keystone of conservation.
- Unashamedly stand up for wild things being good-in-themselves, and therefore for the underlying good of wilderness and wildlife conservation.
- Stand up for strongly warded protected areas as "the most valuable weapon in our conservation arsenal." [10]
- Carefully frame the tale of wilderness and wildlife conservation so it is both winning and true to wild beliefs.
- Acknowledge that the overwhelming plight is the Manmade Sixth Great Extinction, driven by the booming population of Men and further goosed by rising affluence and technology (the Man swarm).
- Set forth and work for a vision that is bold, workable, scientifically believable, and *hopeful*.

These are the steps wildlovers need to climb if we are to take back our clubs and network and to boldly tackle what kills life.

---

10   Michael E. Soulé and Bruce A. Wilcox, "Conservation Biology: Its Scope And Its Challenge," in Michael E. Soulé and Bruce A. Wilcox, editors, *Conservation Biology: An Evolutionary-Ecological Perspective* (Sinauer Associates, Inc., Sunderland, MA, 1980), 4.

TOM PAINE CONSERVATIONISTS

In December of 1776, the American Revolution was in its darkest time. That was when Tom Paine wrote his first "Crisis" paper:

> *These are the times that try men's souls: The summer soldier and the sunshine patriot will, in this crisis, shrink from the service of his country; but he that stands it NOW, deserves the love and thanks of man and woman.* [11]

General Washington had the broadside read to his cold, ragged, hungry, disheartened troops in their frozen winter camps. There was no giving up. Years of hard fighting lay ahead but victory was gained.

We need Tom Paine conservationists in *our* dark time. Let us not be ashamed for loving wild things, for caring about other Earthlings, for speaking the truth. Reach out to others. Make deals when they are good deals. But let us not be frightened and browbeaten into giving in. Let us instead offer a bold, *hopeful* vision for how wilderness and civilization can live together, and be unyielding in keeping and rebuilding wild things and in standing up for the thought and being of Wilderness Areas and other wild havens.

A LAST WORD ABOUT THE BOOK

Take Back Conservation is not a cold-potato, both-sides, academic book, notwithstanding the landslide of footnotes and quotations. It is, instead, a work of straightforward but thoughtful and fair advocacy. I write it as a lover of wild things and a conservationist, not as an aloof, unfeeling watcher and weigher. Therefore, I use the pronouns *we* and *us* when I write about conservationists. I know much about the long work to shield wild things and much about the conservation network. I have well-grounded, unwavering beliefs. I am peeved and unhappy. I have unfathomed love for other Earthlings—for all kinds of life. As the

---

11 Paine, "Crisis."

reader can tell from the many books and articles referenced, I have done scholarly research, and I work to be dead-on truthful. However, what I draw from most deeply in writing this book are my sweeping work as a conservationist since 1971, the wilderfolk with whom I have worked, and my many days and nights with wild things all over the world in their wild neighborhoods.[12]

Some of my conservation friends and mentors go back in our feisty clan far longer than I do, even to the 1920s. Some whom I have known knew well Aldo Leopold, Bob Marshall, Victor Shelford, Will Dilg, Rosalie Edge, Olaus Murie, Howard Zahniser, Sigurd Olsen, Frank Fraser Darling, Rachel Carson, and Wallace Stegner. I know or knew Dave Brower, Ed and Peggy Wayburn, Lowell Sumner, Ed Abbey, Mardie Murie, Paul and Flo Shepard, Clif Merritt, Ernie Dickerman, Harry Crandell, Mike Nadel, Celia Hunter, Charlie Callison, Bob Marshall's brothers, Dolores LaChapelle, Aldo Leopold's children, Arne Naess, Bill Devall, Bob Zahner, Paul Martin, Phil Burton, Stewart Udall, John Seiberling, Ned Fritz, Bill Mounsey, Stewart Brandborg, Rupe Cutler, Mike Frome, Ginny Wood, Polly Dyer, Mike McCloskey, George Schaller, Martin Litton, Katie Lee, Ken Sleight, Huey Johnson, Donald Worster, Vicky Hoover, Hugh Iltis, George Sessions, Brock Evans, George Davis, Max Oelschlaeger, Paul and Anne Ehrlich, Bill Catton, Jack Loeffler, Howard Wiltshire, David Ehrenfeld, Rod Nash, Bob Howard, Michael Soulé, John Terborgh, Doug Tompkins, and Yvon Chouinard, to name just a few of my elders and teachers.[13]

I have listened to hundreds of everyday wildlovers from over ninety to under ten years of age speak at hearings about their love for wilderness overall and for this or that wilderness, and for wolves

---

12 Besides widely in the lower 48 states, I have lived or wandered in wild-lands and -seas in the North America Arctic and Boreal Forest, Mexico, Central America, the Caribbean, the Amazon, Patagonia, Bermuda, northern Scotland, Africa from Lake Malawi south, the Philippines, Indonesia, and Hawaii. Nor am I yet done (leastwise, I so hope).

13 These are my *elders*, not folks of my generation or younger.

and other wildeors. I have read stacks of grassroots conservation newsletters and other publications going back scores of years. It is from this deep-rooted but chummy conservation recall that I best know the conservation network. From this knowledge and understanding I can say that the next-to-heart belief that wild things should be kept and shielded for their own sakes is the bedrock of the conservation mind.

I have also read what many scholars have written about the conservation network and its lore. Sometimes they get it right, sometimes they don't. Those who have been in grassroots fights to shelter wilderness and wildlife, those who row their own dories, have been first on Sierra peaks, heft their own backpacks, shoot their own meat, drive their own dog teams, or have been blown down by the dusty prairie wind write about conservation far better than do those who draw from paper only.

Read on. And stand up for wild things.

CHAPTER 1

The Myth of the Environmental Movement

In the years following Earth Day, environmentalism,
once regarded as the self-serving indulgence of a privileged elite,
became 'America's cause'...

—Phil Shabecoff [1]

THE MYTH IN A NUTSHELL

Earth Day, April 22, 1970, gave birth to the long-in-the-womb overhauling of the American conservation movement into the environmental movement. By 1970 the conservation movement was tired, stodgy, and cut off from a growing and shifting America. Since Rachel Carson's *Silent Spring*, which came out in 1962, folks had grown ever more aware of and worried about the evil banes befouling their air, water, soil, and bodies. With the Santa Barbara oil spill in 1969, thickening smog in coughing cities, and the Cuyahoga River through Cleveland flashing afire on June 22, 1969, the onslaught against our

1   Philip Shabecoff, *A Fierce Green Fire: The American Environmental Movement* (Hill and Wang, NY, 1993), 114.

living space was in everybody's face.[2] The upper-crust conservation movement, which had never found a snug home with Americans, was straightaway made "relevant" with a new target on threats that mainly harmed *people*—smog, poisons in our food, filthy rivers, traffic jams, unsafe Pintos, and thoughtless, uncaring, and even evildoing big businesses. Conservationists had been a band of hikers, bird-watchers, mountaineers, and sportsmen. Environmentalists are mothers, fathers, and children. Deep woods with tall trees rolling on for miles, wildlife, and National Parks are okay, but when you get right down to it, what comes first are human health, safety, and quality of life. Today, the environmental movement has cast its net wider to haul in social justice, anticolonialism, feminism, animal rights, and Green politics, on top of fighting pollution and shielding wilderness.

So goes The Myth of the Environmental Movement. In sundry shapes it is ballyhooed by academics and the news business, and believed in by the public, politicians, and many of those who belong to conservation and environmental clubs.

It is also wrong.

John Muir would sit down beside a blossom new to him and get to know it. Let's sit down here on our path by The Myth of the Environmental Movement, sunder it petal by petal, root by root, and try to tease it out. We can deal out this myth into four belief-heaps:

(1) First and foremost, The Myth of the Environmental Movement holds there is one widespread folk gathering that cares about pollution *and* Endangered Species, urban transportation *and* wilderness, human health *and* "ecology."[3]

---

2   From the late 1800s to the 1950s, it was not odd for industrial rivers to flash afire. The earlier unheard-of hullabaloo over the Cuyahoga in 1969, however, was a beacon for the big shift in Americans' thinking. Christopher Maag, "From the Ashes of '69, a River Reborn," *The New York Times,* June 21, 2009.

3   Endangered and Threatened are legal designations under the Endan-

(2) Earth Day 1970 is touted as when conservation broadened into the lively, likable, and mighty environmental movement. Veteran *New York Times* environmental reporter Phil Shabecoff wrote, "In the years following Earth Day, environmentalism, once regarded as the self-serving indulgence of a privileged elite, became 'America's cause'....'"[4]

(3) Before Earth Day, the Myth says that conservation was waning, unknown to most Americans, and politically weak. In 1971, even mindfully farsighted and canny human ecologist Paul Shepard wrote, "By 1970 the long-standing but obscure crusade for conservation, once dominated by 'nature lovers' and modestly aimed at a mixture of amenities and improved land use, had abruptly graduated to the first rank of national concerns."[5]

(4) Environmentalism is above all about human health. Back in 1994, the founder of the National Association of Physicians for the Environment (NAPE), Dr. John Grupenhoff, said, "Every environmental problem is or will become a health problem. Therefore, pollution prevention is disease prevention."[6] (I don't know where NAPE is today, but it or something like it is sorely needed.)

Let me slice up each of these beliefs, and then we will look more thoroughly at this vampish little myth with our pocketknife, tweezers,

gered Species Act for those Earthlings we are driving to extinction. So, when I write them with this law-book meaning, I will capitalize.

4 Shabecoff, *A Fierce Green Fire*, 114.

5 Paul Shepard, "Preface One," in Paul Shepard and Daniel McKinley, eds., *Environ/Mental: Essays On The Planet As A Home* (Houghton Mifflin Company, Boston, 1971), vii. Shepard became unhappy with conservation clubs in the late 1950s when he felt they did not do enough to fight commercial logging in Olympic National Park. He also believed that conservation had been too shallow in what it fought, that we needed a much deeper look at what was wrong with modernism.

6 Michael Castleman, "Dr. Clean," *Sierra*, January/February 1994, 22.

and hand lens, so we can see how environmentalism and conservation are not the same. In the next chapter we will see further why they are unlike and sometimes clash.

First of all, I do not believe there is an "Environmental Movement." Rather, I see work to keep wildlands and wildlife as *the conservation movement* or *network,* and the job to halt the harm technology does to human health and quality of life as the *environmental movement,* which would be better called the *human health network.* My friend David Quammen, author of *Song of the Dodo* and maybe the best writer on biodiversity, thinks much like me. In a 1999 interview, he said, "The preservation of biological diversity and the cleaning up of the human environment are not a single enterprise....Conservation and environmentalism are not the same thing."[7] In his column for *Outside* magazine, "Natural Acts," he had a few years earlier written, "The term 'environment' implies a set of surroundings for some central, preeminent subject. That central subject...is human life. Therefore the very word 'environment' entails a presumption that humanity is the star of a one-character drama around which everything else is just scenery and proscenium." He went on, "Environmentalism is not in its essence perverted. It's just an understandable campaign of self-interest, by our species, with potentially dire implications for the world at large. What does seem perverted is confusing environmentalism with conservation."[8] I wish more of my conservation friends would take these words to heart and clean up their language. Muddling conservation with the name "environment" is not only wrong, it is harmful to shielding wild things.

The late, steadfast Canadian naturalist John Livingston, thirty years ago wrote in his unyielding book *The Fallacy of Wildlife Conservation* that "'environmentalism'...should not be confused with wildlife

---

7   "An Interview David Quammen," *Wild Duck Review,* Winter 1999.
8   David Quammen, "Dirty Word, Clean Place," *Outside,* August 1991, 25-26.

preservation."[9] Lots of other conservationists nod their heads that conservation and environmentalism are not one thing (though far fewer environmentalists do so). So, I will call the yoked networks "The Environmental Movement" (in quotation marks and capitals to show it is ersatz), shielding wildlands and wildlife *conservation*, and fighting pollution *environmentalism*. Now, to most folks, conservation and environmentalism are the same thing (that's some of why I'm writing this book, after all). I've sparked some warm squabbling with my belief—mostly from a handful of environmentalists and a few academics. Thoughtful conservationists, with a tighter, deeper, and more *inside* understanding, are more likely to see the two as two. Some of these worry, nonetheless, that making too much of the cleavage is harmful. In these bad days, they feel that we wildlovers need all the friends we can find. Seeing the two as others, however, says nothing about how they can work together.

Second, this bit about conservation being an "indulgence" with little to show for it is so much hogwash as I have shown in my books, *The Big Outside, Confessions of an Eco-Warrior*, and *Rewilding North America*. Indeed, over the last one hundred and fifty years it is conservationists who have given America most of what is best about our country on the ground. Conservationists had racked up many wins and had made many gains by 1970. From the early 1950s on, they stopped a dam in Dinosaur National Monument, put away almost ten million acres in the Arctic wilderness of northeastern Alaska, worked the Wilderness Act and the National Wilderness Preservation System through Congress and signing by President Johnson, and started a National Wild and Scenic Rivers System thereby keeping dams off some free-flowing streams. Each of these wins was big, BIG. I do not believe we could pass the Wilderness Act today. In the late 1960s, great fights were won to set aside new National Parks in northern California's Redwoods

---

9   John A. Livingston, *The Fallacy of Wildlife Conservation* (McClelland and Stewart Limited, Toronto, 1981), 19.

and Washington's North Cascades, and to stop dams in the Grand Canyon. These struggles made the news all over America. Even with the white-hot clashes over Vietnam and civil rights filling newspapers and television sets, Redwoods and the Grand Canyon broke through as news.

Widely overlooked by those who sniff at the "irrelevance" of the "elitist," pre-Earth Day conservationists are so-called "wildcat" Wilderness bills by members of Congress for their backyards (and *voters*) from 1965 to 1971. These wildcat Wilderness Area bills were put together and boosted by outdoorsmen and –women who knew the lands, and were fought tooth-and-nail by the Forest Service from rangers in the field to the Chief in Washington. The weight of the wildcats cannot be overstated since they led straight to the Forest Service's roadless areas inventories and at long last to the 2001 Roadless Area Rule, which in one fell swoop did more to keep wild America wild than any other single doing in the Lower 48 states.[10] All of these struggles drew national heed and backing from folks all over the land.[11] See Table 1.1 for a short list of wilderness and wildlife wins *before* Earth Day 1970 to see how conservation was far from dead in the water.

It is also true that Earth Day along with the wrath-wave about pollution led to landmark legislation in the early 1970s for clean air, clean water, and such things. I would love to see that sparkle and gale burst out once again—this time against greenhouse-gas pollution. So, I'm not belittling the 1960s unhappiness over how big business was poisoning us, I only want to show here that public land shielding was chugging along well on its own before and after Earth Day 1970.

10 I'll go into wildcat wilderness bills and these other gains in one of my
    next books, *Conservation vs. Conservation*.

11 The film about David Brower, *Monumental: David Brower's Fight for Wild
    America*, shows how public lands fights in the 1950s and 1960s were
    widely known, as does Roger Kaye's book, *Last Great Wilderness: The
    Campaign To Establish The Arctic National Wildlife Refuge* (University of
    Alaska Press, Fairbanks, 2006).

Table 1.1. Some USA Conservation Wins 1950-1970

1952	SW New Mexico outdoorsfolks fought Forest Service plan to cut Gila Wilderness in half
1956	Echo Park Dam on Yampa and Green Rivers in Dinosaur National Monument stopped, Utah & Colorado
1960	Arctic National Wildlife Range, Alaska
1960	Haleakala National Park, Hawaii
1960	National Grasslands authorized under the U.S. Forest Service
1961	Hawaii Volcanoes National Park
1962	Padre Island National Seashore, Texas
1962	Petrified Forest National Park, Arizona
1962	Pt. Reyes National Seashore, California
1964	Wilderness Act signed and National Wilderness Preservation System set up
1964	Land & Water Conservation Fund Act signed
1964	Canyonlands National Park, Utah
1964	Ozark National Scenic Waterways, Missouri
1965 - on	"Wildcat" Wilderness bills offered by local members of Congress
1968	Wild Rivers Act signed and National Wild & Scenic Rivers System set up
1968	Redwoods National Park, California
1968	North Cascades National Park, Washington
1968	Two big dams in the Grand Canyon, Arizona, stopped
1968	Great Swamp National Wildlife Refuge (NWR) Wilderness Area, New Jersey
1968	Pasayten, Glacier Peak, and Mt. Jefferson Wilderness Areas, Washington and Oregon
1970	National Environmental Policy Act

Moreover, the conservation team was not heavily behind Earth Day. Dr. Edgar Wayburn, Sierra Club Vice-President at the time and even then a wise, never-weary wilderness warrior, warned, "We cannot let up on the battles for old-fashioned wilderness areas," in answer to the call to leap onto the antipollution bandwagon.[12]

Third, the conservation movement before Earth Day had gathered a sweep of Americans. Conservation after Earth Day kept on drawing ever more folks—not only those upset by pollution or jazzed about Earth Day, but by the swelling throngs of backpackers, birders, river runners, and flyfishers fighting to keep their loved spots from harm, and by those roused after learning about widespread extinction of wildlife and wholesale wiping out of ecosystems. In the 1960s, the campaign for the Wilderness Act and to set aside new Wilderness Areas under it became a growing grassroots network, which kept growing throughout the 1970s and early 1980s. The belief that the conservation team before Earth Day was elitist is shallow and overblown. It is held and written about by those who were not there, who have not talked to those who were, and who have not read *The Living Wilderness, Sierra Club Bulletin,* and other conservation writings from the time. The folks I've known who had worked for Wilderness Areas before I came along in 1971 were overall middle-class; any who could be thought of as bluebloods were few and far between. What elitism they had was in woodcraft, goodness, wisdom, and farsightedness, which, truly, is the elitism that means something, the kind of elitism—or *natural aristocracy*—that Thomas Jefferson hoped would rise in the new Republic as it grew.

Fourth, I happen to go along with Dr. Grupenhoff. Environmentalism *is* about human health. Environmentalists should be even more willing to say so. It is not conservation. It is not about wilderness. However, it need not be at odds with sheltering wildeors and letting evolution keep rocking along. *Environmentalism is a big friend of conservation, as is conservation of environmentalism.*

12 Mark Dowie, *Losing Ground: American Environmentalism at the Close of the Twentieth Century* (The MIT Press, Cambridge, MA, 1995), 25.

I am taking on The Myth of the Environmental Movement on a handful of grounds. Foremost, it is wrong, as I have shown. It is a sock drawer full of socks, brassieres, underwear, gloves, light bulbs, screwdrivers.... It is a map that does not draw the land—if you follow it, you're going to get lost. "The Environmental Movement" is not a good way to understand folks working together either to shield wilderness and keep whole threatened wights and worts, or to clean up pollution and make our cities livable.

By cramming two whole-in-themselves movements into one, squabbling follows, as in a bad marriage. So we hear some environmentalists sneering at work for Wilderness Areas and for Endangered Species as paltry and piddling, or worse.

Some consultants, pollsters, and funders, who come from environmental or community-nonprofit instead of outdoor backgrounds, are telling doughty conservation outfits to soften their tongues and to sit down, jaw, and work out deals with other "stakeholders." They tell us to talk about people, not wildlife, and to hide our love of wild things for their own sakes.

By thinking that there is one, seamless "Environmental Movement," those who love wilderness and wildlife have a hard time seeing and understanding trends within "The Environmental Movement" that belittle and thwart the shielding and rebuilding of wild things.

And last, "environmentalist" has a shady if not outright unwholesome name among some who might back much land and wildlife conservation. Among such folks are some hunters and fishers, small town dwellers who like birds and trees, and thinking Republicans and independents who yet believe in prudence and responsibility.

So, as long as conservation is muddled up with environmentalism, I worry that it will become ever tougher to get out the true conservation tale and to keep wilderness and wildlife from being overlooked.

TWO MOVEMENTS

One can see the believed blending of shielding wilderness and stopping pollution in one of at least three ways. In the first, the conservation network widened its cares about the time of Earth Day to take in the Manmade or "built environment" on top of wild things. In this take, "The Environmental Movement" is the conservation network with broader cares. Or, in the second way, two freestanding gatherings, conservation and environmental, wed each other on Earth Day or thereabouts. In this look, "The Environmental Movement" is a tight fellowship between wildlands/wildlife and human-health cares. I look at it in a third way: I see conservation and environmentalism as sister clans. We're kin, sure. However, we don't live together, although we get together for Sunday picnics once in a while.

Now, what we are quacking about here are abstract maps of politics and sociology. Sock drawers. Pigeon holes. Cubbies. I think my map is truer than are those that bunch up environmentalism and conservation into one being. I draw my map out of my many years of working all over in the wilderness and wildlife crowd, wide reading of conservation documents and history, and much listening to campfire tales from old-timers. I also believe to the marrow of my bones that seeing the two as two will lead to better teamwork between them and to stronger conservation and environmental fellowships.

However we map it, we must always keep in mind that the map is never the territory. Some theorists seem to believe that their maps are truer than what they map.

Let's take another look at my map. Along with conservation and environmentalism is another bunch, also often called conservationists: the resourcists. As I wrote this chapter I came to see that if I were to take down The Myth of the Environmental Movement, I first had to take down an even older myth, that of The Myth of the One Big Conservation Movement.

CONSERVATION AND RESOURCISM

From the beginning there have been and yet are two kinds of folks who call themselves conservationists. The nineteenth century in North America was an unbridled slaughter of wildlife and scalping of wilderness. These *landscalpers*, as I call them, had no heed for the morrow and sought only to skin the land for the most short-time gain and then head on to the riches over the next ridge. They carelessly and greedily gnawed Man's wasteful will into wild landscapes and gleefully slew wildeors—forty million bison, thirty million pronghorn, and over one *billion* passenger pigeons in the score of years after Appomattox.[13] Against this wanton wracking, a wave called *conservation* swelled in the waning days of the century to stop the landscalpers, bring scientific management to natural resources, and to shield Nature or, as I'd rather write, wild things.[14] At the same time, a new word came into the English tongue. For the first time in the nine hundred years since the Anglo-Saxon *deor* and *wildeor* were shoved aside by the Norman-French *beast*, which was later elbowed over by the Latin *animal*, a new word grounded in Anglo-Saxon was crafted to mean those Earthlings from sponges to ravens: wild life, then wild-life, and now wildlife. I can't help but see this as tied to the blooming of conservation, answering a need for a name for our fellow deors that was not as abstract, soulless, held at arms-length, or putdown as both *beast* and *animal* seem to me.

This conservation rising soon was riven by blowups over logging and livestock grazing in forest reserves (soon to be called National Forests) and over river-plugging dams in National Parks.[15] Stephen Fox, in his top-notch book *The American Conservation Movement*, saw the two kinds of conservationists as heirs to either John Muir, daddy of the

---

13 I tally the gruesome wounds in *Rewilding North America* and will tell the landscalping tale in *Conservation vs. Conservation* (forthcoming).

14 I'll look at all this and more in my forthcoming *Conservation vs. Conservation* in the *For the Wild Things* series.

15 Roderick Frazier Nash, *Wilderness and the American Mind* (Yale University Press, New Haven, CT, 1967).

Sierra Club, or Gifford Pinchot, father of the U.S. Forest Service.[16] They were widely cleft in how they saw wild things, with the Pinchotians driven to stamp Man's will over the whole world so as to manage it for the greatest "production" of resources or raw goods for the greatest number of Men—in a "scientific" and "sustainable" way, mind you.

Conservation, as I see it, is about shielding wildlife, wilderness, and outdoor loveliness (or scenery—both "monumental" and "sublime") from scalping and being made ugly, and about keeping lands and waters for solitude and nonmotorized recreation for Man. Its key word is the old standby *Nature*. By *Nature* I mean wildlife, ecological doings, and wild neighborhoods—evolution in all its wonder and thrill, as well as our getting into the outdoors with wild things. I do not mean the "built environment" made and willed by Man. Nature is an awfully overworked and fuzzy word, however, and I'd like to give it a rest, so I'll instead write "wild things" for the whole ball of life: wights and worts, flows and upsets, lands and waters, life and death, and the thing that makes it and keeps it going—descent with modification, or evolution. I'll sometimes write "Tree of Life" for the same. There are non-living wild things, too, such as fire and flood, weather and earthquakes, sunsets and moonrises.

Notwithstanding this cleavage, wide in spots, both conservations stood for braking the landscalpers and called for self-restraint and prudence in our dealings with Earth, though resourcism comes with a hearty draught of godlike gall.

Until the 1960s or so nearly everyone still saw one conservation movement, but it was like a flock of house sparrows with lots of noisy squabbles and feather-pulling. As rumbles between government resource agencies and grassroots wilderness and wildlife clubs got hotter, more and more folks began to see the two as sundered. My generation of conservationists was more likely to see the one

16   Stephen Fox, *The American Conservation Movement: John Muir and His Legacy* (University of Wisconsin Press, Madison, 1985).

conservation movement as no longer—if ever—true.

There are yet those, however, who believe in the one conservation movement, and I want to answer their belief. My next book in the *For the Wild Things* series, *Conservation vs. Conservation*, will find its thread in the twentieth-century war between landscalping, resource conservation, and wild (Nature) conservation. Here, though, let's look quickly at four of the ways the two conservations follow their own paths.

One. The resource camp grabs ownership of the name *conservation*. Gifford Pinchot wrote that he came up with the word and sneered at Muir and his allies as *preservationists*. He didn't want to let them in his conservation club. Pinchot shrugged off "preservation" as "sentimental" and "impractical" while his conservation was scientific and practical (Pinchot mellowed out in later years when that spellbinding fellow Bob Marshall was dating his niece).[17] Nonetheless, for much of the twentieth century, both paths, as roughly embodied by the Sierra Club and the Forest Service, were seen by many as part of one conservation movement—owing to how they were both against cut-and-run, rape-and-scrape, run-of-the-mill business on the ground, and how both backed the National Forests and other public lands against undoing. Between the two world wars, squabbles softened, the Forest Service set aside a few *Primitive Areas*, and conservationists had some key jobs in Franklin D. Roosevelt's Administration. Moreover, folks who worked or had worked for the resource agencies were often the leaders of wilderness and wildlife conservation. Even in those days there were some heated wrangles—killing off wolves in National Parks, for one. After World War Two, rifts deepened. The Forest Service scurried to sell, sell, sell timber and to build roads to the moon and back. The Park Service seemed to be following Walt Disney instead

---

17　In the engineering fad one hundred or so years ago, both sentimentality and impracticality were dreadful sins to bear. For Marshall's merry love life (and more), see James M. Glover, *A Wilderness Original: The Life of Bob Marshall* (The Mountaineers, Seattle, 1986).

of John Muir. Young Turks in the Sierra Club led by Dave Brower and Ed Wayburn wanted to take off the gloves and fight the wilderness-wrecking agencies and industries. Others in Washington-housed outfits such as The Wilderness Society were seeing a sharper cleft, too, and came to understand the agencies could not be trusted to take care of Wilderness; therefore, Congress would have to bulwark Wilderness through legislation.[18]

Paul Shepard, a leading conservationist and "human ecology" professor in the second half of the twentieth century, called the resource conservationists *resourcists* in his 1967 book *Man in the Landscape,* and damned resourcism as "the most insidious form of nature hating because it poses as a virtue, as prudent, foreseeing, and unselfish."[19] *Resourcism* is a better name for what Pinchot's followers do than is *conservation.* Therefore, I use *conservation* for Nature or wild conservation and *resourcism* for resource conservation. I acknowledge that darn few if any resourcists would call themselves such; I think most still hold onto being *conservationists* and call my kind *preservationists,* just as Pinchot called Muir one hundred years ago.

I don't call myself a preservationist owing to how it was wielded by Pinchot as a put-down of Muir and to it being rather out-of-date. However, I acknowledge that conservationist is not the best name for those of us who love wild things, but it is likely the best overall for understanding. I write other names for our trail-dusty crowd, too: wildlovers, wilderfolk, wilderness and wildlife network, and Cannots. My mind starts to blur after writing conservation or conservationist time and again.

Two. Stephen Fox clove early conservationists into *amateurs* and *professionals.* Fox sees folk conservation clubs as within the Amateur

---

18 I will follow this in depth in *Conservation vs. Conservation.*

19 Paul Shepard, *Man in the Landscape: A Historic View of the Esthetics of Nature,* Foreword by Dave Foreman (The University of Georgia Press, Athens, 2002 (1967), 236-237.

Tradition (to wit: John Muir and the Sierra Club) and government agencies and professional societies (Gifford Pinchot and the U.S. Forest Service) as within the Professional Tradition.[20] The key to understanding the Amateur-Professional Cleavage is that amateurs do conservation work out of a *calling*; professionals do it for hire as a job or career. It is not mostly about whether one has a job or is hired for conservation work, though, but *why* one does conservation work: for love or money. Nor is it about how much one knows, how hard one works, or how skillful one is. We "amateurs" have more often than not outworked and outfoxed the agency professionals. Moreover, some "professionals" working for the Forest Service and other government agencies are themselves within the Amateur Tradition and some who work for nongovernmental conservation groups may be overmuch in the Professional Tradition—indeed, they are the ones against whom I am warning in this book.

Academics in natural resource management schools, environmental studies departments, forestry schools, and even conservation biology departments often find kinship with the agency resource professionals, and may share their lack of understanding of the amateur citizen conservationists (*some* not *all* by any means). This tie leads many such academics to see conservation work as being done by professionals working for agencies, not by folks working together in clubs. (On the other hand, college faculty from all academic fields have made up much of the backbone of grassroots clubs.) Truth be told, the 107-million-acre National Wilderness Preservation System is much more the child of folk conservationists than of the government agencies managing the lands. I think some academics without ties to grassroots conservation would gainsay this, but I dare them to show me wrong. Academics and others who work mostly on international conservation find a conservation network much more made up of professionals from

20   Stephen Fox, *The American Conservation Movement: John Muir and His Legacy* (University of Wisconsin Press, Madison, 1985).

agencies, academia, international agencies, and big international conservation organizations, with little if any grassroots conservation on the ground (though even in the third world I think there is more grassroots conservation than they would guess—India, for one, has a true grassroots conservation network, as does Belize). They bring this frame back with them to the United States, Australia, Canada, and elsewhere where strong folk "amateur" nonprofits are foremost.

There are professionals working for government resource agencies, by the way, who embody the Amateur Tradition in conservation at the highest rung, and work out of love for wildeors and wildernesses, and not just for a paycheck and career furtherance. I have been blessed to know a campground-full of such worthies.[21] Two of the best conservation outfits were started by and are for agency staffers: Forest Service Employees for Environmental Ethics (FSEEE) and Public Employees for Environmental Responsibility (PEER). Another is for retirees: the Coalition of National Park Service Retirees.[22]

One chunk of what's wrong with today's conservation network is the over-the-top "professionalization" of even small conservation clubs and the loss of the Amateur Tradition among staffers. Along with this professionalization is a weakened standing for unhired folks—the grassroots. I'll go into this more later.

I will call nonprofit conservation outfits *clubs* or *teams* depending on whether they have active volunteer memberships (clubs) or whether they are mostly a staff bunch with no membership or a mostly inactive membership (teams). *Organization* strengthens the corporate institutionalization of conservation nonprofits, which is what I want to

---

21 For starters amongst retirees: U.S. Fish & Wildlife Service, Dave Parsons; National Park Service, Kim Crumbo; Bureau of Land Management, Shaaron Netherton, the late Jeff Jarvis; Forest Service, Don Hoffman; Bureau of Reclamation, Dave Wegner; Natural Resources Conservation Service, Randy Gray; state game & fish departments, Jeff Davis....

22 See www.fseee.org, and www.peer.org. I have to say, though, that no group has a worse acronym than FSEEE. Try pronouncing it. Then again, maybe it shows their outdoor skill in reading sign, such as scats.

undercut, whereas *club* or *team* gives a much more amateur feeling.

Three. Another cleft is how conservation and resourcism see the good of Nature—what I call wild things but they call natural resources. Here we get into the true split—the underlying belief gap between conservation and resourcism: Conservationists believe in keeping wild things for their own sakes.[23] Resourcists believe in managing natural resources for products and uses for Man. "Multiple-use" is their watchword. Conservationists believe that many lands and waters should abide wild (free of Man's will); resourcists believe that Man should tame nearly all lands and waters. There is a lot of room between these two beliefs and much wandering about in between. This is a map, after all. Lines in the true world are seldom razor-sharp.

It is also true that most of the *public* arguments made by wilderness and wildlife lovers are grounded in recreational, aesthetic, utilitarian, and, more lately, ecological and scientific values. Nonetheless, since at least the time of Henry David Thoreau, many wilderness and wildlife conservationists have spoken out about how they care for wild things *for their own sakes*, seeing them as good-in-themselves, which is where ethics begin.[24] This belief has been stated in many ways. The late Canadian naturalist John Livingston wrote in 1981 that wildlife conservation is "The preservation of wildlife forms and groups of forms in perpetuity, for their own sakes, irrespective of any connotation of present or future human use." He went on, "In essence, wildlife conservation is the preservation of nonhuman beings in their natural settings, unaffected by human use or activity, uncontaminated by human antibiosis, emancipated from human serfdom."[25] In this, I

---

23 I know that all of those who call themselves "conservationists" and who study conservation do not go along with me here. I will answer the naysayers throughout this book.

24 *Encyclopaedia Britannica* Vol. 8 (William Benton, Chicago, 1959), 757-58.

25 John A. Livingston, *The Fallacy of Wildlife Conservation* (McClelland and Stewart Limited, Toronto, Ontario, 1981), 17-18.

believe he spoke for most of us who would not want to live without wild things, whether or not some shier wildlovers would put it so bluntly to their father-in-law.

Set against Livingston, a Bureau of Reclamation cheerleader wonderfully set out the innermost belief of hard resourcism when the heyday of dam-building was getting underway: "The destiny of man is to possess the whole earth, and the destiny of the earth is to be subject to man. There can be no full conquest of the earth, and no real satisfaction to humanity, if large portions of the earth remain beyond his highest control."[26] Such is the gap between the two bands that call themselves conservationists. A more enlightened statement of how resourcism *can* bestow worth on wild things comes in a 2007 article in *Science*, "The case for biodiversity conservation can be argued on economic, sociocultural, and aesthetic grounds."[27] Yet even here there is no acknowledgement that wild things may be good-in-themselves; biodiversity is worthwhile only for what good it offers Man, even if in our hearts and eyes and not in our pocketbooks. We hear the same from those who call on conservationists to uphold biodiversity by highlighting how wild things give Man "ecosystem services" and who tell us not to talk about the inborn worth of other beings as such talk will put off politicians and the public. Such "conservationists" are in truth a kinder, softer stripe of resourcist, who see aesthetics, biodiversity, and ecosystem services as natural resources worth many dollars just as timber, minerals, water, and other raw goods or "multiple uses" are worthwhile in dollars. They may well work for the same on-the-ground goals as we own-sake conservationists, but not as doggedly or steadfastly, as I will show.

---

26 J. Widtsoe, *Success on Irrigation Projects* (New York, 1928), 138. Quoted in Donald Worster, *Rivers of Empire: Water, Aridity & The Growth of The American West* (Pantheon, New York, 1985), 188.

27 S. J. Butler, J. A. G. Vickery, and K. Norris, "Farmland Biodiversity and the Footprint of Agriculture," *Science, 315,* 2007, 381.

Aldo Leopold saw wilderness as the theater for "the pageant of evolution."[28] Biologist Michael Soulé, founder of the Society for Conservation Biology and The Wildlands Project, has written much the same thing. Evolution embodies wild things being for their own sakes. Evolution is good-in-itself. In the early 1950s, National Park Service biologists Lowell Sumner and George Collins called for setting aside what is now the Arctic National Wildlife Refuge in northeastern Alaska as wilderness where evolution could go on without meddling from Man. Historian, bush pilot, and Arctic National Wildlife Refuge wilderness manager Roger Kaye writes, "Collins brought to northeast Alaska the belief that the highest experiential values of wild areas derived from understanding that natural processes 'are ongoing, they are evolving, they are beyond good and bad. They are "right" because they are right unto themselves and can evolve naturally without the medium of man.'"[29] Kaye also writes, "Sumner expressed the hope that this place might always have the 'freedom to continue, unhindered and forever if we are willing, the particular story of Planet Earth unfolding here... where its native creatures can still have the freedom to pursue their future, so distant, so mysterious.'"[30]

Evolution is wild. It is wild in the deepest meaning of the word, and thus is the hallmark and the highest good of wilderness.

If we are to be good neighbors, if we are to let beings be, if we are to fit in with other Earthlings for the long haul, then we must step back somewhere—many somewheres—so evolution is free to unfold for wild things in its own unhobbled, murky way.

The most needed and holy work of conservation is to keep whole the building blocks of evolution along with sweeping landscapes

---

28   Aldo Leopold, *A Sand County Almanac: And Sketches Here and There* (Oxford University Press, New York, 1949), 199.

29   Roger Kaye, *Last Great Wilderness: The Campaign To Establish The Arctic National Wildlife Refuge* (University of Alaska Press, Fairbanks, 2006), 17.

30   Kaye, *Last Great Wilderness*, 21.

such as Arctic National Wildlife Refuge where that unforeseeable, unfathomable wonderwork can play out unhindered. We need to bring evolution back to the fore as the highest good to be shielded by conservation; sadly, it has faded from sight since its heyday in the 1950s.

I do not belittle how we find happiness in wild things and how we seek to keep whole other Earthlings out of wonder and love for them, thanks to what key players some are in keeping wild neighborhoods healthy, and so on. I wallow in that glee in my own life. But when it comes right down to it, we conservationists want to keep wild things for their own sakes without thinking that they must have a dollar, aesthetic, or even ecological worth. The weight of conservationists with whom I have worked over the years would go along with this belief, as Sumner and Collins did sixty years ago. Such wildlovers are the true wits on the conservation network and its lore, beliefs, and Weltanschauung.[31] I readily acknowledge, though, that some wilderness and wildlife conservationists seldom think about such lofty lodestars as inborn worth and seem only to work to save their best hideaways or to shield their most loved wildeors. Sheltering wild things for their own sakes is for many something unsaid deep inside. A given. I think, therefore, from the hundreds of folks with whom I've worked over forty years, if nudged most would acknowledge that wild things should be kept from harm for ought but being.

Four. The beliefs of resourcism and conservation come to life in policy and in on-the-ground management, protection, and restoration. In the twentieth century in the United States and Canada, I believe, federal, state, and provincial resource agencies snuffed and yoked more wild things than did resource industries, poachers and their ilk, and other landscalpers. In shoving wildlife to the brink, the agencies have

---

31 Alack, a *wit* today is taken by most to mean cleverness in a funny or bit-ing way. A *wit* also, though, for hundreds of years, has meant those who are knowledgeable and wise.

been as bad as the landscalpers. Most of the work of conservationists on the public lands (also Crown Lands and Parks in Canada) has been to thwart agency wilderness-taming "development" and wildeor-killing work.

Far from keeping things wild as they should, federal and state/provincial land and wildlife managing agencies work mostly to help timber, mining, livestock, energy, commercial fishing, trapping, outfitting, tourism, downhill ski, and other industries rip-out raw goods from wildlands (and seas) and build resorts and other developments in wildlands. In Canada, federal and provincial agencies have lately been even worse than their U.S. mates, helping landscalpers slaughter wildlife on land and sea as badly as anywhere in the world today. We must understand that resource agencies have an agricultural mind-set. In some state and provincial wildlife agencies, things are slowly shifting thanks to "nongame" wildlife and Endangered Species programs and to the kind of "wildlifers" coming in to work for and even run such programs. Elsewhere, through the hammer of political will, state wildlife agencies (such as in Alaska, Idaho, Wyoming, and the Dakotas foremost) have flipped back to the early 1900s to kill off wolves, mountain lions, prairie dogs, and other "pests" (the same is happening in Canadian provinces—Alberta is a standout).

I am weighing here the beliefs and deeds of institutions. Folks working for land and wildlife agencies since the beginning have been widely spread in how they think about and work with wild things. In other words, agency staffs in the U.S. and Canada have been made up of landscalpers, resourcists, and Cannots. Some have loathed mountain lions, lands without roads, and uncut big woods. Others have done what they think is a good job caring for wildlands and wildlife while overseeing taking raw goods from wildlands. Yet others have taken bold, sometimes job-ending stands to keep wilderness and wildlife hale, and to fight sloppy, over-the-top logging, livestock grazing, commercial fishing, and slob hunting wanted by the economically and politically strong.

Getting new National Parks and Wilderness Areas named by government and shielding and bringing back threatened wildeors have been at the heart of the struggle between conservationists and resourcists. In the United States, Wilderness Areas are by law federal lands that have no permanent human dwellings, no permanent roads, no use of motorized or mechanized equipment or vehicles (except for emergencies or vital administrative needs), and no commercial logging or other development.[32] Wilderness Areas are on the whole open to nonmotorized, nonmechanized recreation, as well as to lawful fishing and hunting, and for scientific study. [33]

In the clash over Wilderness Areas (and other wild havens) between the Forest Service and other land-managing agencies on one hand and wilderness clubs on the other, the cat fights swirl about choices such as: how many new Wilderness Areas or other wild havens should be set aside; which landscapes should be set aside as havens; how much of such landscapes should be kept wild; where should boundaries of such havens be drawn on the ground; how many "cherrystem roads" and other "intrusions" should be left open into the Wilderness;[34] should any dollarable trees or other raw goods be "locked up" in the Wilderness; should playgrounds wanted by off-road-vehicle, mountain-bike, and

32 Some states—foremost New York, California, and Michigan—have designated Wilderness Areas by state law on some state-owned lands, such as state parks.

33 Jay Watson and Ben Beach, eds., *The Wilderness Act Handbook* Fourth edition revised (The Wilderness Society, Washington, D.C., August 2000). This eighty-four-page booklet not only has the full text of the 1964 Wilderness Act but meaningful slices from other key Wilderness legislation and agency regulations. It's chock-full of needed explanations and resources for understanding the National Wilderness Preservation System. Everyone working for Wilderness Areas should have it and look at it often.

34 A *cherrystem road* is a dead-end road going to some spot within what is otherwise a roadless area. Whether to make a non-Wilderness corridor for such roads thereby leaving them open for motorized driving or to close them wholly or at some spot before they end is a run-of-the-mill question in drawing Wilderness Area boundaries.

snowmobile thrill seekers be carved out of the Wilderness; and so forth.[35] These are technical quandaries, yes, but they get to the heart of clashing beliefs about wild things. More often than not, the agencies work for "the less the better" and "the weaker the better."

Nonetheless, resourcists can caretake land for Wilderness and work to help Endangered Species, too—I do not say that one has to be a truehearted believer in wild things for their own sakes to shield them. Nor do I say that conservation over its 150-year life has been driven straightforwardly by belief in the inborn worth of other Earthlings. Some resourcists work now to help biodiversity. They do a more middling job of keeping from harm wild things than would conservationists, and they do it mainly for the good it gives Man: recreation (wildlife watching), aesthetics, economics, pharmaceuticals, DNA prospecting, ecosystem services, and so on. We can learn how resourcists have mostly thought about Wilderness Areas by how the Forest Service and other agencies have put wilderness management in their recreation divisions. Furthermore, *management* was and is the working mind-set of resourcists when it comes to wild things. Management is too often the stamping of Man's will over will of the land, even if it is meant in a warmhearted, motherly way.

What is *good* is key here. Mull over protected areas set aside and cared for on "utilitarian" grounds alongside those set up and shielded for the inborn goodness of the wild things therein, or for what lies ahead in evolution. It is much more likely that the first kind of havens will be undermined for a whole slew of grounds. The same holds true for wildlife. In a bungling that rides next to my heart, bringing back the Mexican wolf in southwestern New Mexico and southeastern Arizona is coming to naught owing to how the U.S. Fish & Wildlife Service seems to have lost its soul and now lacks champions for the lobo for

---

35 Although I write Wilderness Areas, I mean all kinds of set-aside wild
    havens such as National Parks and Wildlife Refuges. Moreover, I capital-
    ize Wilderness when it is for lands designated by government, whereas
    "small w" wilderness is for roadless, undeveloped lands not yet set aside.

its own sake (as it had when Dave Parsons and Wendy Brown ran the undertaking). Therefore, having only utilitarian and aesthetic good, Mexican wolves nearly always come in last in any run-ins with cattle, which also have economic and political good, even on National Forests. When wildlands and wildlife are shielded for their own sakes, or for their own sakes along with utilitarian, recreational, and aesthetic goods, such warding is far less likely to be weakened.

Some hardcore conservationists, who believe in Wilderness and who believe that other beings have inborn worth, work for resource agencies—once in a while even near the top. When agencies do the right thing, it is often because of such staffers. I've often wondered if Mexican wolves would ever have been freed into the wild in 1997 if conservationist Dave Parsons had not been the U.S. Fish & Wildlife Service's team leader for the lobo.[36] Too often, though, agency staff have dark tales of browbeating from their bosses to open lands to logging, mining, grazing, oil & gas exploration, and willy-nilly off-road-vehicle hooliganism—never mind the harm or if the work sometimes stretches the law.[37] Sadly, you could fill a sprawling feedlot with the resourcists on the job with a blinders-on drive to build roads, get out the cut, graze cows, kill wolves, stop wildfire, and tame every acre of land. Thanks to better agency heads picked by President Bill Clinton, the Forest Service, Park Service, Fish and Wildlife Service, Bureau of Land Management, and others overall got much better in the 1990s, even though Clinton himself didn't show much feeling for wild things. But those good steps forward were more than backtracked under Bush/Cheney as good folks were manhandled out or took early retirement from the agencies. The

---

36   Parsons, now retired from FWS, is Carnivore Conservation Director for The Rewilding Institute.

37   Todd Wilkinson, Foreword by David Brower, Introduction by Jim Baca, *Science Under Siege: The Politicians' War on Nature and Truth* (Johnson Books, Boulder, CO, 1998). Wilkinson's book was written before Bush/Cheney took over, yet rattles your brain that such repression could go on in the USA.

Bush Junior Administration also cunningly slipped political commissars into federal resource and science agency offices to burrow in a heavily antiscience ideology. Shades of Uncle Joe and Trofim Lysenko.[38] Barack Obama has been a saddening, disheartening letdown as President, but nowhere so much so as on conservation. He's kept on the Bush track.

Conservationists acknowledge that careful, fair resourcism is needed on some lands. *Fair,* though, well might not mean the same to the Forest Service and Center for Biological Diversity. The ongoing struggle over stewardship of public and private lands in the U.S., Canada, Australia, and other countries swirls around what is even and fair. However, there is no way that even the most thoughtful and careful resourcism can get seven billion men, women, and children what they need to live from Earth. It becomes even more hopeless as the Man swarm keeps swelling. [39]

Wildlovers also hail all the good that men, women, and children get from being in wilderness (or near wilderness) and from sundry, tangled, and overflowing wild things. I love watching families from all walks of life standing in awe and wonder outside their cars as a few thousand Sandhill Cranes and Snow Geese fly into a pond at dusk in Bosque del Apache National Wildlife Refuge. Folks can't help being enthralled by the skyslide of big noisy birds. Wilderness Areas are good for our health. Roderick Nash shows in his chapter "The Wilderness Cult," in *Wilderness and the American Mind*, that what we find in wilderness   being alone, enlightenment, lack of gall, and daring of mind and body—has long been touted as needed for our health.[40] In his

---

38   Carl Pope and Paul Rauber, *Strategic Ignorance: Why the Bush Adminis-tration Is Recklessly Destroying a Century of Environmental Progress* (Sierra Club Books, San Francisco, 2004); Chris Mooney, *The Republican War on Science* (Basic Books, New York, 2005). Both of these are top-notch, eye-opening, and well documented.

39   Dave Foreman, *Man Swarm and the Killing of Wildlife* (Raven's Eye Press, Durango, CO, 2011).

40   Roderick Nash, *Wilderness and the American Mind* (Yale University Press, New Haven, CT, 1967), 141-160.

books, Paul Shepard writes that cutting ourselves off from wildernesses and big wildeors freezes us in "adolescence" (a mood illness) and brings on further mood illnesses.[41] Having spent the last ten years too lame to hike or backpack in wilderness owing to a gimpy back, I know more than ever how thoroughly I need the freedom of the big outside for my happiness and health. I am blessed to have a wife who is a wonder at putting together long canoe or raft trips on the wildest rivers of the West and in the far north. Though hard and painful for me to do, I'd be at a full loss without Nancy's trips. I am thankful for the handful of paddling friends, most of all John Davis, who help me or put up with me on these long river trips.

To get to the heart of the cleavage between resourcism and conservation, we must go back in time to the first written English. The earliest meaning of wilderness in Old English, let us recall, is "self-willed land." Likewise, *wildeor* meant "self-willed beast." Wilderness can also mean "home of self-willed beasts."[42] Being self-willed strongly says that something is its own thing and not a belonging of another. So. In a nutshell: Conservationists work to keep Man's will from taming all of Earth. Resourcists work to stamp Man's will over as much of Earth as they can, even in designated Wilderness Areas through "management" of some kind. *Whose will?* is the bedrock question behind conservation battles.

Environmentalism (And Enviro-Resourcism)

Environmentalism, as I see it, is a widespread, grassroots care about how industrialization and technology harm our health and run down the urban quality of life. Once population growth was among

41 Paul Shepard, *Thinking Animals* (University of Georgia Press, Athens, 1998) and *Nature and Madness* (University of Georgia Press, Athens, 1998).

42 Roderick Frazier Nash, *Wilderness & The American Mind* Fourth Edition (Yale University Press, New Haven, CT, 2001 (1967)), 1.

these worries, but political correctness has made population work taboo for many.[43] Environmentalism also tackles "consumption" and lifeways, thereby swallowing the consumer protection movement or "consumerism." Over the 1990s, environmentalism looked more at rural life, and helped to prop up family farms against the onslaught of agribusiness and foreclosure, and backing Appalachian neighborhoods shielding their homes from mountaintop removal by coal companies. These are only some of what environmentalism has taken on of late.

Environmentalism is a much needed good in today's world. I hate to think of what America and other countries would be without it. I can look from my back deck to Mt. Taylor sixty-six miles away. Some 800,000 folks and their trucks and SUVs and cars in the Albuquerque metro area are between us. In the 1970s with many fewer folks and cars in Albuquerque, I would not have been able to see Mt. Taylor most days. It's thanks only to environmentalism and the Clean Air Act that the air I breathe and look through is so much cleaner today. Nor am I belittling Earth Day; it was a wonderful happening. I wish we could regain the fireworks and feeling of citizenship it birthed. Indeed, environmentalism should be seen as good citizenship, while the foes of environmentalism have done an amazing flip in getting many to think that their bad citizenship is patriotic. I wish environmentalists would wrap themselves in the flag more and talk about the true meaning of good citizenship. Greedy big business that skirts the law and winks at unneighborly behavior is one side of the coin of bad citizenship today. The other is the tax-whiners and childish anarchists of the Tea Party. Both are key foes of environmentalism and conservation today.

Ralph Nader's early fight to protect people from death-trap automobiles was the environmental movement. Stewart Brand and the *Whole Earth Catalog* were the environmental movement. The American Lung Association's war on smoking is the environmental movement. The Sierra Club's work against sprawling industrial hog farms and

43   Foreman, *Man Swarm*.

their waste is the environmental movement. Fighting nuclear power plants is the environmental movement. Wrath at putting toxic dumps or polluting factories in forlorn or minority neighborhoods is the environmental movement. Seeking clean alternative sources of energy is the environmental movement. The struggle to stop global weirdness from greenhouse gases is the environmental movement. Folks from all walks of life being arrested in the summer of 2011 in front of the White House over the tar sands pipeline is the environmental movement. The environmental movement's key word is *people*. On the other hand, some of these threats also harm wild things and conservationists work on them, too.

Conservationists are nearly always also environmentalists, but environmentalists are not *always* conservationists. When environmentalists look at wild things, they can be either conservationists *or resourcists* or switch between the two (Men are maddeningly flighty and are fuzzy thinkers most of the time). I must underscore that environmentalists can be either conservationists or resourcists. We can't understand the kinship between conservation and environmentalism without it. And it is key to what this book is all about.

Since it is bedrock, I'll say it again: *Conservationists are nearly always also environmentalists, but environmentalists can be either conservationists or resourcists.* This is why I earlier showed that Nature Conservation and Resource Conservation are so unalike. I have hammered out on my word anvil a rather ungainly new name—*enviro-resourcist*—for those environmentalists who have a resourcist outlook on Nature or wild things. Although they are mostly well meaning, when enviro-resourcists come into leadership or are listened to within the wilderness and wildlife world, they weaken and undercut forthright wild conservation—they are *resourcists*, after all. Other enviro-resourcists are against much of what wilderness and wildlife conservationists want to do and against how we see the wild world. Some don't get our love for wild things or our belief in keeping wild things for their own sakes. Unlike Aldo

Leopold, they can live without wild things. Showing the breadth and depth of this plight and laying out what we wildlovers can do are the meat of this book.

Understanding how enviro-resourcism is remaking conservation is key for why the conservation network needs to stand on its own, away from the environmental movement.

In the next chapter, I'll look more deeply at how environmentalism is more than a new step for conservation, but also at how it can, at times, work against conservation.

CHAPTER 2

It's Not Just About Whales Anymore

It's not just about whales anymore.

—An environmentalist

THERE IS A HEAP OF WAYS one could show how unlike environmentalism and conservation are. One of the best I've heard, though, likely wasn't meant to be heard as such; indeed, I'll bet that the fellow being quoted in the newspaper wasn't even thinking about environmentalism and conservation being unlike cares. I'd say he was only looking for a snappy way to tell everyone how bad the threat from greenhouse gas fouling had become.

It's not just about whales anymore, he said.

How dead on and to the point! How pithy. *It's not just about whales anymore.* I'll bet he thought he had come up with just the right zinger to say how grim our climate tomorrow was going to be if we didn't do something about it *now*. For that environmentalist, it would seem that so long as a threat is about whales or other fellow Earthlings, it's not so bad. But when it at last threatens Man, then it becomes a big deal.

Environmentalism is about Mankind. And about what most think is Man's habitat—the *built environment.* That is well and good. But many of its stalwarts believe it therefore shoves aside conservation, which, after all, is only about wildlife. Lots of them don't understand what drives us—that we cannot live without wild things. They are dumbstruck when they at last come to grips with the understanding that we care most about wild things. Such an outlook is a thumping big "why" we should see the two as sundry paths. Many of those who care about the welfare of children, women, and men find it hard to understand how we can weep over other Earthlings ("animals") when our own kind are being killed in wars and such. I recall a cartoon from my town's afternoon newspaper *The Albuquerque Tribune,* alack now gone owing to money woes. The cartoonist, Glasgow, was a progressive and overall a booster for conservation, but his cartoon shows Death, in a black cassock holding a body of what is tagged "Innocent Iraquis Dead," asking a weeping animal welfare activist at a tombstone for prairie dogs killed at the airport, "Have you some tears left?"[1] A cartoon by another artist had a demonstrator with a sign that read "Dar Fur." She was saying, "Maybe if they think it's about a cute, fuzzy, little animal, they'll care." In other words, how the hell can some worry about just *animals* when people are being hurt? There is nothing wrong with caring about the plight of other humans, but it needn't clash with caring about the plight of wild things, nor should it override caring about other Earthlings. After all, only about 2 percent of charitable contributions in the United States go to help wild things—so it's not as though everyone cares about cute animals instead of starving children. What is telling, though, is that some think there is something wrong with caring about other Earthlings when others of our kind are needy.

John Muir had it right. When it came to a war between beings, he was on the side of the bears. So am I. Though, to be truthful, I'd rather run with the big cats.

1   Glasgow, "Glasgow's View," *Albuquerque Tribune,* March 21, 2007.

Not the Same

The cares and work of conservationists and environmentalists overlap somewhat but are not the same. Look at the ongoing work by Defenders of Wildlife, the Center for Biological Diversity, The Rewilding Institute, WildEarth Guardians, Grand Canyon Wolf Recovery Project, New Mexico Wilderness Alliance, and others to bring back the Mexican wolf to the wild in Arizona and New Mexico, and then at the Environmental Working Group's spotlighting of the bad chemicals in Teflon.[2] Sundry things and sundry players. No clash.

Environmentalism and conservation are mostly made up of unlike folks. Even in the Sierra Club, which works on both environment and conservation, the folks who work on each are seldom the same. Conservationists are mostly outdoorswomen and -men—hikers, mountain climbers, birders, naturalists, canoeists, river runners, hunters, and fishers, although some other conservationists are happy to stay home and only know that wilderness and wildeors *are*. While some environmentalists are outdoorsfolks, more are not, at least not hardcore. The two streams flow out of their own watersheds—and thoughtsheds. They have their own folk heroes, classic books, and lore. Their leaders are most often not the same and, although there is more overlap here than elsewhere, clubs mostly belong to one network or the other, not to both. Those that truly work in both fields are fewer than a handful of big national outfits: Sierra Club, Natural Resources Defense Council (NRDC), and Environmental Defense Fund (EDF) foremost. Some state or citywide outfits, such as those that call themselves an "environmental" or "ecology center" or that come out of PIRG (the Public Interest Research Group) also work on both environment and conservation though they nearly always lean one way or the other.

2   "Sticking It To NonStick," *Sierra,* November-December 2004, p. 11; "BushGreenwatch," email alert from info@bushgreenwatch.org, January 13, 2005.

SANITARIANS: THE GRANDPARENTS OF ENVIRONMENTALISTS

Scholars have shown that the environmental network, far from popping up in the 1960s as a broadening of conservation, has its own history almost as long as that of conservation. Robert Gottlieb, an urban planning lecturer at UCLA, in his book, *Forcing The Spring*, tracked environmentalism back well over a hundred years to such things as worker safety, urban planning, food safety, and pollution. Instead of conservation widening its arms to bring in human health cares, Gottlieb showed that environmentalism has its own past as a working network for public health and the urban quality of life. Let's mosey down a little side street through the open sewers, slaughterhouses, tenements, and smoky factories of yore to look at the lore of early environmentalism. Watch where you put your feet, though. North American and European cities were pretty nasty in the last half of the 1800s. Dickens knew well about what he wrote. We need to take this walk to learn that unhappiness about how industrialization harms folks' health was not something new that popped up in the 1960s, and thereby we will better understand that conservation and environmentalism were each running on their own tracks for a hundred years or more before Earth Day. We find they are about the same age.

Gottlieb held up Alice Hamilton as "this country's first great urban/ industrial environmentalist." From the 1880s to the 1920s, she was "the premier investigator of occupational hazards in the United States." She was at last made an assistant professor of industrial medicine at Harvard in 1919 and wrote a pathbreaking book, *Industrial Poisons in the United States*.[3] Environmentalists should get to know her and uphold her just as conservationists uphold John Muir from the same time. We should have a party for some key hundredth or other anniversary in her life and work. She is truly a great American and citizen of the world.

---

3   Robert Gottlieb, *Forcing The Spring: The Transformation of the American Environmental Movement* (Island Press, Washington, DC, 1993), 47-51.

Hamilton was not the first physician in occupational or environmental medicine, though. In the 1690s, Eberhard Gockel, a physician in Ulm, Germany, found that a widespread and sometimes deadly colic came from "sweetening" bad wine with a white oxide of lead. Maybe the first consumer protection legislation came when the Duke of Wüttemberg banned all lead-based wine additives after hearing of Gockel's study. Lead poisoning from wine dates back to Roman times. Gockel drew insights from the work of a Harz Mountains physician, Samuel Stockhausen, who, forty years earlier, found that the *Hüttenkatze* disease among mine and smelter workers came from lead dust or vapors.[4]

While Hamilton looked mostly at the ills of the workplace, others in the early public health drive (or "sanitarians," as they called themselves in the 1800s) worked on toxics, sewage, smoke, and solid wastes fouling where folks lived in cities.[5] In 1907, the International Association for the Prevention of Smoke was set up to lessen air pollution.[6] Gottlieb showed how the muckraking journalists of the Progressive Era and labor unions fighting for safer working conditions were also key players in the early environmental network.

While Gottlieb underscored the class-struggle side of the sanitarians, overall, public health was mainstream or one could even say Main Street. I believe that we should see the whole of public health, not just smoke control and bettering unsafe sweatshops, as a forebear to environmentalism and also as a framework for how today's environmentalism could be more winning and draw a broader swath of Americans. Indeed, we need to frame environmentalism as good citizenship and show that the anti-environmentalists are tearing down the standards of citizenship and want to take us back to the sights,

---

4   Josef Elsinger, "Sweet Poison," *Natural History* 7/96, 48-53.

5   Thanks to Prof. Robert Brulle, I have a copy of the logo of The New York Sanitary Association "Instituted 1859."

6   Gottlieb, *Forcing The Spring*, 51-59. "Smoke" was the word for smog or air pollution back in the early years of industrialization.

smells, and health of Dickensian London. Antiscience corporations and the Republican hacks who do their bidding need to be so framed. A mighty television ad for progressives would be footage from black and white movies of Dickens's books with the warning that if the government- and regulation-hating Republicans get their way, this is where we will go.[7]

Another side of early environmentalism was urban planning. Gottlieb wrote, "The radical[8] environmental critique of the workplace was complemented during the early part of the [twentieth] century by a developing environmental critique of urbanization, initiated by movements seeking to address questions of planning and urban form." The City Beautiful Movement in the decades before and after 1900 set off this urban planning campaign.[9] Again, Gottlieb highlighted the class-struggle side of it, but overall it was also Main Street. Indeed, it was wealthy conservatives who came up with zoning to keep their tony neighborhoods free from blight. And, although Gottlieb did not bring it up, in 1894 Theodore Roosevelt started the National Civic League "to promote citizen involvement in cities."[10]

Gottlieb well showed that there was an environmental network in the United States long before Earth Day. I think he also showed that the sanitarians were not the same as those working to set up the first National Parks and to shield egrets and other birds by banning plume hunting and feathered hats for Gibson girls. (There were ties through the Regional Planning Association of America, however.[11])

7   Chris Mooney, *Republican War on Science* (Basic Books, NY, 2005).

8   When Gottlieb and other leftists say "radical," it means class struggle or Marxist.

9   Gottlieb, *Forcing The Spring*, 71.

10   Scott Smallwood, "Jemez Had Unique Approach in Contest," *The Albuquerque Journal*, June 18, 1998.

11   Paul S. Sutter, *Driven Wild: How the Fight Against Automobiles Launched the Modern Wilderness Movement* (University of Washington Press, Seattle, 2002).

Two Networks

Rachel Carson's *Silent Spring* in 1962 played matchmaker between the backwoods hiker and birdwatcher of conservation and the city lawyer of environmentalism. In 1966, four years after *Silent Spring*, Victor Yannacone, a Long Island lawyer, sued to stop the spraying of killer pesticide DDT because of the harm it did to birds and to people. Yannacone's suit led in 1967 to the setting up of the Environmental Defense Fund (EDF) in New York City. Philip Shabecoff calls EDF "the first of the new-style national environmental groups."[12] *Silent Spring*, the Environmental Defense Fund, Earth Day... Shabecoff and others have written how these widened the work of conservation so it became environmentalism; but I don't see it that way. True, there was a strong linkage between conservation and environmental cares in the DDT lawsuit. Some shared worries, yes, but "new-style national environmental groups" were mostly about the "built environment" or Man's world instead of wild neighborhoods. I believe EDF, Barry Commoner, Ralph Nader, and most of Earth Day were a renewal of Hamilton's sanitarians and politicized public health. The "new-style national environmental groups" did not care much or even think about self-willed land, but about how industrialization harmed human health and quality of life. A key linkage was that we shared corporate and political foes, which made us friends—but being friends does not make two the same. And, I believe, Commoner and Nader were nearer to resourcism than to wilderness and wildlife keeping. The same could be said of Stewart Brand of *Whole Earth Catalog*. He has always been high on gadgets, techno-fixes, and cutting-edge management techniques, not on wild things. Another linkage was that conservationists cheered on the new environmentalists since outdoorsmen and –women lived mostly in cities and choked on smog and hated cram-packed streets, too.

---

12   Shabecoff, *A Fierce Green Fire,* 104.

Early on many environmentalists did not care that much about wildlife and wilderness, though, other than in a fuzzy "Mother Earth" way. Gus Speth, a founder of the Natural Resources Defense Council (NRDC) and later chairman of the Council on Environmental Quality for President Jimmy Carter, said that "unregulated discharge pipes, fish kills, urban air pollution, all kinds of industrial pollution—those were the issues that originally turned my head. It was not establishing new wilderness areas in Montana."[13] John Adams, the longtime head of NRDC, said in 1989, "In 1970 there were no environmental laws."[14] Well...maybe. But there sure as heck were *conservation* laws—The Wilderness Act (1964) and the Wild & Scenic Rivers Act (1968) for starters. Adams's words show that he did not see wildlands and wildlife work as in his environmental movement.

Leafing through a stack of books by leading environmentalists like Commoner, I find nothing about Wilderness Areas, National Parks, National Forests, John Muir, or Aldo Leopold in the indices. And why should there be? Commoner was fighting pollution and did a good job of waking up Americans to the banes around them. In the spate of books that came out at the time of Earth Day 1970, wildlands and wildlife got little heed. And Denis Hayes, the organizer of Earth Day, recalls that "by and large, there was, I think, a pretty deep amount of ignorance of all of that and even some tendency to sort of distance themselves from the rest they termed 'the birds and squirrels people.'"[15] Many environmentalists are environmentally sensitive but ecologically naive. However, I have to say that we birds and squirrels people are

13   Shabecoff, *A Fierce Green Fire*, 117
14   Shabecoff, *A Fierce Green Fire*, 133.
15   Shabecoff, *A Fierce Green Fire*, 119. Today Speth and Hayes are much more knowledgeable about conservation. What they said in the 1970s, however, shows how environmentalists then thought about wildlife and wildland work. Speth is now Dean of the Yale School of Forestry and a leader on environmental and conservation work. Hayes now runs the Bullitt Foundation in Seattle, which funds many conservation groups.

amazingly sophisticated and well-dressed, at least after we brush off the seed and nut hulls.

Now, I am not roughing up any of these environmentalists for not working on conservation. Their work has been needed, and I am thankful for it. I am only showing that their environmental movement was and is about Man's health and not about wild things.

Just as environmentalists often overlook conservationists and our wildlife and wildlands work, so do conservationists often not give heed to environmentalists and to the plights of cities and factories. The best books about conservation—such as Rod Nash's *Wilderness and the American Mind,* Michael Frome's *The Battle for the Wilderness,* and Max Oelschlaeger's *The Idea of Wilderness*—do not have Earth Day in their indices and bypass pollution worries. Phil Shabecoff wrote, "The older conservation groups—the Sierra Club, the National Audubon Society, the National Wildlife Federation, the Izaak Walton League, and others—played little or no role in Earth Day….Still preoccupied by traditional land and wildlife preservation issues, most—although not all—of the old guard had remained blind and deaf to the growing national anger over pollution and other environmental threats to human health."[16] Threats to human health, the Vietnam War, and civil rights were not work for conservationists whose calling was caring for wildlands and wildlife. I am not saying that human health, the Vietnam War, and racial discrimination were piddling things—only that they did not come under the wing of conservation. Throughout his book, Shabecoff seems to think it is a given that the needs of Man outweigh those of other Earthlings; indeed, I think he can't understand how someone could care more for wild things than for Man. This is a never-ending drumbeat from environmentalists about conservation. This is why "It's not just about whales anymore" wraps up the Weltanschauung of environmentalists so well when it comes to weighing the worth of Man and everyone else. Environmentalists like Shabecoff do not

16   Shabecoff, *A Fierce Green Fire,* 118.

acknowledge that Man is but a flicker in the unwinding of evolution and a flyspeck in the whole of life.

In his book, Shabecoff seems to say that the new work on pollution and urban woes led to the 1970s membership jumps in the "old-line conservation clubs and societies."[17] Far from it. Tens of thousands of hikers, birders, river runners, and hunters were drawn into The Wilderness Society, Sierra Club, Montana Wilderness Association, Oregon Wilderness Coalition, Southeast Alaska Conservation Council, and other fighters for the big outside not thanks to worries about pollution or city-life betterment, but for thrilling grassroots struggles to set aside more National Forest Wilderness Areas throughout the U.S. and millions of acres of new National Parks, Wildlife Refuges, Wild and Scenic Rivers, and Wilderness Areas in Alaska. Far from being dead in the water and needing a strong draught of pollution fighters or urban reformers, conservation clubs were bubbling over thanks to their stodgy, hidebound, old cares. New conservation clubs—international, national, regional, state, and local—have sprung up from the late 1960s to today without letup. Heck, I've helped start a handful or two. There are hundreds of such outfits. This is not the mark of a tired old bunch that has needed to draw new backers by broadening its sweep of cares. And, like me, other new conservationists since 1970 have been "preoccupied by traditional land and wildlife preservation issues."[18]

Indeed, Mike McCloskey, executive director of the Sierra Club from 1969 to 1985, wrote that "the pollution issues, which were at the heart of the modern movement, struggled for a constituency. In the early 1970s, they were top-down issues. They were pushed by the national leadership as an exercise for intellectual commitment, but it was hard to build excitement in the ranks." He went on to say that "the issues that captured the hearts of [the Sierra Club's] members were

17   Shabecoff, *A Fierce Green Fire*, 121.
18   The Rewilding Institute website at www.rewilding.org links to more than one hundred wildlands/wildlife conservation groups.

protecting wilderness, defending Alaska's wildlife, saving old-growth forests...."[19] I gave an early draft of chapters 1 and 2 of this book in a talk to the Environmental History Society in 2002. Mike McCloskey was asked to give his thoughts about what I said, and pretty much backed me up: "Basically I agree with Dave Foreman's thesis that there is a limited bonding between the older conservation movement and those concerned with pollution issues. I agree that most activists are focused on one set of issues or the other and their folklore, literature and myths are different." He also said "there is an intellectual case for combination. The environmental movement in theory wanted to be all embracing..."[20] This is true, but I don't think the "all embracing" want worked well.

Historian Samuel Hays, author of the best book on this time of "The Environmental Movement," *Beauty, Health, and Permanence,* writes, "The wilderness movement was the most successful organized citizen effort in the Environmental Era.... Much of the environmental movement was shaped by the ideals and inspiration embodied in the drive for wilderness."[21]

So. Conservation has never needed environmentalism for bounce, bucks, and bodies, nor for doers, leaders, and thinkers. However, as Hays writes, environmentalists drew on strong leadership from conservationists to show them how to build their network.

Yes, some of the growth in the Sierra Club was from those who wanted to clean up pollution and make cities more livable, but the wild bunch has more than pulled its own weight.

---

19   Michael McCloskey, "Twenty Years of Change in the Environmental Movement. An Insider's View," in Riley E. Dunlap and Angela G. Mertig, eds., *American Environmentalism: The U.S. Environmental Movement, 1970-1990* (Taylor & Francis, Philadelphia, 1992), 80.

20   Michael McCloskey, "Notes on Dave Foreman Paper: The Myth of the Environmental Movement," March 15, 2002.

21   Samuel P. Hays, *Beauty, Health, and Permanence: Environmental Politics in the United States, 1955-1985* (Cambridge University Press, New York, NY, 1987), 120-121.

Yes, too, there is overlap. John Muir told us that everything in the universe is hitched together. Rachel Carson showed how chemicals such as DDT killed birds *and* threatened human health. Some folks bridge conservation and environmentalism well. The late David Brower, founder of Friends of the Earth, was one. Paul and Anne Ehrlich are two others. Former Senator Gaylord Nelson, father of Earth Day and then Counselor to The Wilderness Society until his death in 2005, was a great environmentalist and a great conservationist—and a forthright leader calling for population stabilization. Mike McCloskey has led in both fields. A few clubs such as the Sierra Club and professional teams such as the Natural Resources Defense Council work on both.

That conservation and environmentalism sometimes overlap and work together does not mean, however, that they are the same. Likewise, environmental justice activists bridge the civil rights and environmental houses, but this does not make civil rights and environmentalism the same network.

Unyoking Helps Both

I do not put a bundling board between conservation and environmentalism to stir things up, to cheapen the need to clean up pollution, or as a thought game, but rather to show that by acknowledging conservation and environmentalism as two networks with sundry folks, cares, and goals, with their own beginnings and paths, each can work better alone and together. In no way do I mean to rub sand between the two, at least no more than is already there. Instead, I want to still those roily waters. I think I have drawn a truer map. Let me spread it out again: The Wilderness Society, Endangered Species Coalition, Panthera, Center for Biological Diversity, Defenders of Wildlife, The Rewilding Institute, New Mexico Wilderness Alliance, Friends of the Bitterroot, WildEarth Guardians, Grand Canyon Wildlands Council, RESTORE: The North Woods, Wilderness Watch, and many other bunches are conservation clubs and work on wildlife and wildlands.

The Environmental Working Group, Environmental Defense Fund, Center for Science in the Public Interest, Citizens Clearinghouse for Hazardous Waste, National Toxics Campaign, the American Lung Association, Clean Air Task Force, and Citizens for Clean Water are environmental outfits and work on pollution—they don't worry about bringing home wolves to the Blue Range Primitive Area.

In asking whether conservation and environmentalism are one, I am not alone. Gottlieb asked, "Is it a movement primarily about Nature or about industry, about production or about consumption, about wilderness or about pollution, about natural environments or about human environments … ?"[22]

I answer that it is not a movement; it is two movements. We will work better together if we are not hissing and clawing to be top cat in one tree. If each is straight about its goals and home, there may be less fuss and fur flying.

The Sierra Club stands out as the most thorough wedding of conservation and environmentalism. "The Sierra Club is leading the effort to protect America's public lands and public health at the federal, state, and local levels," said then-Executive Director Carl Pope in 1997.[23] The Sierra Club's volunteer framework is split into three broad campaigns, though, which show the sundering. The Wild Planet Strategy Team deals with wildlife and wildland; the Environmental Quality Strategy Team with pollution and toxics; and the Sustainable Planet Strategy Team with population, international trade, and global warming.

Now, many things overlap conservation and environmentalism. Clean water can be worked on out of worry over pollution harming fish and stream ecology *and* over worry about the health of children, women, and men. Samuel Hays writes, "During the years from 1965 to

22   Gottlieb, *Forcing The Spring*, 315.
23   1997 membership letter (undated) signed by Carl Pope, Executive Director.

1972 threats of pollution had been thought of primarily in terms of their impact on the larger biological world rather than on human health." The Fish and Wildlife Service led the antipollution fight among federal agencies back then. Later in the 1970s, pollution fighting became more focused on human health and "the [Environmental Protection Agency] became a human-health agency."[24]

In the early 1980s, Earth First! fought putting the United States' national nuclear waste dump near Canyonlands National Park in southeastern Utah. We did not do so because we were an antinuke bunch or worried about radioactive pollution in Los Angeles's drinking water from the Colorado River. Rather we were fighting a big industrial plant in one of the wildest landscapes in America, we were shielding a National Park, and we were working to keep a wild neighborhood free from pollution. We worked with antinuke and environmental groups, yes. We each had our own thrust but we worked together against a shared foe. This is how conservationists and environmentalists should work together.

Man's overpopulation is something on which conservationists, environmentalists, *and resourcists* have worked together. The shame of "The Environmental Movement" is that lately it has pretty much shied away from the thorny threat of the Man swarm and dwindling carrying capacity for all Earthlings.[25]

THE ENVIRONMENTAL TUSSLE WITH CONSERVATION

Trying to shoehorn conservation and environmentalism into one box raises hackles. From the beginnings of "The Environmental Movement" in the 1960s to today, some of its spokesmen and -women have shouted, "Environmentalism is about human health," and have churlishly shouldered wildlands and wildlife aside. They want conservationists to sideline our cares and take on theirs.

24   Hays, *Beauty, Health, and Permanence*, 205.

25   Dave Foreman, *Man Swarm and the Killing of Wildlife* (Raven's Eye Press, Durango, CO, 2011).

Environmentalists sometimes struggle against conservationists for dollars, staff, and standing in shared clubs.

There are also times when environmentalism can clash with conservation. Years ago working to cut air pollution in southern California led to coal-fired power plants being built in the Four Corners Region—once the cleanest airshed in the U.S. and an off-the-beaten-track wild landscape. Now the Grand Canyon fills with smog. Acid precipitation in the wild lakes of the Adirondack Mountains in northern New York is from tall smokestacks on power plants and factories in the Ohio Valley. "The solution to pollution is dilution," we were told back in the 1970s. What they were truly saying was, "Let's get this air pollution high enough so that it doesn't come down here in the populated regions that make it but drifts hundreds of miles to come down in unpopulated wild places."

Today there is a clash as some environmentalists work for "alternative energy sources" (anything but oil!), such as big wind farms sprawling for miles along highland ridges, looking for all the world like the Martians in H. G. Wells's *War of the Worlds*—and as deadly if you are a bird. Bird lovers warn that the spinning blades of these giant windmills kill thousands upon thousands of migrating birds, bats, and flying insects. Some one thousand federally protected hawks and owls are killed every year at the Altamont Pass wind farm in California alone.[26] In England, conservation clubs like the Council for National Parks are fighting unsightly wind farms next to the Lake District National Park; environmental clubs like Greenpeace and Friends of the Earth back the wind farm.[27] Some environmentalist backers of wind power shrug off its downsides with the same careless gall we heard from PR hacks for the nuclear industry when threats from nuke plants were first brought up in the 1960s and 70s. I've been happy to hear that

26   Frederic J. Frommer, Associated Press, "U.S. Government Investigators Urge More Federal Involvement in Wind Farms," September 20, 2005.

27   "Argument Over Wind Farm," *National Parks and Protected Areas International Bulletin*, May 2005, 22.

under the browbeating from conservationists, the wind power industry has come up with blades that are less deadly to birds and bats. I don't know about insects. After all, who cares about them? Who knows what new devils may then pop up? Moreover, the loveliness of landscapes and seascapes, such as Long Island Sound, are not piddling things. Beauty is good in and of itself, and not something to be carelessly given up for new ways to make energy.

With strong backing from sun power boosters and the solar energy industry, the Obama Administration through Secretary of the Interior Salazar and the Bureau of Land Management are going all out to lease many thousands of acres of desert managed by BLM for either solar photovoltaic panel "farms" or mirror and tower energy plants. Notwithstanding many better settings for solar plants, a team of environmental/conservation outfits is working to help Salazar and BLM pick the best sites on public lands for this industrial development. Make no mistake, it is industrial development and will lead to tens of thousands of acres of wild desert plants and ecosystems being bulldozed away for panels or mirrors. Moreover, there will be thousands of miles of new power lines from these back-of-beyond spots to where the power is wanted. This is another struggle between an environmental Weltanschauung and a conservation one.

I've written in my "Around the Campfire" internet column about much better spots for sun energy development, which meet two needed standards: (1) make the power where folks live so there is no need for long transmission lines; and (2) harm no wildlands or croplands by landscalping for solar factories. Among the kinds of acres that meet these two standards are parking lots; flat rooftops of big-box stores, shopping malls, schools, government buildings, and so on; home roofs; irrigation ponds, reservoirs, and canals; wastelands such as old strip mines, brownfields, and landfills; and solar cells sandwiched between two-paned windows on skyscrapers. Targeting these spots first before any public wildlands would give us more than enough room for making sun power so that we would never have to trash the deserts. Conservationists need to call for a full moratorium now on any leasing or building solar energy plants on public lands.[28]

Another clash between alternative-energy environmentalists and biodiversity conservationists is over biofuels, the making of which is likely to be worse than wind power. How many thousands of tons of crop leftovers will be hauled off the land for biofuel instead of drizzling organic richness back into hammered agricultural soils? How much wild forest—most of it in the tropics—will be torn up for oil palm, sugar cane, and other biofuel plantations? In southeastern Asia and Indonesia, Borneo foremost, some of the last tropical forests are being uprooted for biofuel-producing palm-oil plantations. Flying over Borneo and driving through the off-the-beaten-track Indonesian island of Halmahera in March of 2012, I saw patch after patch of forest cleared and planted in oil palm. In Iowa a state-of-the-art plant went on line in 2005 to get ethanol out of corn. One little stumble: it burns 300 tons of greenhouse-gas-belching coal a day to do so.[29] In years past, millions of acres of so-so soils on the high plains have been taken out of farming and given over to stopping erosion and giving wild birds much needed neighborhoods. Now they are being plowed back to corn for biofuels with the loss of the new bird habitat. Where is the wrath—heck, where is the *prudence*—among environmentalists? As I was writing this, biofuels were no longer everyone's darling and a wide sweep of folks was beginning to ask about the growing worries.

Conservationists and environmentalists sometimes line up against each other on herbicides to fight invasive species. Environmentalists have often knee-jerked against herbicides anytime, anywhere, while conservationists and biologists are willing to think about the need for herbicides to shield native species against invasive exotics.

28   Dave Foreman, "Urban Solar Now," *Around the Campfire with Uncle Dave*, No. 27, April 6, 2011, www.rewilding.org/rewildit/432/dave-foremans-around-the-campfire-urban-solar-now/

29   Mark Clayton, "Carbon Cloud Over a Green Fuel," *The Christian Science Monitor*, March 23, 2006.

California mountaineer and philosophy professor George Sessions warns that "environmentalists whose concerns are directed primarily to anthropocentric urban pollution problems fail to grasp the full dimensions of the ecological crisis and its philosophical implications."[30] He wrote in 1992 that "the most serious threats to the integrity of the biosphere are the exponential growth of the human population, the greenhouse effect, ozone layer depletion, and species extinction as a result of habitat loss. Various forms of urban pollution and pesticide poisoning, usually focused upon by the Environmental Protection Agency (EPA), the general public... and many anthropocentric reform environmental groups, have a much lower risk factor."[31] Nicholas Kristoff of the *New York Times* wisely took a like stand in one of his columns: "Given the uncertainties and trade-offs, priority should go to avoiding environmental damage that is irreversible, like extinctions, climate change and loss of wilderness."[32] Bully for Nick.

ANTICONSERVATION ENVIRONMENTALISTS

To see how environmentalism and conservation can be strongly at odds, we need to go to Canada and Norway. Both lands are believed to be among the most civilized in the world and leaders in sustainability, healthy cities, and pollution control.[33] The 2004 Environmental Sustainability Index (ESI) named Norway second and Canada fourth out of 142 nations (the United States was a lousy 45th) on twenty "core indicators of environmental progress."[34] In 2005, the ESI put Norway

30   George Sessions, "Radical Environmentalism in the 90s," in Max Oelschlaeger, editor, *After Earth Day: Continuing the Conservation Effort* (University of North Texas Press, 1992), 21.

31   Sessions, "Radical Environmentalism," 19.

32   Nicholas Kristoff, "I Have a Nightmare," *The New York Times,* March 12, 2005.

33   Gene Johnson, Associated Press, "Canada beckons unhappy Americans," *Albuquerque Tribune,* November 13, 2004. This article lists ten ways Canada betters the U.S. on progressive issues.

34   "EarthTalk: Scandinavia leads world in environmentalism," *E/The Environmental Magazine,* January 15, 2004.

second and Canada sixth.[35] The *New York Times* calls Norway a "redoubt of welfare capitalism and strict environmental laws."[36] In 2006, the ESI was made over into the EPI (Environmental Performance Index), but little has shifted in the six or seven years since the switch. The Pilot 2006 EPI put Canada 8th and Norway 18th out of 133 nations. Niger was dead last. In the 2012 EPI, Norway had climbed to 3rd while Canada slipped to 37th, though still in the rank of "strong performers."[37]

Canada still has the good-guy, Dudley-Do-Right flashing teeth and strong chin the world loves. Folks at home, though, know Canada's good world citizen standing is a sham. David Suzuki, biologist, author, and host of the television show "The Nature of Things," has polled as the fifth "Greatest Canadian," ahead of all others yet living. Now he is ashamed of how Canada has backed off on greenhouse-gas-reduction commitments. "Canada has coasted on a reputation far beyond its merits," says he.[38]

Both Norway and Canada have frontier thinking on logging, dams, and mining, and have shoot-'em-up wildlife slaughter policies from the nineteenth century. Canada carried out the greatest slaughter of large mammals anywhere in the world these days by killing 975,000 seals in three years on their Atlantic shores.[39] That is nearly one million big wildeors. Back to the glory days of the buffalo slaughter! And who is buying the "products" of the bloodbath? Why, Norway and Denmark, stars of environmental holiness. Even the United States bans "imports

---

35   Felicity Barringer, "Nations Ranked as Protectors of the Environment," *The New York Times*, January 24, 2005.

36   Simon Romero, "The $6.66-a-Gallon Solution," *The New York Times*, April 30, 2005.

37   http://epi.yale.edu/epi2012/rankings

38   Jonathan Spicer, "Canada Not Listening to Leading Environmentalist," *Reuters*, October 14, 2007.

39   Clifford Krauss, "New Demand Drives Canada's Baby Seal Hunt," *The New York Times*, April 5, 2004; David Ljunggren, Reuters, "Canada Says Seal Populations Growing Despite Hunt," May 25, 2005.

of seal products."[40] A ban on importing all seal products at last became law in 2010 in the European Union. The harp seal slaughter did not end, though. Every year since 2006, between 224,745 and 468,200 (in 2011) harp seals have been killed.[41] Canada keeps bludgeoning to death about one million harp seals every three years. There is no end in sight. And Canada is thought the standard-bearer of what a civilized country should be.

Iceland has always done well in these rankings. For the 2012 EPI, Iceland was 13th. And yet, and yet.... Besides overfishing, Iceland slaughtered "125 endangered fin whales in 2009 and 148 in 2010...."[42] The fin whale is the biggest being on Earth after the blue whale. I recall seeing one in the Bay of Fundy. The back rolling up above the sea kept going and going and going. Nancy and I were left in awe. What a wonderful being with which to share Earth! And yet the überenvironmentalist Icelanders are slaughtering them as if they were Black Angus. Even President Obama—who has shown little care for wild things—is upset and ordered U.S. "agencies to ramp up pressure on Iceland to end its slaughter." In a Message to Congress, Obama wrote, "Iceland's actions threaten the conservation status of an endangered species and undermine multilateral efforts to ensure greater worldwide protection for whales."[43]

The peace-loving, bicycling Norwegians are doing full-on commercial whaling years after the world came together to free the great-minded giants of the sea from hunting. However, the health-conscious Norwegians no longer eat fatty blubber, so it is tossed overboard. Nothing but the lean cuts for the fit, outdoors-loving

40   Associated Press, "Canada's Spring Seal Hunt Opens," *The New York Times,* March 29, 2005.

41   www.harpseals.org

42   Andrew C. Revkin, "Obama Presses Iceland Over Fin Whale Hunt," *New York Times,* September 16, 2011.

43   Revkin, "Obama Presses Iceland."

Scandinavian environmentalists![44] Folks in Sweden, number four in the 2005 ESI and 9th in the 2012 EPI, mostly back hunting the pitifully small handful of wolves hanging on there.[45] Norway also kills most of the wolves that sneak into their mountains and tundra. So much for these "redoubts of strict environmental laws," and the world's leaders in peaceful, just, progressive civilization. When it comes to wolves, Scandinavian countries are as bad as Alaska, Idaho, and Wyoming, whereas Spain, Italy, and Eastern European countries are much more forbearing. Canada is also death on wolves. Let's hear it for wonderful, healthy built environments for people with wild things killed off and gotten out of the way.

Oil companies, governments, and all who are hooked on black gold are thrilled at how much oil and gas may be lurking under the Arctic Ocean. As the Arctic ice melts thanks to greenhouse gas fouling of the atmosphere, drillers are beside themselves in the dash to sink their shafts in the new energy bonanza. Who is out front? Why, no other than the überenvironmentalist Norway. Tim Dodson, executive vice-president of Norway's Statoil said, "The race is on for positions in the new oil provinces." Norway is drilling gas further north than anyone else today but will leapfrog closer to the North Pole with wide-open extraction in the Barents Sea—from which they hope to suck out gas "equivalent" to one million barrels of oil a day by 2020. The Norwegian minister of petroleum and energy, Ola Boten Moe, reliving a little of the old ransacking Viking mood, said, "There's an ocean of new opportunities that we will grasp with both hands."[46] They will be grasping more than

44   Alister Doyle, "Oslo wants more whaling to boost fish stocks," Reuters, May 19, 2004; Doug Mellgren, Associated Press, "Norway's Disputed Whaling Season Opens with Higher Quota than Last Year," *Environmental News Network*, April 19, 2005.

45   Goran Ericsson, Thomas A. Heberlein, Jens Karlsson, Anders Bjarvall, and Anders Lundvall, "Support for hunting as a means of wolf *Canis lupus* population control in Sweden," *Wildlife Biology* 10:4 (2004), 269-276.

46   Quirin Schiermeier, "The great Arctic oil race begins," *Nature,* January 31, 2012. www.nature.com/news.

opportunity with an oil spill in the rough, unforgiving, faraway waters of the high Arctic.

If there was a Nobel Prize in "environmental hypocrisy," I think either Norway or Canada would win it every year, though Iceland would give them a good run.

Let me again underline that I do not think that there has to be squabbling between environmentalism and conservation. Hard feelings come from two neighboring networks hissing to be boss cat in their shared "Environmental Movement." There will be less of this clawing if we acknowledge how we are unalike and that both movements are needed, work together when we should, and let the other be as we go about our own work. Wildlands and wildlife conservationists should not call themselves environmentalists or let the news business do so. I've found that telling reporters at the beginning not to call me an environmentalist is a good opening for a more thoughtful interview.

Put-downs of conservation by environmentalists notwithstanding, I have seen very little shunning of environmentalism by conservationists other than when environmentalism backs resourcism over conservation. Most conservationists, like me, strongly back cleaning up urban air pollution, stopping toxic dumping, and making our cities livable and clean. These are just not things on which we mostly work. I may be misunderstood, so let me be straightforward here. Human health is important. We need to clean up air pollution. We need to stop making toxic wastes. We need more mass transportation such as light rail. We need to work for environmental justice. Furthermore, conservationists understand well that industrial pollution, industrial agriculture, atmospheric ozone depletion, and anthropogenic global climate change are all threats to wildlife and wildlands, as well as to human health.

I want a strong and hearty environmental network.

But I do not want it to keep working to take over the conservation network, nor do I want to be targeted with the harmful stereotype that some environmentalists bear.

Nonetheless, what truly is highest at this late hour is the worldwide biodiversity crisis, made bigger and even more awful by global weirding from greenhouse gas pollution. As I showed in *Rewilding North America,* Man is waging wholesale murder against our fellow Earthlings.

It is about the whales.

CHAPTER 3

How Enviro-Resourcism Undercuts Conservation

*Above all we do not want in our ranks people whose
first instinct is to look for compromise.*

—"The Wilderness Society,"
four-page printed statement, January 1935[1]

A NOT-SO DISTANT MIRROR

Thus far on our hike through the Myth of the Environmental
Movement, I've been poking at an anthill with a stick. There are good
environmentalists and conservationists who will shake their heads
"no" at my splitting environmentalism and conservation into two
standalone but friendly networks. Some will shudder and bristle at
how I cast environmentalists. And resource conservationists, such as
Forest Service "timber beasts," put-and-take game and fish managers,
and the kind of hunters and anglers they make happy, will cuss me up
one side and down the other for filching *their* name as conservationists.

---

1   Quoted in James M. Glover, *A Wilderness Original: The Life of Bob
Marshall* (The Mountaineers, Seattle, 1986), 182.

Resourcists and some environmentalists will steam over how I make caring for wild things *for their own sakes* the heart of conservation.

But now I'm going to take my stick and thoroughly rile the anthill by spelling out how the conservation fellowship is heading down a wrong path. I know a swarm of ants is going to come crawling and biting up my legs. Alack, I can't help but to come down on missteps I see in my old conservation gang—it seems to be who I am, as it was for Rosalie Edge, who I think of as my conservation great-grandmother. And I am a believer in the old slogan, "To thine own self be true." Keep in mind, though, that I am not alone now or before. I am not keening a lonely Jeremiad from a split-rock spire in the dryland sun. Along with my own, I am handing on irked grumbles rising up from a crowded trail of conservationists from the 1920s on who come from all over our playing field: staff of national and local clubs, outdoorsfolks, board members, funders, scientists, academics, staff with federal and state agencies, retired land and wildlife managers.... While some have spoken out, many can't take the soapbox since they need funding, jobs, and goodwill from some of those whom I take to the woodshed here.[2]

Moreover, what I am doing is nothing new. For one, I am following the sturdy steps of Rosalie Edge, a forthright, unyielding wildlover, who worked tirelessly to clean up the National Audubon Society and to free it from weakening by the firearms and other businesses. She started the Emergency Conservation Committee with her own wealth and sent out blistering alerts on a sweep of conservation issues from the 1930s to 1950s. She also bought Hawk Mountain in Pennsylvania and hired a warden to shield migrating hawks from gunners.[3]

Most of all, I sizzle about sell-outs the same way the founders of The Wilderness Society did in 1934-1935. Those founders were a small, hard knot of the toughest, most visionary conservationists of the time.

2   Owing to this need, I quote some here without giving names.

3   Stephen Fox, *The American Conservation Movement: John Muir and His Legacy* (The University of Wisconsin Press, Madison, 1985), 174-182.

My gripe is lifted straight from one of my high elders and lodestars: Bob Marshall. When Bob and a few others started The Wilderness Society in 1935 (with Bob's money), he wrote that the new outfit wanted "no straddlers." Benton MacKaye, the visionary father of the Appalachian Trail and one of the founders of The Wilderness Society, may have been even more scathing, but then he was older than Marshall and had seen more undercutting of brawny conservation by milksops, as well as the takeover of some clubs by big business (such as happened to the Audubon Society).[4] MacKaye snorted, "I have in mind a long list of people who should NOT be admitted. We want those who *already* think as we do; not those who have to be shown."[5] Marshall, MacKaye, and the others would be downcast and glum to learn how many fence-straddlers today cram The Wilderness Society and its sibling clubs and teams, and how some once-stalwart outfits such as The Nature Conservancy (TNC) have been so upholstered with fast-buck businessfolks and wheeler-dealers that they have fallen off the fence onto the other side into the mud-bog of resourcism. Oh, how Rosalie Edge would steam the corporate flunkies who have taken over The Nature Conservancy! Out of the trail-dusty lore of the old gang that worked hard to shelter wild things, my wild bunch buddies and I are echoing the words of Bob and his wild bunch buddies from nearly eighty years ago.[6] To borrow from historian Barbara Tuchman, the mid-1930s are a "distant mirror" in which we see the plights of today's

---

4   Fox, *The American Conservation Movement.* Fox does a matchless job of telling about early fights for the soul of conservation. *The American Conservation Movement* is a must-read book for anyone who wants to understand the conservation movement.

5   Quoted in Fox, *The American Conservation Movement,* 211: Marshall letter to Harold Anderson, October 23, 1934; MacKaye letter to Robert Sterling Yard, June 25, 1935.

6   If you don't know much about Bob Marshall, you need to learn. He was Mr. Personality of conservation in the 1930s. James M. Glover, *A Wilderness Original: The Life of Bob Marshall* (The Mountaineers, Seattle, 1986).

conservation network reflected.[7] For those who want to look into this distant mirror of early fights for the soul of conservation clubs, read Stephen Fox's *The American Conservation Movement: John Muir and His Legacy*. There is likely no better sidekick book to *Take Back Conservation* than Fox's. I've learned as much from it as from any book I've read.

CONSERVATION ON THE ROCKS

Julianne Newton and Eric Freyfogle at the University of Illinois write in *Conservation Biology*, "Sustainability's popularity among conservationists ought to give us pause because it provides telling evidence that conservation is on the rocks, intellectually speaking.... If conservation had a sound overall focus, sustainability would not enjoy the popularity it does."[8] They offer Aldo Leopold's Land Ethic as the bedrock for conservation, rather than the shifting sand of sustainability. They rightly see how Leopold's Land Ethic works for lands from the wilderness to the farm.[9] Wilderness is the land I love, but I also back the Land Ethic on the farm and ranch by being on the advisory board for the Wild Farm Alliance.[10]

I think that enviro-resourcism is the gale that has driven our boat onto the rocks of so-called sustainability. In this chapter and the next three I'm going to look at how enviro-resourcism has undercut and weakened the conservation network through sundry plays and players. In the last three chapters of the book I'll get back to these plights with a work sheet for how we can warp the *USS Conservation* off the rocks (*HMS Conservation* in Canada.).

7   Barbara W. Tuchman, *A Distant Mirror: The Calamitous 14th Century* (Alfred A. Knopf, New York, 1978).

8   Julianne Lutz Newton and Eric T. Freyfogle, "Sustainability: a Dissent," *Conservation Biology*, Vol. 19, No. 1, February 2005, 24.

9   Julianne Lutz Newton, *Aldo Leopold's Odyssey: Rediscovering the Author of A Sand County Almanac* (Island Press, Washington, DC, 2006) is an eye-opening study of Leopold's life from the standpoint of his work on how folks can live on the land without wrecking it.

10   See www.wildfarmalliance.org

In my "Nature's Crisis" broadside in early 2005 (which I rewrote as the "Introduction" to this book), I set out some woes in the wilderness and wildlife network.[11] A big slab of what is wrong is that it has slipped its moorings away from its holdfasts, away from what it holds dear, its freedom, its quirky selfhood, and its pluck. Much of why it has drifted away from its historical berth is the sway—now growing into the hand on the rudder—of enviro-resourcists.

Field Marks of Conservationists

Before I can throw out lifelines for conservation, I must first answer: What are the field marks of wilderness and wildlife conservationists? Aldo Leopold spotted the heart-most when he wrote in the first line of *A Sand County Almanac*, "There are some who can live without wild things, and some who cannot."[12] Conservationists are the "Cannots" and together we are the Cannot Club. We should wear that badge proudly for it speaks to our deep-rooted mood-health and merry righteousness. We have a mighty tie to wilderness and wildlife. Some of us are roused more by the derring-do, insightfulness, and happy loneliness that we find with being in the big outside; others by the lovely, often-breathtaking landscapes and little blossoms that make up wild neighborhoods. Yet others of us are caught up in the frolicking rough-and-tumble of wildeors in the theater of evolution. Many of us need to get out and dirty in the wild; others are happy to know it dashes and twirls in the National Park outside the lodge picture window from the coziness of their overstuffed leather chairs and warm brandy

11   Willard Van Name, of the American Museum of Natural History and a gadfly reformer of the National Audubon Society and other straying conservation clubs, wrote "a pamphlet, *A Crisis in Conservation,* in the summer of 1929." Fox, *The American Conservation Movement,* 174. It is what remade birder Rosalie Edge into a "hellcat" for conservation.

12   Aldo Leopold, *A Sand County Almanac: And Sketches Here and There* (Oxford University Press, New York, 1949), vii.

snifters. The matchless Will Dilg, founder of the Izaak Walton League, wrote in 1927:

> *I am weary of civilization's madness and I yearn for the harmonious gladness of the woods and of the streams. I am tired of your piles of buildings and I ache from your iron streets. I feel jailed in your greatest cities and I long for the unharnessed freedom of the big outside.*[13]

Mighty Bob Marshall, who ate trail-miles like lumberjacks ate flapjacks, wrote:

> *A small share of the American people have an overpowering longing to retire periodically from the encompassing clutch of a mechanistic civilization. To them the enjoyment of solitude, complete independence, and the beauty of undefiled panoramas is absolutely essential to happiness. In the wilderness they enjoy the most worthwhile or perhaps the only worthwhile part of life.*[14]

However we wish to see or to play in the big outside, it comes down to loving and holding high wild things. Whether we are fully aware of it or not, I think what we conservationists are enthralled by are *self-willed* lands, waters, worts, deors, and happenings...even when such wild things are threatening. We need to know that there are things untamed, carrying on their evolutionary wanderings and stumblings without need for Man. We see the wildwood, not two-by-fours; we see wildeors, not meat or pests; we see rivers, not "clean" hydroelectric power. At our deepest we believe that other Earthlings should be shielded for their own sakes, whether they have worth of any kind for Man, or even if they are a threat or a bother.

---

13   W. H. Dilg, *Outdoor America,* Izaak Walton League, October 1927. For more on Dilg, see Fox, *The American Conservation Movement,* 159-172.

14   Robert Marshall, "The Wilderness as a Minority Right," *U.S. Forest Service Bulletin,* 8/27/28, 5-6.

The first editor of *Conservation Biology* and author of one of the few must-read conservation books, *The Arrogance of Humanism,* David Ehrenfeld, calls this the "Noah Principle": ecological communities and species "should be conserved because they exist and because this existence is itself but the present expression of a continuing historical process of immense antiquity and majesty."[15] Philosopher Martin Heidegger said much the same with "Let beings be."[16]

So, whether we wild folk think about it or not, *most* of us want to keep wild things—lands and wildeors—for their *inborn worth.*[17] Arne Naess, the gristly yet playful Norwegian philosopher and mountaineer who fought the Nazis and then became a leading thinker on Gandhi and an amateur boxer, worked out a formal philosophical framework for the inborn worth of other lifekinds: Deep Ecology.[18] But even for university philosophers like Naess, marking the goodness-in-itself of all

---

15　David Ehrenfeld, *The Arrogance of Humanism* (Oxford University Press, New York, 1978), 207-208.

16　Bill Devall and George Sessions, *Deep Ecology* (Peregrine Smith, Layton, UT, 1985), 99.

17　I am not saying that every wilderness backer for the last ninety years believes in the inborn worth of wilderness and wildlife. I've known some who couldn't care less about Endangered Species or self-willed land. They only want to be alone or they want to hike where there are no vehicles or roads or other signs of Man. Most hikers, backpackers, horsepackers, climbers, rafters, canoeists, backcountry hunters and fishers, and other wilderness recreationists have not helped conservation, I'm sad to say. (However, not being an active conservationist does not mean that one doesn't believe in wild things for their own sakes—there may be other things that keep such a one from the struggle.) Others have helped only out of their own selfishness to keep their roadless playgrounds. Such work is needed and welcome, nonetheless. A core job for conservationists is to make wilderness folks understand that it is for their own good to keep their wilderness playgrounds or gymnasiums unscathed. Working with such fair-weather friends does not clash with loving wilderness for its own sake.

18　Arne Naess, "The Deep Ecology Movement: Some Philosophical Aspects," in George Sessions, editor, *Deep Ecology for the 21ˢᵗ Century* (Shambhala Publications, Boston, 1995), 64-84.

wild things comes first and foremost from the evolutionary heart—just as it does for all kinds of wildlovers. We love self-willed life, we need it to be whole, we need it to be hale, we would not want to live without it; therefore we hold it as good-in-itself. This is the only true love, whatever the target of our love.[19]

Our work is grounded in these goods. We work to keep the back of beyond *forever* locked away from ransacking—as lawful Wilderness Areas or as other well-warded wild havens. We shield Endangered, Threatened, and at-risk species. We bring back wolves, lynx, black-footed ferrets, bolson tortoises, humpback chubs, California condors, and peregrine falcons to their former homes. We fight dams on rivers that yet flow free. We stand for the hallowedness of National Parks. We say "enough!" athwart more roads; try to block the feckless glee of off-road vehicle hooliganism; sue against careless logging, mining, and energy tearing-out in wildlands; work to outlaw "recreational" trapping and irresponsible hunting;[20] give dollars to those who take on whale-killers on the high seas; appeal sloppy, land-withering livestock grazing....

FIELD MARKS OF ENVIRO-RESOURCISTS

It is here we have stood. But now there are those in the wilderness and wildlife network—some executive directors, staff, board members, foundation staff, consultants, and "trainers"—who do not fully share our loves, goals, and wiles; who are not wholly wild themselves. Well-

---

19 I make my own sweeping, bedrock stand for the inborn worth of wild things in my long chapter "Five Feathers for the Cannot Club" in Patricia Hasbach and Peter Kahn, editors, *Rediscovery of the Wild* (MIT Press, Boston, 2012) forthcoming; and in my chapter "Wild Things for Their Own Sakes" in Kathleen Dean Moore and Michael P. Nelson, editors, *Moral Ground: Ethical Action for a Planet in Peril* (Trinity University Press, San Antonio, 2010), 100-102.

20 Many good hunters work against hunting bears with dogs, spring hunting of female bears and mountain lions, and other kinds of slob hunting.

meaning, clueless, or just looking for a settled career, these are the folks who are undercutting true conservation with creeping enviro-resourcism and even outright resourcism. Some are suits, some are wee cowerin' mousies, some are sidewalk folks, some are careerists, some like the smell of sawdust, some want to have a friendly cup of coffee with good ol' boys....

In Chapter 1, I spelled out my belief that conservation, environmentalism, and resourcism are stand-alone but neighborly networks, often less neighborly between conservation and resourcism. There is much back and forth under the sheets, even with longstanding feuds and clashes. In this chapter and the next three, though, I will look at how enviro-resourcism undercuts conservation in seven ways, which are not always linked (I'm sure there are more ways). One is the growing chiding to *downplay wild-things-for-their-own-sakes.* Two is to *shoulder aside protected areas for sustainable development and ecosystem management.* Three is to *downplay doom-and-gloom with smiley-face Pollyannaism.* Four is to *thrash out with other "stakeholders" "win-win" deals.* Five is to *get some kind of outcome as soon as can be done and call it a big win even if it's an overall loss.* Six is to *lift the conservation organization over its mission.* Seven is the dream that *technological fixes can make everything rosy.* These seven jumble together like bunnies and I know I'm showing them in a somewhat tangled way, but that's the way things work out in the dirt. Nor do all enviro-resourcists hop with all the bunnies. Some may hop with only one or two. See Table 3.1.

WARNINGS

Tarry with me for a bit here. I need to make four warnings about the winds that follow, lest I be misunderstood. Some folks are bothered or even upset by my doggedness that our belief in the inborn worth of wild things must be the core of how we talk about conservation. They see my unyielding stand as spurning any kind of political give-and-take and as putting down all utilitarian grounds for conservation at any time.

Table 3.1. Enviro-Resourcist "Jumbled Bunnies"

Downplay wild-things-for-their-own-sakes

Shoulder aside protected areas for sustainable development and ecosystem management

Downplay doom-and-gloom with smiley-face Pollyannaism

Thrash out "win-win" deals with other "stakeholders"

Get some kind of outcome as soon as can be done and call it a big win even if it's an overall loss

Lift the conservation organization over its mission

Technological fixes can make everything rosy

When you take on or have to deal with enviro-resourcists in any way, keep these seven bunnies in your mind so you can better understand what you are fighting.

Others worry that I am running off likely friends who may not believe in wild things for their own sakes.

First, I am waving harmful *trends* in wilderness and wildlife conservation, and dealing out an overall path for wildlovers to tread; there will always be outliers, fuzziness, and other worthy paths to take. Second, I am not against all resourcism or taking raw goods out of the land and sea for Man's needs. Third, cutting deals on set issues (Wilderness Area boundaries, say) is not the same as cutting deals about what is good (whether Wilderness Areas are good, say). Fourth, utilitarian grounds for conservation can be given alongside those rooted in the own sake of wild things; this is done often (even by hard-asses like me) thanks to it often working for true wins. The same goes for aesthetic, historical, literary, recreational, ecological, and health grounds. I call for a wise wedding between what is right and what works. Indeed, I do not think of myself as an idealist at all; I am a bruised, world-weary pragmatist. I like what works. I do not think wholehearted surrender works. I do not think enclasping the values of Nature haters or fastbuck exploiters works. I think being thoroughly straightforward on why we want to keep and restore wild things works, but does not keep us from acknowledging or wielding other grounds for sheltering and restoring wild things. I think well-warded wild havens of sundry kinds work. I do not think conservation without strong protected areas works; I do not even think that it is conservation.

I must ask you to read this chapter and the next three (forsooth the whole book) as though every paragraph drips with qualifications like a honey-stuffed sopapilla: most enviro-resourcists are not bad folks, they mostly want to do good, they have sometimes helped conservation clubs, and so on. I will not goo up every paragraph for you, though, since that would make an unreadable mush of shilly-shallying. The price of brevity is loss of nuance. Nor do I wish to be personal, even when I name folks, nor am I going to write a grand-jury indictment. (Okay, okay, I don't always live up to this—I'm truly not sweet.) Furthermore, I write this to do good. I would like those whom I name as enviro-resourcists to think about what they do and to instead help conservation be conservation—*or at least to step aside and let conservationists be conservationists*. And I call on wildlovers to stand up for true conservation. Let us all renew our tie to the sheltering and rebuilding of wild things.

Resourcism at its heart is agriculture (Gifford Pinchot wrote that forestry was tree farming), and agriculture is how we live today. I go along with careful, thoughtful resourcism on *many* of the lands and waters *already* tamed. I am against resourcism that is not careful and trustworthy, which likely and sadly holds for most resourcism today. I'm for the path of the Wild Farm Alliance, farming and ranching on private lands that fits with shielding and giving homes to wild things, and even with rewilding. I'm against resource extraction and industrial use on lands and waters that are mostly wild. And I'm against resourcism that does not have room for hefty wild havens and big wild-hunters over a wide landscape.

In the wildlands networks I've helped to draw, so-called "compatible-use areas" outside of the "core protected areas" are a key chunk of the whole wildlands network. In *Rewilding North America,* I lay out the way wildlands networks are made up of both hands-off wilderness and lands where careful, light logging, livestock grazing, and so on can be done. Published wildlands network visions also have much more about how compatible-use areas fit in with a wildlands network. These wildlands network visions show well that rewilders back careful, evenhanded resourcism on the right lands.[21]

Within our wild bunch there is room and need for sundry games, dodges, and ways. Some conservationists want more Wilderness Areas set aside than do others. Some are willing to cut deals earlier than others. Such stands come from how folks weigh "political reality" or how to get the best deal. It is craft, not one plus one equals two; therefore wilderness lovers can see the best deal in sundry ways. The mid-2000s rift within the wilderness crowd over the Central Idaho Economic Development and Resource Act (CIEDRA), while sometimes heated, was mostly between good conservationists; I have friends on both sides, though I didn't think the bill was a good deal (this tussle is still going on).[22]

---

21   Dave Foreman, *Rewilding North America* (Island Press, Washington, DC, 2004); Dave Foreman, Kathy Daly, Barbara Dugelby, Roseann Hanson, Robert E. Howard, Jack Humphrey, Leanne Klyza Linck, Rurik List, Kim Vacariu, *Sky Islands Wildlands Network Conservation Plan* (The Wildlands Project, Tucson, AZ, 2000); Dave Foreman, Kathy Daly, Reed Noss, Matt Clark, Kurt Menke, David R. Parsons, and Robert Howard, *New Mexico Highlands Wildlands Network Vision* (The Wildlands Project and New Mexico Wilderness Alliance, Richmond, VT, 2003); Brian Miller, Dave Foreman, Michelle Fink, Doug Shinneman, Jean Smith, Margaret DeMarco, Michael Soulé, and Robert Howard, *Southern Rockies Wildlands Network Vision* (Colorado Mountain Club Press, Golden, CO, 2003). Only the Southern Rockies document is for sale. The others are on CD from kim@wildlandsnetwork.org.

22   The White Cloud Mountains are dear to me, not only for themselves and their wonderful wilderness (wherein I saw a wolverine), but also because Nancy and I were married at the 1986 Round River Rendezvous on the edge of the proposed Wilderness Area.

Brian Miller writes that compromise is not the same as concessions. Compromise can be helpful even when painful if it shuffles you along toward your goal. That is how I saw the highly compromised 1980 New Mexico Wilderness Act; it left out key wildernesses and had weak boundaries for others, but it was better than what we would have gotten the next year. That's why I worked hard for it over more than a month on Capitol Hill the fall of 1980. Miller also teaches that one can only compromise with those that acknowledge that there are grounds for conservation. We must always ask: What are we getting? What are we giving up? How does this get us nearer our long-term goal? How does it weigh when all is said and done?

Other times, however, "conservation" clubs have stepped over a worrisome line, such as a 2006-2007 deal in which a few "conservation" outfits in Montana made a thoroughly unneeded give-away by working with off-road vehicle clubs to open up roadless areas to motorized use.[23] I am becoming more and more worried about what some conservation groups are willing to give up for a small Wilderness bill or to get along with big shots in small towns and the hinterlands. When this happens, I think we can fairly ask whether the leadership of the conservation group has been taken over by enviro-resourcists or worse. When that happens, true conservationists need to openly oust the sell-out bunch from our team.

Utilitarian arguments for shielding lands or caretaking wildlife are okay with the right background and when given carefully. They dig pitfalls when they are overplayed or when they shoulder aside

23   In Montana, nearly all conservation clubs have been forthright about shielding all National Forest roadless areas in a way that would keep out motorized vehicles. The governor of Montana backed this stand in 2006-7. But, the once-proud, now hapless Montana Wilderness Association (MWA) along with the National Wildlife Federation undercut the rest of the conservation network and the governor by cutting a deal with the off-roaders to open motorized vehicle trails in roadless areas on the Beaverhead National Forest. From this and like stunts, I think MWA has written itself out of the conservation team.

outspoken beliefs grounded in inborn worth. There are three ways in which someone might offer utilitarian arguments for wild-thing conservation: (1) They don't believe in the inborn worth of wild things; (2) They believe in the inborn worth of wild things but are afraid to talk about inborn worth, or they are callow and not yet thoughtful; and (3) Without hiding or gainsaying inborn worth, they find utilitarian arguments to be workable, sound, and needed with some folks we want on our side for, say, a Wilderness Area we offer. The first wheeler-dealer is not truly a Cannot—they are an enviro-resourcist or resourcist. The second greenhorn dealer has been led to believe that the truth will be harmful and hasn't the grit or worldliness to know otherwise. The third conservationist is thoughtfully and wisely wielding sundry tools without shunning the underlying good.

CONSERVATION HAS FAILED

Overall, the big shift enviro-resourcists want wilderness and wildlife conservationists to make is also the most harmful. Their reckoning goes like this: (1) Conservation is failing at protecting biodiversity; (2) We are mostly failing because we ground our work in our belief that we should save biodiversity for its own sake; (3) Therefore, conservationists need to drop their own-sake beliefs and talk, and say that conservation is to help people. In short, enviro-resourcists say that our straightforward loving of wild things spawns our political stumbles and shortcomings. The enviro-resourcists say the wilderness and wildlife network fails at getting folks to understand or care about the big plights besetting Earth owing to how we talk about how industrialism harms wild things (scenery and bugs) instead of how it harms the economy, ecological services, and the health and livelihoods of children, women, and men. Conservation will work, they say, only if it is straightforwardly about helping Mankind live healthier and better. Biodiversity is a resource for Man.

Some tout this earthquake of a shift as only pragmatic. We can still love wild things for themselves, but we will better keep and shelter them if we talk only about how Nature is good for Man and needs to be wisely managed for Man's good. But when we look deeper, we find those coaxing us to this new path truly do not love wild things for their own sakes. Many of them are not outdoorsfolks; some have never been camping. Few of them are naturalists—they don't live to bird or name wild blossoms or read tracks. They are not trying to only flip over our arguments; they want to flip over what conservation holds as good. As one of my friends write, they do not bring wild things into their thinking about the ethical community or neighborhood. They spurn Aldo Leopold's Land Ethic.

Moreover, their reckoning of why conservation is failing is thunderingly wrong, as I'll show elsewhere in this book. Tarring our good-in-themselves beliefs for our "failures" overlooks the sweeping strength our foes have. Given all that is against conservation, maybe we've done pretty darn well. After all, we are working against the 50,000-year-long takeover of Earth by *Homo sapiens*. Forsooth, sometimes when I sit back and think about it, I am boggled at how well we lovers of wild things have done, given the nature of Man and the overwhelming strength of those who see Earth only as our warehouse. I think those who fault conservationists have not been in the fight enough to understand the strength of our foes. Even with the setbacks today, it is amazing to conservation old-timers that we restored wolves anywhere in the cowboy/slob hunter West.[24]

The call for a new Man-first path for conservation comes mostly from those working in international conservation and holds up what are said to be conservation stumbles in the third world to underline

---

24   This is not to say that we have won by any means. It's only to say that it is a little amazing, given all that has been and is against us, that we have been able to set aside any big wild havens closed to money grubbing. And we have done this on every continent, big island, and ocean on Earth.

the need for a shift. The Nature Conservancy also touts this new path in the United States, as we'll see in Chapter 5. I'll knock down this chiding of wildloving conservation more in *True Wilderness*. But, for now, I'll say that without our long work for protected areas and wildlife protection policies and enforcement all over the world, the state of wild things (biodiversity) would be far, far grimmer than it is. Would there be any wild tigers left in India? I think not. Would there be growing pods of great blue whales in the world's seas? I think not. Would mountain gorillas yet roam the Virunga Mountains without National Parks and armed wardens? I think not. Without the deeds and gains of wildlovers through the last hundred-and-fifty years, mass extinction and landscalping would be much worse.

WILD THINGS FOR MAN

Some well-known environmentalists and conservation biologists back wild havens and the work to bring back threatened wildlife, but shun the thought that wild things are good-in-themselves. They mean well, but chip away at the righteous strength of the wilderness and wildlife network. Robert F. Kennedy Jr., of the Natural Resources Defense Council and maybe America's best-known environmentalist after Al Gore or Bill McKibben, takes this path in his speeches: he does not want to keep wildlife and wilderness for their own sakes, but for his children and for the economy. In his talk at the September 2005 Sierra Club Summit in San Francisco, he said, "We're not protecting the environment for the sake of the fishes and the birds. We're protecting it for our own sake because we recognize that nature enriches us. It enriches us economically, yes to the base of our economy." He said the same two more times in that one rambling talk.

Jared Diamond, an early conservation biologist and protected-area thinker, says much the same in his best-seller *Collapse*: "I'm more interested in environmental issues because of what I see as their consequences for people than because of their consequences for birds."[25] Diamond has done darn good fieldwork on birds in New Guinea, but seems blind to the wildness that he has found there. Folks often puzzle me; I don't have all the answers on how our overtangled and twisted brains work. Some other well-known and listened-to conservation biologists have taken like stands, while others bet the farm on the economic worth of biodiversity from bioprospecting to ecosystem services.

I believe Kennedy, Diamond, and others in their camp have done good for wild things—but I do not want their soft path drowning out that of hardcore wildlovers. To put all good in Lord Man brushes aside and forsakes everything the wild world tells us. It forgets how short a time Man has been a leaf in the Tree of Life: Think of the time of complex lifekinds as a 550-page book; each page then is a million years in the span since the Cambrian Explosion of Life.[26] Behaviorally modern Man doesn't show until the last two sentences on the last page (the last 50,000 years). Read that again: *Behaviorally modern Man doesn't show until the last two sentences on the last page of a 550-page book.* Does that help you see how big we truly are? Does that help you see how much the world should twirl about us? Yet those who should know better think all other life is good only for what it does for us? Was nothing good until we evolved?

Diamond is widely read and Kennedy is widely listened to, so it is key that wildlovers be straightforward that, Kennedy and Diamond notwithstanding, we *do* back keeping birds and fishes for their own sakes whether or not they are good for the economy or for our children. Conservationists must never let others think that environmentalists or enviro-resourcists such as Kennedy and Diamond speak for us about what we hold high. David Johns warns against "goal shift, that

25   Jared Diamond, *Collapse: How Societies Choose to Fail or Succeed* (Viking, New York, 2005), 16.

26   About 550 million years ago, nearly all of the known phyla of animals show up in the fossil record for the first time. Stephen Jay Gould, general editor, *The Book of Life* (W. W. Norton, New York, 2001).

is, efforts to move conservation away from eco/biocentric goals, to make conservation subservient to other social goals. These efforts will destroy conservation."

Now, some folks who believe in the inborn worth of other Earthlings hide their true feelings to make utilitarian arguments for keeping wild things so they will seem more mainstream and believable. This path sucks the strong marrow from the words of the wilderness and wildlife team and flips one into a guileful wheeler-dealer. Strong utilitarian arguments may be good to sling about—so long as we do not hide the bedrock good of wild things for their own sakes. I will get back to this tug-o'-war between the good and the utilitarian in chapters 4, 12, and 13.

Talking only about the dollar worth of biodiversity or the good of other Earthlings thanks to how they make us smile are not the only come-hithers to get us to talk narrowly about how conservation is good for Man. It comes, too, in the eagerness for a "techno-fix" and in the keenness for "ecosystem services."

TECHNO-FIX

William McDonough, "green" architect, has gained much heed. I've heard him at a Conservation Biology Conference and the 2005 Sierra Summit. He is the kind of public speaker who holds his listeners in his hand, and his path is hopeful, fair-minded, and get-the-job-done. It is engineering in a bighearted, caring way. Big businesses, such as Ford, PepsiCo, and Nike, are listening to him that we can "design" our way out of our "environmental" turdhole. The *Washington Post* writes, "He argues that a 'diverse, safe, healthy and just world with clean air, water, soil and power' is attainable by redesigning the way we make things, without waste and in harmony with nature."[27] No doom and gloom here, but the let's-get-it-done hopefulness Americans love to hear. It's also an outlandish flight into make-believe land. Such technical-fix

27   Linda Hales, "An Environmental Problem Slipping Through the Quacks," *Washington Post*, August 27, 2005.

gimmicks can be helpful, *but are not enough.* And they can be harmful if they further undercut our understanding that Man's population growth and rising gobble-gobble drive the Sixth Great Extinction and that technology won't—can't—pluck us out of the whirlpool of our own making.[28] On my bad days, I worry that these lipstick paths only put off the day of reckoning. In his gruffly true book, *The Spirit in the Gene,* Reg Morrison warns that the longer we put off crash, the worse it will be.[29]

Under the leadership of Carl Pope from the 1990s up until 2010 or so, the Sierra Club did steadily less on conservation and slowly shifted its oil-tanker bulk to another way—that of McDonough's techno-fix. Many who speak for "The Environmental Movement" don't talk about wild things anymore. Alternative energy sources, greater resource efficiency, better design, and so on get their hearts beating faster. The 2005 Sierra Summit in San Francisco, which drew a few thousand Sierrans, did not offer one conservationist as a plenary or highlighted speaker. Even Doug Scott, a gripping speaker and one matchless in knowledge about the Wilderness System and its lore, as well as a leading Club staffer in the 1970s and 1980s, was shuffled off to a short meeting up against other talks. The same for yours truly. McDonough and Kennedy were star speakers. From the lineup, one would have had no inkling that Man is driving a mass extinction, or that our population growth is still blowing up and is the bedrock woe. There were lots of hybrid cars on show, though, from the whale-killing islands of Japan. On the other hand, the last big Sierra Club get-together in 1989 was much more given to the wild.

The July/August 2005 issue of *Sierra* magazine (which was tied to the Sierra Summit) underlies my worry. The cover and leitmotif of the

---

28 See, for example, James Howard Kunstler, *The Long Emergency* (Atlantic Monthly Press, NY, 2005).

29 Reg Morrison, Foreword by Lynn Margulis, *The Spirit in the Gene: Humanity's Proud Illusion and the Laws of Nature* (Cornell University Press, Ithaca, NY, 1999).

issue was "Can Technology Save the Planet?" Carl Pope, then-executive director of the Club, wrote in his opening column:

> *The planet cannot sustain 6 billion humans aspiring to better lives without 21st-century solutions. We need the services of science and technology, and the skills of engineers. We need to enlist human genius to solve problems, not merely to increase profits. Our role as environmentalists increasingly will be to make sure the appropriate rules and incentives are in place, and then stand back and let the engineers get to work.*[30]

I find this a mind-boggling statement, and also find it hard to believe that Carl truly believed it. He is a sharp politico and he and I have shared friendly drinks and wrangles over the years, but here I think he was doing his utmost to take the Sierra Club into new and stormy waters: those of efficient cornucopianism. It is the way cursed years ago by David Ehrenfeld in his landmark *The Arrogance of Humanism*—the belief that clever, streamlined, technological answers will take care of our woes.[31] Another article in that *Sierra* began with, "For almost every environmental ill, scientists are working on a technological solution—or three."[32] This should make us happy, but we should also be afraid of what it means: that our network's leaders think there are technological answers for every "environmental ill." Every conservationist or environmentalist bewitched by the songs of the techno-fix sirens should have *The Arrogance of Humanism* stuffed in their ears so they can't hear the sweet come-ons that will crash us on the rocks.[33]

30   Carl Pope, "Let's Get Technical," *Sierra*, July/August 2005, 11.

31   Ehrenfeld, *The Arrogance of Humanism*.

32   Sean McCourt and Reed McManus, "The Perfect Fix: Simple And Sophisticated Solutions For Some Of Our Most Vexing Problems," *Sierra*, July/August 2005, 42.

33   I look at how technology works in raising our carrying capacity and thereby our "impact" on wild things (I=PAT) in Dave Foreman, *Man Swarm and the Killing of Wildlife* (Raven's Eye Press, Durango, CO, 2011), 139-143.

With his dogged campaign on global weirding, I think Al Gore has become America's foremost environmentalist. But even he has fallen for the techno-fix, telling us that we have the answers and tools; all we need more is the political will to use them. How I wish it were so. As economics columnist Robert Samuelson (of all people!) writes, "the available technologies promise at best a holding action against greenhouse gas emissions."[34] Snubbing the Ehrlich-Holdren formula I=PAT (Impact equals Population times Affluence times Technology) and the need to freeze then lower population and how much we "consume," the techno-fixers are just pissing in the wind.

The kind of techno-fixes Carl Pope and the Sierra Club were going for came out in early 2012. As the alternative to dirty coal, the Club pushed "clean" natural gas, even if it came from the dirty method of fracking. Felicity Barringer writes in the *New York Times* that the Sierra Club took $26 million in secret donations from Chesapeake Energy from 2007 to 2010 "for its Beyond Coal campaign...." At the same time, the Sierra Club was paid $1.3 million from 2008 on by Clorox "for the right to display the Sierra Club logo on a new line of 'Green Works' cleaning products." When he heard of these deals, the Sierra Club's new executive director, Michael Brune, killed them both—as well as another $30 million in the pipeline from Chesapeake, even though the Club was in the middle of a big shortfall in dues and donations.[35] Wow. How about that? The Sierra Club has a new executive director with stone-hard righteousness.

As it now stands, the Club's targeting alternative energy is to stop or slow greenhouse gas belching. In the spring of 2007, I was glad when Bruce Hamilton, the Club's staff leader on conservation, met with the leaders of the Spine of the Continent Initiative to tell us how the Club would be doing more work on landscape-level conservation to

34 Robert J. Samuelson, "No Movie Fix for Global Warming," *Albuquerque Journal,* March 23, 2007.

35 Felicity Barringer, "Answering for Taking a Driller's Cash," *New York Times,* February 13, 2012.

deal with the dread outcomes climate weirding will have on the wild world. Under Bruce's leadership, the Sierra Club now has a "Resilient Habitats" Campaign to seek ways to shelter wild things in the gale of global weirding from greenhouse gas pollution. I'm on the listserv and a lot of good things flow between the Sierrans—staff and members. Carl Pope is at long last gone from the Club, and it sounds like many are not sorry to see him out the door. Although I fret about the Sierra Club, I also know that it is the only big conservation or environmental outfit that is still a grassroots club overall.

Nonetheless, we, even environmentalists and, alack, conservationists, will always be soft prey for cool technology. Josh Quittner, the technology writer for *Time* when I still subscribed, nailed why this is so: "Great technology, today as always, renders us as gods."[36] So it was when one of our forebears first kindled a fire. So it is today.

Ecosystem Services

Lately, some leading enviro-resourcists, conservation biologists, and resource managers have been calling for biodiversity arguments to be grounded in what they call "ecosystem services"—such as how forests clean the air and make oxygen. They have reckoned sky-high economic benefits from these ecosystem services. Some also say that the ecosystem-services grounds should elbow aside any talk about wild things for their own sake, that selfish grounds are the only ones that work for most Men.

The New York Times and others acknowledge Stanford University's Gretchen Daily as a leader "in the growing worldwide effort to protect the environment by quantifying the value of 'natural capital'—nature's goods and services that are fundamental for human life—and factoring these benefits into the calculations of businesses and governments." Daily and Stanford University helped start the Natural Capital Project

---

36   Josh Quittner, "Who Will Rule The New Internet?" *Time,* June 16, 2008.

with some other universities and The Nature Conservancy and World Wildlife Fund. It goes beyond older work to bolster conservation through the economic value of wildlife and wildlands in a much more sophisticated and high-tech way. It also goes beyond old reckoning that a marsh was worth dollars thanks to the ducks and geese it grew that brought in hunters who spent money locally. Natural capital or ecosystem services seeks to keep wildlands for the "benefits from nature—like flood protection, crop pollination and carbon storage— [that] are not part of the traditional economic equation."[37]

Long ago, though, Aldo Leopold warned that if we make conservation "easy," we make it "trivial." He also wrote, "One basic weakness in a conservation system based wholly on economic motives is that most members of the land community have no economic values....When one of these non-economic categories is threatened and if we happen to love it, we invent subterfuges to give it economic importance."[38] He wrote that economics wasn't the why for conservation anyway, it was "whether a hawkless, owl-less countryside is a livable countryside...."[39]

So-called "ecosystem services" is a new, clever, and well-meaning take on the old wildlands-and-wildlife-are-good-economically kettle that Aldo Leopold warned about in the 1930s as it was first steaming up. I'm glad that, unlike some pushing ecosystem services, Gretchen Daily says she cares about wild things and acknowledges that there are other values. She says, "The beauty of the natural capital approach is it leaves the vast, immeasurable aspects of nature in their own realm while focusing in a very practical way on environmental benefits that we can

---

37 John Moir, "An Economist for Nature Calculates the Need for More Protection," *New York Times,* August 8, 2011.

38 Aldo Leopold, *A Sand County Almanac* (Yale University Press, New Haven, CT, 1949), 210.

39 Aldo Leopold, "Conservation," in Luna B. Leopold (Ed.), *Round River: From the Journals of Aldo Leopold* (Oxford University Press, New York, 1953), 150.

and should incorporate into our current decisions."[40] Good words, yes, but what I've seen is that those who plug ecosystem services shove wild-things-for-their-own-sakes into a dark hole where it is never brought up again—indeed, most of the ecosystem-services boosters I've read say conservationists should shut up about wild things being good for themselves. Wildlovers need to be sharp-eyed and loud watchdogs to keep this new economic reckoning from elbowing the inborn worth of wild things out of the conservation argument.

VISION

The way conservation work is framed these days is another shift to enviro-resourcism. The word *environment* itself sketches our talk in an abstract, Man-targeted way, instead of in a wild-hearted way. Weighing the good of wild things by economics, such as ecosystem services, chips away at the belief in the inborn good of wild things. When they put economics up front, wilderness and wildlife clubs fall into how resourcism and wilderness exploitation frame what is good, then the talk shifts to tradeoffs between wild things and fast bucks, cutting off hope of even stating our goals and what we hold high. The fight for wild things quakes rhetorically. Our bedrock shifts to sand beneath our feet.

Not only does enviro-resourcism drain the fire and boldness of conservation groups, it drains their vision as well. Most outfits whip in to fight development threats and to fight backtracking on already gained shelters and tools, *as they must,* but seldom anymore offer sweeping visions for tomorrow. In *Rewilding North America,* I set out the key way vision has worked in earlier conservation gains and wins. Big visions such as the Alaska Lands Act (1980) have not been the work of mainstream conservationists for the last thirty years.[41] Today, when

40   Moir, "Economist for Nature."
41   The California Desert Protection Act in 1994 was a pretty big vision, but it was driven by grassroots Sierrans and desert rats. After Senator Alan Cranston came on board, the national conservation groups did, too.

a conservation club calls for something visionary—a three-million-acre Maine Woods National Park, say—they find themselves standing almost alone. Funders and big conservation outfits slight such great steps out of fear they are too hot.[42] The Maine Woods National Park proposal from a scrappy New England team, RESTORE: The North Woods, has been snubbed by many national and regional conservation groups—and not for it being a crackpot or new thing. Forsooth, it was foreshadowed by Thoreau and is well within the mainstream of earlier conservation proposals—such as Arctic National Wildlife Refuge (1960), Redwoods National Park (1968, 1978), North Cascades National Park (1968), the Eastern Wilderness Areas Act (1975)—and rests on stone-hard ethical, ecological, recreational, and economic grounds. Its lack of backing owes mostly to enviro-resourcism meekly narrowing the frame of our dreams.

THE IRON LAW OF OLIGARCHY

Among the ways enviro-resourcists sway and weaken the work of conservation is since they believe Man is the meat and potatoes of "conservation," not wild things, that therefore squabbles should be worked out by all the stakeholders (only the *Homo sapiens* ones) trying to find "consensus" for "win-win solutions." These people want to log their trees and yet keep the forest.

However, in some way it is unfair to scorch the men and women and the teams who make this happen. David Johns, who teaches political science at Portland State University, tells me that they are only following Robert Michel's "Iron Law of Oligarchy" (1915), the process by which organizations "reify" as they grow. This reification of conservation clubs, where the organization becomes more important than its mission, is what I am lashing in this book.

---

42   To my unhappiness, even the Vermont office of the Wildlands Project held the Maine Woods National Park proposal at arm's length.

Enviro-resourcism overlooks The Big Thing in the world today: the Sixth Great Extinction. It also shrugs its shoulders at the key driver of this wholesale loss of life: the population explosion of Man.[43] Enviro-resourcism also backs away from tough wild havens. It buys into what David Ehrenfeld calls the "Arrogance of Humanism," the belief that all plights can be worked out by Man, that Man is at bottom good and can be made better, that political institutions are reformable, and that our civilization is everlasting. It mostly shuns biology, evolution, and hard edges for how much there is and how far we can go. It does not acknowledge that other Earthlings are good-in-themselves nor the earnest health need we have for wilderness and wildeors.

The conservation network must shake off enviro-resourcism and get back to its true self. Wildlovers must stand up and take back *their* conservation network. I'll look at ways to do this in chapters 11, 12, and 13. In the next chapter, I'll line up some of the enviro-resourcists and show how they have undercut and weakened our work and our network.

---

43   Foreman, *Man Swarm.*

CHAPTER 4

Meet the Enviro-Resourcists

Even within the conservation movement there are too few people, including those in leadership positions, who come from the ranks of avid backpackers, river runners, horsepackers, hunters, anglers, backcountry skiers, etc. And it is my opinion that it has begun to show. 'Just knowing that it's there....' does not form the foundation of a strong movement. A commitment to 'progressive politics' doesn't either. Direct experience and knowledge of the wild does.

—a canny Washington, DC, conservation staffer

AS ENVIRO-RESOURCISTS THICKEN THEIR SWAY over the conservation network, I think it likely that they neither understand our love for wild things nor how we see other Earthlings as good-in-themselves. Lumping together environmentalism and conservation rears high for why Man-first enviro-resourcists have been freer to take over the wilderness and wildlife network.

ENVIRO-RESOURCISTS

Although I've slopped together the word "enviro-resourcism," the same kind of threat has been known by hardcore wildlovers throughout the last hundred years and by many of my friends lately. After all, we started Earth First in 1980 owing to how conservation clubs were shifting.[1] (See Table 4.4.) Bob Marshall knew well the threat in 1935 when he wrote that the new Wilderness Society wanted "no straddlers."[2] My friends have told me most of the tales upon which I ground my worries in this book. They have asked me to write this warning about where the conservation network is headed and its loss of craft and to call for getting back to where we should be. In 2007 one flinty leader of a wilderness club emailed me: "Currently we can barely respond to any issue without a bevy of media specialists trying to make people think of... other value[s] that in some cases [are] peripheral of what the issue really is.... [In response to the Bush Administration's attacks on conservation] we have responded in a weak and technical manner, void in many cases of emotion, or more appropriately outrage.... [We must] be willing to say what we believe. If we continue to move with caution we will have little left to fight for."[3]

Steve Capra, the stalwart, wild-hearted Executive Director of the New Mexico Wilderness Alliance (NMWA), backs up this conservation leader's words. As Barack Obama was putting together his cabinet, conservationists pushed hard for Representative Raul Grijalva of Arizona to be appointed Secretary of the Interior. Grijalva may be the most upstanding fighter for wild things in Congress today and is much liked by conservationists throughout the United States. Instead, Obama went for Senator Ken Salazar of Colorado, who was far weaker on public lands and wildlife in Congress than Grijalva and who had been out-and-out bad—not just weak—on Endangered Species protection. So, the tougher conservation group leaders, such as Capra,

---

1   The exclamation mark (!) did not get tacked onto Earth First until later.

2   Quoted in Stephen Fox, *The American Conservation Movement: John Muir and His Legacy* (The University of Wisconsin Press, Madison, 1985), 211: Marshall letter to Harold Anderson, October 23, 1934.

3   I do not cite sources in this chapter where my source wishes to be anonymous.

came out strong in newsletters against Salazar and for Grijalva.[4] The day the NMWA newsletter with Capra's thumbs-down editorial on Salazar came out, he got a phone call from a top funder ripping him up one side and down the other for any gainsaying of Obama.

Too few have been giving heed to how Man-first enviro-resourcists have been seeping into the wild-things-first wilderness and wildlife network. This creeping enviro-resourcism is not always willful or even thought-out. Sometimes it is meant to be shrewd—some seek to shield wild things by wielding Man's welfare and happiness as the overall goal. The pitfall here is that such cunning players can get further sucked down such a path to forget what they love, and end up seeking to shield a bloodless abstraction, whereas Cannots fight with a burning love for wild things they know well, bewitching wild things with an inner being unknowable to Man's mind but yet well known and loved in the hearts of Cannots. Enviro-resourcists may understand how to cross the "t" and dot the "i" in policy and for issues about wild things, but they likely do not truly *know* the living wildeors and their wild neighborhoods, even if they can sling their names about. Such is an upshot of the fading of natural history in biology and conservation.[5]

In Table 4.1, I list some of the ways conservation is being jounced into enviro-resourcism. The words I field are a mishmash of values, buzzwords, and quirks, but as a whole they give a feeling for how resourcism is redoing the conservation mind-lair. I am framing enviro-resourcism in a mussy, helter-skelter, sprawling way in this chapter, but

---

4   Stephen Capra, "Notes from the Executive Director," New Mexico Wilderness Alliance, December 18, 2008. Grijalva represents the same Arizona congressional district as Stewart Udall, who became Kennedy's and Johnson's Secretary of the Interior in the 1960s. Salazar has shown himself to be the weakest Democratic Party Secretary of the Interior in a hundred years.

5   Thomas Lowe Fleischner, editor, *The Way Of Natural History* (Trinity University Press, San Antonio, 2011). Fleischner and others are boosting a campaign to show how key natural history is for conservation. I look at this in Chapter 13.

Table 4.1. Some Trends in the Conservation Network

WILDERNESS AND WILDLIFE CONSERVATION	ENVIRO-RESOURCISM
Wild Things	Man
Wild Havens	Ecosystem Management
Wild Havens	Sustainable Development
Armed Wardens	Weak Enforcement
Unyielding Watchdogging	Resource Extraction
Vision	Compromise
Limits	Cornucopianism
Truthfulness about Human Nature	Political Correctness
Realism about Political "Friends"	Serving "Pet" Politicians
Daring	Pandering
Fight	Negotiate
Toughness	Softness
Mission	Organization

that's the way I see the doings of Man, not as tidy and mindful, however much we might wish to sing "Glory to Reason in the Highest." In Table 4.2, I list some of the players that are dragging or nudging wilderness and wildlife clubs into enviro-resourcism. And in Table 4.3, I list some of the ways enviro-resourcism has sway.

So, who are these enviro-resourcists bridling the wilderness and wildlife network? (See Table 4.2.) Among them are *some* staffers and board members of foundations that make grants to conservation clubs. Most of these funders belong to the Environmental Grantmakers Association (EGA) and the Consultative Group on Biological Diversity (CGBD). There are also a few wealthy men and women who link their gifts with nudges (wink!) for politically correct behavior. (Other lone givers and foundation leaders are hard-core conservationists unhappy with today's trends, thank goodness.) Many "trainers" and consultants who help nonprofits with "organizational effectiveness" come from outside the wilderness and wildlife network. They are enviro-resourcists or progressive political players, as are most media consultants and pollsters.

Some, maybe most, leaders of big conservation clubs and a growing cast of hired staffers of conservation clubs from big to little are enviro-resourcists. They come to the wilderness and wildlife network right out of environmental studies or natural resources programs in colleges, after working for social-justice or other progressive outfits, from having worked on "The Hill" for members of Congress or congressional committees or the Administration, after retiring from land and wildlife managing agencies, or from business (some conservation staffers from all such backgrounds, however, are Cannots and darn good fighters for the wild). Another downside to the link of conservation and the progressive political movement is that there seems to be a swinging job door between all kinds of outfits in progressivism and the Democratic Party (just as there is on the right with the Republican Party, but somehow the Republican *apparatchiks* seem tougher and meaner). As we'll see in the next chapter, the leadership of some big international organizations (The Nature Conservancy, Conservation International) has gone even farther away to work hand in glove with resource-extraction businesses and to put business-linked sustainable-development ahead of shielding threatened wildlife and ecosystems.

Most conservation friends in politics—office-holders, candidates, staff, pollsters, media consultants—lean to enviro-resourcism or have weak backbones. There are some senators and representatives who know and care about wild things, who backpack and run rivers, but some of them seem afraid to be out in front to fight for good bills. Many social scientists, foremost anthropologists and economists in both universities and think tanks, who work on resource and poverty issues, are enviro-resourcists (they might call it "political realism" or "justice" or "anticolonialism"). These folks are mostly left of the middle. Slightly to the right internationally, the World Bank, International Monetary Fund, and other financial institutions are behind much of the shoving for sustainable development instead of for wild havens that have rifle-toting wardens. I'll look at international sustainable development in more depth in *True Wilderness* in this series.

In the United States and Canada, rural elites (county commissioners, miners, loggers, big ranchers, beguiling good ol' boys and gals) and sobbing "victims" nudge gullible, greenhorn, and softhearted conservationists into working together which then seems to flip conservationists into being enviro-resourcists or wimps. Canadian

Table 4.2. Enviro-Resourcists

Spread: Some to All:

Foundations and other funders
Consultants and trainers
Leaders and staff of clubs
Club board members
Friendly politicians
Organizational effectiveness consultants
Political/media consultants
Pollsters
Social scientists
World Bank and other international lenders
News Business*
Businesses*
Rural elites*

* Some of these, however, are strong foes of any kind of wilderness and wildlife shielding and of any hobbling of resource exploitation. Some are out-and-out landscalpers, not even resourcists.

Table 4.3. How Enviro-Resourcists Have Sway

Funding and other backing

Organizational effectiveness training

Media strategy and backing

Training for collaboration and negotiation

Indoctrination in the "stakeholder" frame of decision-making

Lifting Man's selfishness over wild things

Professionalization and institutionalization

Steady career with fat salary

Draw of being a "player" with the big boys and girls

Subtle shifts in language (framing)

Must be optimistic and problem-solving

Stay away from doom and gloom and scaring folks

friends tell me this is even worse in Canada than in the States. The next step comes when the goal becomes having a friendly cup of coffee with hinterland leaders at the regulars' table in the town café instead of sheltering wildwood and grizzly bears. *High Country News* began as a scrappy little newspaper for Rocky Mountain conservationists in the 1970s. Today it sits at the regulars' table calling wildlovers over and asking, "Can't we all get along?" "Can't we solve the wilderness (or predator) problem for all the stakeholders?"

Enviro-resourcists can be worthwhile friends; indeed they are needed fellow workers for conservationists. The pitfall, though, for which we must watch, is two-fold: who runs the show, and whether conservationists and enviro-resourcists understand themselves and each other and their right bond.

Some kinds of enviro-resourcists lead in pulling big and little conservation clubs away from steadfast sheltering of wild things. Let's look at these and how they work.

FUNDERS

Foundations and wealthy backers have every right to say where their dollars are going and to whom they are giving. What I am seeing, however, is that more and more staffers for conservation funders lean to enviro-resourcism in values and policy more than do the board members or the wealthy philanthropists behind the foundations (not the old robber barons who set up some hoary foundations, but their offspring). Today, unlike a score of years ago, many staffers come from outside the conservation kinship; they have been shaped in the environmental and social-change worlds, or in progressive politics instead. They don't yearn to get out of New York, Seattle, or San Francisco to the big outside whenever they can. Moreover, I think some of these staffers get a kick out of bossing about heads of wildlife and wilderness groups and calling the shots on political deal-making in a state. Holding the purse strings gives one might over others. On the other hand, I do know a few foundation staffers who work well with grantees, even coming to strategy meetings and playing like a peer, not telling others what to do.

In 2005, the Environmental Grantmakers Association (EGA) put on some "salons" for their foundation members in key cities in the United States to talk about where the grantmaking clan should be going. I was asked to come to the San Francisco Salon and talk about the lay of the land and where tomorrow might lead. Folks, mostly staffers, came from a score or more foundations. In the ten minutes I was given, I brought up wholesale extinction and how our still bursting population bomb was driving it. My talk went over better (I think) than if I had farted loudly, but that's about the best I can say.

At the end of the evening, I offered a complementary copy of my book, *Rewilding North America*, to anyone who wanted one. Two or three folks already had it, but only one other out of twenty-some asked me for one. Some friends with ties to the foundation crowd in San Francisco were not taken aback—nor was I. Earlier I had sent *Rewilding*

North America to folks at more than ten foundations I thought would find it worthwhile. No one wrote back acknowledging the book. That the foundation staffers who oversee picking conservation clubs for grants didn't care about *Rewilding North America* does not mean they are bad folks. Their lack of heed only shows how little some conservation-grantmaking staff now truly care about wilderness and wildlife. In the mid-1990s, I spoke about extinction to an EGA meeting and found many keen listeners. Today, I fear that too few hirelings of the foundations that back conservation outfits have spent any time in conservation clubs or in the big outside (though there are some standouts).

Foundations also sow plights by the kinds of things they fund and don't fund and in what they want from funded groups organizationally and behaviorally. In 2004, David Orr of Oberlin College and the late Peter Lavigne of the Rivers Foundation of the Americas and on the faculty of Western Colorado College wrote "Rethinking Green Philanthropy" to look at what is wrong with how foundations help conservation groups. They wrote, "Environmental giving from private foundations misses the boat when it comes to systematically addressing the major problems we face." They went on to weigh how "environmental" funders work against the far more skilled way right-wing foundations work.[6] Insofar as I can tell, their review went straight to the recycling bin even though Orr and Lavigne were well thought of in the wilderness and wildlife network. Lavigne and Orr highlighted the following things as being wrong with how foundations fund conservation clubs:

- A "myopic emphasis on project funding and on measurement of those projects. General support and infrastructure funding is nearly impossible to come by."
- The "environmental grantmaking community barely supports research and idea generation."

6   Peter M. Lavigne and David W. Orr, "Rethinking Green Philanthropy," *OneNorthwest,* September 8, 2004.

- They don't fund books, films, policy papers, and public speakers.
- They don't fund "people and leadership."
- They don't fund systemic approaches and groups and individuals that "cross boundaries."[7]

I've heard like raps from others knowledgeable with grantmakers. Making things worse, many conservation grantmakers are fickle and switch what they want to fund much too often, thus tripping up the growth of deep knowledge and high skill in targeted fields and careful building of long campaigns. One big foundation built up a national network of regional coalitions to work on National Forests and keeping old-growth and other healthy forests. After a few years, though: Bingo! We're bored with this. There will be no more money from us for the forest campaign. Not only did this hurt conservation work on forests, it hurt some folks who had put themselves into the work only to be cut off at the ankles with nowhere to go. This case of fickleness is the worst of which I know but there are a bunch of lesser funding switches pulled by foundations.

Some foundations shove wilderness and wildlife clubs into more bureaucracy by asking for detailed, analytic reports on outcomes, improvements needed, lessons learned, and so on. To handle the paperwork, some non-profits end up having more overhead staff than program staff. Executive directors spend more time pushing paper than leading fights to shelter wild things. Moreover, foundations fund clubs and teams that "behave." Roy Beck and Leon Kolankiewicz, in their cutting "The Environmental Movement's Retreat from Advocating U.S. Population Stabilization," show that foundations became unwilling to fund population freeze work after such became politically incorrect, or fund clubs for anything if they took a tough stand on overpopulation. This led some wilderness and wildlife outfits that had acknowledged

7   Lavigne and Orr, "Rethinking Green Philanthropy."

how population growth drove wounds to wild Earth to shut up about population.[8]

The outstanding tale is how one billionaire offered $100,000,000 (that's one hundred million dollars) to the Sierra Club but told Carl Pope that the Club wouldn't get a penny if they spoke against immigration. Moreover, the donor did not want to be known. Carl kept the giver unknown even to the Sierra Club board and worked hard (one could say worked dirty) to kill the Club's stand on keeping immigration to what would give the U.S. no population growth. I don't knock the wealthy giver—he had the right to put strings on his big money. I do, however, knock Carl and the Sierra Club leadership for taking the money with those strings and then running a dirty campaign (worthy of Karl Rove) against good Sierrans and upstanding conservation leaders who called for a member vote on immigration policy (it lost).[9]

One seasoned conservation leader wrote me,

> *Foundations are not willing to invest in the long-term. Their measurements of success are formatted in a way that forces organizations to move away from campaigns that take a long time to implement. As an example, if Group X wants to get a one-million-acre reserve designated, they need the first nine years to organize and then have it designated in Year 10. Foundations want 100,000 acres a year, which may be impossible to achieve. Foundations generally lose interest in a project after two years or so and look for the next new approach.*

---

8   Roy Beck and Leon Kolankiewicz, "The Environmental Movement's Retreat from Advocating U.S. Population Stabilization (1970-1998): A First Draft of a History," *Journal of Policy History,* Vol. 12, No. 1, 2000, 150-151. An abridged version was reprinted in *Wild Earth,* Summer 2001, 66-67. Also, see Foreman, *Man Swarm,* Chapter Nine "The Great Backtrack," 119-138.

9   Dave Foreman, *Man Swarm and the Killing of Wildlife* (Raven's Eye, Durango, CO, 2011), 164-167.

A fundraising consultant for nonprofits tells me that "most foundations are obsessed with the need to have a measurable, tangible 'product' as the 'outcome' of their funding." Hooked on such "products" keeps wilderness and wildlife clubs from doing the kind of careful, step-by-step, long-haul work that will give bigger "products" years from now.

I have some understanding, by the way, of how foundations work. For the early years of Doug Tompkins's Foundation for Deep Ecology (FDE), I gave guidance on how much sundry clubs should be given out of FDE's wilderness and biodiversity pot of greenbacks. I read the grant proposals, talked to folks, and then drafted who should get what out of about two hundred thousand dollars a year. John Davis was later hired to do this job and he often asked me about grants. Thinking about how we worked, though, makes me understand how unlike the Foundation for Deep Ecology was from most foundations today—and how it was a more helpful donor. John and I were both as inside conservation as insiders can be and we knew from our own hunger what folks in tiny, hard-hitting outfits were up against. From those days, I also recall Peter Bahouth, who ran the Turner Foundation, Inc. He was tough, caring, and true to both wild things and grassroots conservation clubs. The EGA could use his leadership again today. Alack, both FDE and Turner wound down their granting work about the same time (on unlike grounds) and little grassroots outfits took a bad hit in their funding, which put some out of business. These were good teams and their shutting down was a loss to the work of the wilderness and wildlife network.

Trends in the EGA are picking up speed in the wrong way. Notwithstanding Don Weeden's work to have me talk about population stabilization and our need to keep wild havens in answer to those who think they should be dropped for sustainable development, the EGA would have none of it at the September 2007 meeting in New Mexico. Indeed, there was much talk of dropping the "Environmental" from the EGA name. This might not be a bad thing to do. At least it would end the phoniness. The foundations still true to funding wilderness and wildlife work (population, too) should break away to start a new network of true conservation funders.

A deeper woe with foundations is how they seem to have fallen for the new path of The Nature Conservancy as lined out by their head scientist Peter Kareiva. His way downplays protected areas of all kinds as well as any thought that wild things should be kept for their own sakes. I'll rip into The Nature Conservancy and Kareiva in the next chapter. For now, though, Don Weeden, fearless head of the Weeden Foundation, is worried that many if not most of the foundations making up the Consultative Group on Biological Diversity are leaning to the no-protected areas strategy of Kareiva and his followers. We could begin to see some foundations leaning on conservation clubs and teams to back down.

Another mudslide comes from some (not all!) who work as fundraisers for conservation clubs. Lawrence Noble of the Center for Responsible Politics warns, "The problem is that eventually many fundraisers come to view the issues as commodities with a monetary value separate and apart from the societal cost of the outcome."[10] Enviro-resourcists think that way more so than do wildlovers, but such thinking lurks within the job to raise money. I think it would behoove many folks in the conservation clan to sit under their dearest wilderness tree with a good bottle of wine, and chew over that insight until the wine is gone. *The issues as commodities with a monetary value.* Think about it. Sip the wine. Watch the sun go down. Stumble home with a better outlook and new steadfastness and grit.

Another curse thrown at wilderness and wildlife clubs by the work of raising money is that clubs begin seeing others as rivals, if not as foes, for dollar-chasing. Conservation clubs working against each other on fundraising puts deep cracks into how they can work together to shield

---

10   Lawrence Noble, "Dividing Citizens Lucrative for Special Interests," *Albuquerque Journal,* November 14, 2005.

wild things. This truly has become a threat to skillful conservation. I'll look at it more in Chapter 12 when I get back to the dollar chase and how we might make it less harmful.

CONSULTANTS

A rather new thing in the conservation network is how consultants and trainers have become players for the nonprofit world. Since 1992 or so, I reckon I have been a trainer and consultant bringing conservation biology and a big, hopeful vision to wilderness and wildlife clubs, as have the teams I've helped start: *Wild Earth,* The Wildlands Project, and The Rewilding Institute. Another who learned organizing from Clif Merritt at The Wilderness Society in the 1970s is Bart Koehler. Bart honed to Bowie-knife sharpness grassroots-organizing and Washington-politicking skills from his years leading clubs in Wyoming, Alaska, and Montana. Some younger but otherwise top-of-the-heap organizers, Melyssa Watson and Brian O'Donnell, along with Bart, started the Wilderness Support Center (WSC) in the late 1990s out of Durango, Colorado, to work with state and regional wilderness groups. Rural organizing, working with members of Congress and their staffs, media relations, campaign strategy, and fundraising are where WSC staff have most helped wilderness groups. WSC, which became a wing of The Wilderness Society (but mostly free flying), has been key to the rebuilding of the wilderness network. Their staff was made up of true experts—and wilderness lovers who got into the wilderness. Bart, Melyssa, and Brian are now gone from WSC, though Brian tells me that the new head, Jeremy Garncarz, works to keep it on "grassroots empowerment and getting wilderness bills enacted." I hope the Wilderness Support Center keeps on through the rough shift at The Wilderness Society.

Another outfit that offers good training is Patagonia, Yvon and Malinda Chouinard's standard-setting outdoor clothing company.[11]

---

11   Yvon Chouinard, *Let My People Go Surfing: the education of a reluctant businessman* (The Penguin Press, New York, 2005) gives an inspiring overview.

Patagonia gives operating grants to a score or more grassroots clubs and runs a Tools Conference every few years, where thirty or forty upcoming conservation leaders are given three or four days of workshops on all kinds of handy and needed skills and background. Patagonia also helps clubs with design of brochures, T-shirts, and multimedia shows. I've worked with them over the years.

Then there is Great Old Broads for Wilderness, the most grassroots wilderness club left and the bunch I like best. They run all kinds of hands-on training for their broads and guys old and young. If a wildlover wants to be a player in wilderness-keeping without being a hired staffer for some bunch, Great Old Broads is where to go. They build wilderness lovers into highly skilled wilderness shielders.

What makes the training from the above outfits so helpful and needed is that the folks behind them come right out of the American wilderness kinship; they have the lore and knowledge of the wilderness fight and a deep love for wild things burned into their souls. And they have the wrinkles and the limps, the scars and the quick wittedness from the big outside. They are conservationists first and foremost, just as I am.

Since the 1990s, though, nonprofit-group coaches, *most often from outside the conservation kith,* have begun working with many small clubs at the behest of funders, or to boost their businesses. Such consultants are widespread in business, agencies, and throughout society, so conservation club board members and staffers get the thought that their clubs should bring them on also. It's become a bandwagon. Some of such help is worthwhile and leads staff, board members, and grassroots folks to sharpen fundraising, management, media, and other skills. Other consultants work as "facilitators" to help clubs cobble together organizational "strategic plans." "Organizational effectiveness" is the top goal. Grassroots conservation clubs need nonprofit management skills and need to be trustworthy and well-run, but the drift of "organizational effectiveness" is to lift the nonprofit corporation over its calling and its network; to deal out hired staff, volunteer board members, and volunteer members and activists into walled-off jobs; and to water down wilderness and wildlife outreach and to steer talk away from wild things for their own sakes so it will seemingly better speak to Main Street or back-roads folks. The health and soundness of the *organization* becomes higher than its work for wild things.

Let me be straight here. For nearly forty years I've been leery of organizational consultants and trainers. Back when I worked for The Wilderness Society with my buddies Bart Koehler and Susan Morgan, the executive director of TWS was taken in by a psychologist/preacher who was one of the first of the "people-process" trainers. At best, this guy was a showman on the gravy train; at worst he was a flimflam man. I won't go any deeper here than to say Bart, Susan, and I got shanghaied to work with him.[12] I likely learned from watching him with a crowd, but for the real meat and potatoes it all turned to gooey tofu for me when he earnestly told me that there were no true cleavages between folks on issues. Moreover, there truly weren't issues, it was only folks not understanding each other and our job was to get everyone talking to each other whereupon the plights of conservation, no mind how hot, would work out. While he was on the edge for this kind of drivel, I think that many organizational consultants and trainers lean in such a way. So I have an underlying mistrust of such work.

Most of the organizational-skills trainers I've met do not have ties to nor do they understand the lore of the wilderness and wildlife kinship. Foremost, they don't know that folk conservationists have been at the head of leadership, policy, strategy, beliefs, and so on more than have board members and volunteers for, say, urban soup kitchens. The thrust of such training targets hired staff instead of volunteers. This trend of professionalization is harmful to the makeup and being of the conservation clan.

---

12   Bart and I spent a week holed up at the 4-H Center near Washington, DC, writing a how-to booklet on his pyramid organizing methods for The Wilderness Society staff and cooperators. I can't recall what became of it.

Staff and board members from a few grassroots clubs have griped to me how such consulting groups try to work their way into every little nook and cranny of the outfit. They grumble that the consultants call all the time, ask inapt questions, offer to help when help isn't needed or wanted, and work to take over policy. "I want to tell them, 'Don't call me, I'll call you when I need help. I know how to do my job,'" said one financial manager to me.

They bring a cookie-cutter for how conservation-group boards should be framed after those for run-of-the-mill urban nonprofits. Such a frame doesn't fit for wilderness clubs. I know conservationists who have left club boards after they have become fed up with consultants. I'm one of them. Folks who don't like this new institutionalization and professionalization are winnowed out by their own disgruntlement, so the trend has a positive feedback loop—boards become overloaded with those who like the path driven by organizational consultants. On the other hand, I know of one wilderness club that spurned the draft organizational effectiveness audit one such team did. Why do clubs put up with this? Well, they are sometimes made to do so by funders whose dollars they need. Elsewhere staff of such consulting/training businesses get themselves on a club's board of directors.

The kind of teaching and the outlook of trainers also draw conservation down the path of enviro-resourcism and away from Brower-like true grit. Much of the drill is what you would have for any kind of nonprofit organizational effectiveness. It's vocational-technical, nuts and bolts. The soul and selfhood of conservation is shunned: its history, lore, philosophy, and science. It's shunned owing to the trainers not knowing it and not caring about it.

Organizational and media consultants nudge doughty conservation clubs to work with other "stakeholders" to find middle ground, get along, and build happy little towns in the wide-open spaces, whether the sagebrush hinterlands of the Great Basin or the backwoods of New England and upstate New York. This plight rides high in the work to fight giant energy businesses looting the public lands with big winks from the federal government, even under Obama, who, I believe, couldn't care less about wild things. (As for so many politicians, the great outdoors to Obama is where you hit little white balls.) Back in the mid-2000s, a media-consulting group, which worked with outfits funded by the Rocky Mountain Energy Coalition (RMEC) to fight scalping of the public lands, told wilderness club leaders to back off on grazing lest they upset some ranchers who are our friends on energy, even if foes on wilderness and wolves. The media outfit told wildlife clubs not to talk about Endangered Species since such talk can become heated and may nettle other foes of drilling. This happened early in the fight over drilling on the Otero Mesa grasslands in New Mexico— conservationists were told not to talk about how Otero Mesa is a key wild neighborhood for the aplomado falcon. The media outfit also wanted the man or woman in front of microphones to be a rancher or some such talking about how energy businesses have ruined their land or livelihood or "way of life." Wilderness folk were told to stand on the sidelines. The coalition and media folks work to get all drilling foes speaking with one voice and mood about energy threats—most often a wishy-washy one about families, not wildlife. The upshot is that the frothy-mad fleecing of fossil fuels from the public lands is not being shown as a conservation care so much as an environmental and social one, when it should be shown as *all*. Wilderness and wildlife clubs in the coalition should be free to talk about what they care about so that the whole depth of woes with energy landscalping is brought out. I do, by the way, believe that wrecked ranchland and livelihood are strong tales and should be brought out; they just shouldn't keep the conservation side from being told, too. I am told that, while RMEC is gone, "the concept remains with large funders."

I fear some clubs are not so free anymore, as they more and more hang onto the dollars that come with being on the team.

Overall, these consultants and trainers are not bad folks, but they don't understand how the wilderness clan stands out from city nonprofits, nor do they have fire in the belly for the inborn worth of wild things. They might be helpful now and then, but only for unmistakable chores *under our leadership*.

There is a deeper plight with how widespread consultants are in American life today. Conservation clubs lag politicians and industry in trends such as consultants. There is now sweeping awareness that as for the money-treadmill, leaning on political consultants is a big chunk of what's wrong with politics and governance today. Joe Klein's April 16, 2006, column in *Time* is must reading for anyone who cares about the health and integrity of the conservation clan. His title is, "*Pssst!* Who's Behind The Decline Of Politics? [Consultants.]" The front-page pull-quote reads, "Consultants have drained a good deal of the life from our democracy…Specialists in caution, they fear anything they haven't tested." He warns the Democrats that "there is a demand for leadership, as opposed to the regurgitation of carefully massaged nostrums."[13] I write this in 2012, more than five years later, and Obama and his team are poster children for the truth of Klein's warning. What is it with the Democrats and progressives that they can't learn?

Now, the consultants, news-spinners, pollsters, and marketers who work for conservation and environmental outfits are mostly better folks than the hacks running political campaigns (though some of these political whizzes have edged into the conservation world), but much of what Klein lays on pols shows what is wrong with the conservation and environmental networks. Klein's article and the book from which it is taken should be read and chewed over by conservation leaders lest we become ever more thralls of dithering and pussyfooting like John Kerry.[14] (I do wish Al Gore had been as bold with his tongue in 2000 as he is today.)

Wilderness and wildlife lovers should not spin. We should lay out our thoughts as winningly as we can, but we should not spin.

13   Joe Klein, "*Pssst!* Who's Behind The Decline Of Politics? [Consultants.]", *Time,* April 17, 2006.

14   Joe Klein, *Politics Lost* (Doubleday Broadway Publishing Group, New York, 2006).

Conservationists need to be conservationists. We do not need mousy consultants holding us back. We must not let focus groups tell us what our values are and where we should stand—as some of our organizational "leaders" and consultants would have us do. We know what is right. We know what is wrong. We know what Earth and its wild things need. Focus groups and polls can't tell us such things; at best, they might give us insights on how to make our words more winning. Foundations should put their money into those who work for wild things, not into consultants. Consultants killed Al Gore in 2000. Consultants killed John Kerry in 2004. Let's not let them kill conservation. The last thing conservation needs are "Specialists in caution, [who] fear anything they haven't tested."

STAFF

When my Wilderness Society-Friends of the Earth-Sierra Club friends and I started Earth First in 1980, we did so somewhat owing to the growing "professionalization" in conservation clubs.[15] A few years later, I wrote about such pitfalls in *Earth First!*, and later rewrote it for my 1991 book, *Confessions of an Eco-Warrior* (see Table 4.4). In the years since, the woe of professionalization has gotten worse than what I lambasted then. Today there is a pool of liberal or leftist professionals who work for progressive nonprofits, environmental and many conservation clubs and teams among them. They bring their Man-first Weltanschauung and cares to their new jobs with conservation nonprofits and to foundations that fund conservation clubs. They bring their beliefs of what is doable and workable from their political work with the Democratic Party or progressive world. They bring their fretfulness from the world of consultants. Instead of a burning love for the symphony of evolution and a fear for its tomorrows, they worry about their careers and next job up the ladder. Some don't "get"

---

15 Dave Foreman, *Confessions of an Eco-Warrior* (Harmony/Crown, NY, 1991), 11-23.

Table 4.4. Problems Of Professionalization In Conservation Groups

- Many of the people who work for [conservation] groups today are not conservationists but technicians
- Until the mid-1970s, the route to a job with a [conservation] group was by proving oneself first as a volunteer
- Conservation groups look for potential employees who will fit smoothly into the cubbyholes of their particular organization
- Fewer and fewer staff members of conservation groups are outdoorspersons
- Staff members of conservation groups today often are career-oriented
- Many people working for [conservation] groups today have a higher loyalty to the political process than to conservation
- The viability of the group itself has become more important than the conservation mission of the group
- Efficient operation has become the main concern of [conservation] groups [rather than effectiveness]
- Professional staff are frequently unfamiliar [and uninterested] with the intellectual discussions going on in the movement
- There is a growing breach between grassroots volunteer activists and professionals

Quoted from *Confessions of an Eco-Warrior*, 1991.[1] Additions or edits are bracketed.

---

1   Foreman, *Confessions of an Eco-Warrior*, 201-207.

wilderness and the wildeor. On the other hand, the trends in Table 4.4 don't hold for all wilderness and wildlife staffers. There are still some great hellions for wild things working for clubs big and little.

Note that the rungs in Table 4.4 were written in 1991 or earlier, more than twenty years ago. This plight has been steadily getting worse for a long time.

Top staffers of big conservation groups nowadays often have less of a feeling for wild things than do the members. Some leaders have jumped from wild things into the bigger political world of progressivism and the Democratic Party. Conservation and environmentalism have become too small of a pond for them. Even if they once were wild-thing conservationists, they have become more enviro-resourcist as they have hopped into the bigger puddle. They don't have time for wilderness backpacking or canoeing. Others have never been conservationists or outdoorsfolk but were always environmentalists (or resourcists). Some wilderness and wildlife outfits have hired heavy hitters from outside the conservation team, who when they set policy and cut deals for the clubs which they now lead hearken back to their resourcist outlook and training to find middle ground. Oftentimes they are hired mostly for their fundraising skills, but get to call the shots on all else whether or not they know much about conservation. Also, conservation and environmental clubs had welcome mats out for many Clinton administration staffers after the "election" of Bush Junior in 2000 and after the defeats of congressional Democrats since then. Should Obama get smothered in tea bags in 2012, the welcome mats will be put out again. Some of these government folks fit in and have been good; many, however, are the problem about which I am writing.[16]

Now, somewhat through the sway of funders and consultants, and somewhat through shaping by socially more-diverse boards for

16 Having congressional and agency staff come to work for conservation clubs has been going on since the 1930s. Such folks in the past, though, were already hard-core wildlovers.

conservation clubs, we are seeing folks from outside hired to run smaller grassroots conservation groups, too. Too many executive directors of local, state, and regional groups today have backgrounds in management and fundraising from other social-change groups or from business but lack the fire in the belly for wilderness—believe me, I know from talking to job seekers for executive director of clubs with which I've worked, and from meeting executive directors as I gadabout. Such executive directors drive policy and public relations for their groups. Wilderness and wildlife conservation gets shoved aside for enviro-resourcism. Not only do such group directors work with enviro-resourcists in foundations, consulting groups, and in politics, they bounce among them. They are building a new in-crowd within the conservation kinship, much like the old in-crowd up until the seventies, but so, so unlike it in not being at home in the wilderness. This trend began with big national groups in the late-seventies and has been spreading since. I am glad that many executive directors for smaller wilderness and wildlife bunches don't fit into this business-framed coffee klatsch, but some do and their ranks are growing.

Under the goad of organizational effectiveness, we see the same trends in how members of boards of directors of small wilderness and wildlife clubs are picked. An old western wilderness warhorse, who's been at it more than forty years, tells me that the board of the wilderness group he started (and from which he is now gone) is shifting to folks with no wilderness background or feeling. We hear from our funders and consultants that our boards need to be "socially diverse" and should have spots for those with organizational strengths, even if such folks don't have fire in the belly or have never been camping. Sooner or later, conservation group boards get watered down to look like nonprofit community boards—and then they hire executive directors and other staff for their management and fundraising skills and not for their conservation background, knowledge, and toughness.

One of the best of the Washington, D.C., conservationists writes me,

> *Even within the conservation movement there are too few people, including those in leadership positions, who come from the ranks of avid backpackers, river runners, horsepackers, hunters, anglers, backcountry skiers, etc. And it is my opinion that it has begun to show. 'Just knowing that it's there....' does not form the foundation of a strong movement. A commitment to 'progressive politics' doesn't either. Direct experience and knowledge of the wild does.*

Read the above again. It is likely the biggest "why" for what is wrong with the wilderness and wildlife network. It underlies all the other plights I write about in this book. My friend has hit the bull's eye. His word "avid" is key. It's not enough to take one's family to a National Park campground for a week or even to do a guided river trip. Or to go fly-fishing in Montana or downhill skiing in Colorado once a year. In my dog-eared dictionary, *avid* means "desirous to the point of greed; urgently eager; characterized by enthusiasm and vigorous pursuit." We're talking about having a burning yearning to be outside in the home of the wildeor away from the works of man. Recall what the matchless Will Dilg, father of the Izaak Walton League after World War One, wrote, "I am weary of civilization's madness and I yearn for the harmonious gladness of the woods and of the streams. I am tired of your piles of buildings and I ache from your iron streets. I feel jailed in your greatest cities and I long for the unharnessed freedom of the big outside."[17] Can you dream of any head of one of the big conservation clubs writing something like that for publication today? Heck, can you dream of one *thinking* that? (If there is such a one, please let me know!

17   W. H. Dilg, *Outdoor America*, Izaak Walton League, October 1927,
     quoted in Stephen Fox, *The American Conservation Movement: John Muir
     and His Legacy* (University of Wisconsin Press, Madison, 1985 (1981)),
     159.

I want to meet them.[18]) And dare not forget Leopold's first words in *A Sand County Almanac*, "There are some who can live without wild things, and some who cannot. These essays are the delights and dilemmas of one who cannot."[19]

Instead, let's look at some words from a Wilderness Society staffer today:

Commenting on calls from WildEarth Guardians to set aside more Wilderness around New Mexico's flagship Gila Wilderness Area: "It's about protecting the community and the way of life, looking really at the entire landscape around an area like the Gila and saying you can't divorce people from the landscape. They are part of the landscape just as the landscape is part of them. It's what make the character of places like this."[20] Uhh, whose side is this fellow on? To my ears this sounds like something a county commissioner or local rancher would say in an anti-wilderness community as a jab at wilderness. Now, the staffer may have thought such words would be a clever way to make a bigger Gila Wilderness smell better to "avid" wilderness-haters, but to say it to a reporter only gives ammunition to the other side.

On the other hand, the only dyed-in-the-wool legend working for TWS of late has been Bart Koehler. Fired from TWS thirty years ago by the businessman who had been hired to redo The Wilderness Society (and did he ever), Bart was hired back ten years ago by Executive Director Bill Meadows as the Wilderness Support Center was brought under TWS's wing. Meadows has been one of the best heads of national conservation groups and had enough true vision to be on The Wildlands Project board for a few years. But TWS had a big shortfall in income the

---

18　Mark that I said "big." This leaves out heads of state groups (such as Steve Capra of NMWA) or small national groups (such as Ronni Egan of Great Old Broads for Wilderness).

19　Aldo Leopold, *A Sand County Almanac: And Sketches Here and There* (Oxford University Press, New York, 1949), vii.

20　*Associated Press*, "Group pushes for more Western wilderness," March 23, 2009.

winter of 2011-12 and the governing council blamed Meadows. So he is fired and forty other staffers were booted, as well. One of these was Bart Koehler, who many feel should have been the last staffer to go. I daresay no one else in the outfit knew half as much about wilderness as Bart. So much for the goodness of TWS, which once upon a time was a family. Now it sounds like something Mitt Romney would take over and loot. I hear The Wilderness Society's board hired Jamie Williams from The Nature Conservancy to be their new executive director. I can only hope for the better. You will read about today's Nature Conservancy in the next chapter.

I'm looking at a many-leafed advertisement for *Backpacker* magazine. One sheet reads, "Our editors log hundreds of days on the trail each year furiously testing the latest gear in the most adverse weather and trail conditions." I'd like to see membership and donation pitches from conservation groups reading, "Our staff and board members log hundreds of days on the trail each year checking on threats and seeking the wisdom and insights of the wilderness in the most adverse weather and trail conditions."

There should be one overall, unbreakable law in working for a conservation club: *Our Calling to Keep Wild Things Wild Comes Before Your Career.* A pretty, eye-catching sign with those words should be hung where it can't be missed in every conservation club office. Anyone who doesn't like that bidding should not be hired. *Our Calling to Keep Wild Things Wild Comes Before Your Career.* If you don't like that, hit the road. Please. We don't need you. We don't want you. It goes for board members, too.

The social-change, enviro-resourcist hold on the conservation network arm-twists conservationists to mushy soft-talk about how "conservation is for people," to shy away from talking about wild things for their own sakes. Overall, enviro-resourcists tell wilderness and wildlife keepers to:

- Talk about people and their needs and wants
- Downplay wild things for their own sakes
- Show that Wilderness Areas draw economic growth to counties nearby
- Talk how Nature freely offers "ecosystem services," such as clean water, that would otherwise cost trillions of dollars
- Shut up about doom and gloom—Cassandra should be gagged
- Sideline biology
- Don't worry; be happy
- And—STAY ON MESSAGE (the above)

Now, some of these can help further conservation goals as steps in a carefully thought-out strategy. But if followed alone without acknowledging that we need to keep and shelter wild things for their own sakes, they are harmful. I will further go into the pitfalls of overstating utilitarian arguments for conservation in the last two chapters.

First, though, we need to look at a worse threat to the conservation network.

Enviro-resourcism straddles the fence; the conservation clubs under its sway are still conservationists even if weak of heart and meek of mind. But some of the once-greatest conservation lodges no longer straddle the fence. They've fallen off. *Onto the wrong side.* They have become straightforward resourcists. They've gone to the other camp. If they had to fall off the fence onto the wrong side, I wish they had broken like Humpty Dumpty and their yokes had drizzled into the dirt. Instead, they remade themselves and may now do more harm than good. While enviro-resourcism is mostly an ill from the progressive or social-change camp, the resourcism that now grips The Nature Conservancy and a few other big international conservation organizations comes from the right. Cleverly working to shift giant resource-extraction businesses into green do-gooders and hefty funders, instead The Nature Conservancy and others have sold themselves to logging, mining, and energy multinationals. In the next chapter, we'll see how TNC and some others have stepped away from protected areas to "working" forests, grasslands, and wetlands. Crack the whip over wild things. Make 'em work for us. Biodiversity is now a working resource for Man.

CHAPTER 5

Jumping Off the Fence:
The Nature Conservancy

We need to move past the place where we see people as essentially enemies of nature. We need to break down the barriers between urban and rural, between set-asides and sustainable use, between "us" and "them."

—Steve McCormick, President of The Nature Conservancy, 2005[1]

Conservation strategies that lack meaningful core areas are naive, arrogant, and dangerous.

--Reed Noss and co-authors[2]

THE NATURE QUISLING

Along with the murky pull of enviro resourcism away from wild things-for-their-own-sakes conservation, I see some once-leading

---

1   Steven J. McCormick, "Beyond 'Man Versus Nature,'" *Nature Conservancy, Spring 2005, 5.*

2   Reed F. Noss, Eric Dinerstein, Barrie Gilbert, Michael Gilpin, Brian J. Miller, John Terborgh, and Steve Trombulak, "Core Areas: Where Nature Reigns," in Michael E. Soulé and John Terborgh, editors, *Continental Conservation: Scientific Foundations of Regional Reserve Networks* (Island Press, Washington, DC, 1999), 105.

conservation outfits tiptoeing away from protected areas or wild havens. Tiptoeing? I wrote that a few years ago; I fear it is no longer the right word. Now it is more of a trot, or even a gallop. Here the wonderful old Nature Conservancy (TNC) stands out as a quisling to the "Nature" it once shielded on scores of matchless hot spots of biodiversity all over the United States. The chapter-heading quote above from Steve McCormick, then-President of The Nature Conservancy, forsakes the underlying beliefs and work of conservation; instead it states the beliefs and work of resourcism. The shift began about 1990 under John Sawhill, who was TNC's President before McCormick.

I was on the founding board of trustees for the New Mexico Chapter of the Conservancy in the 1970s and think I've been a member since the Late Stone Age. I long had a credit card that backed TNC. But I dropped my membership a few years ago after I saw that big business had more or less taken over TNC, and that TNC had hired top staffers who were resourcists, not Cannots, who saw Nature not as the Tree of Life to be loved and sheltered, but as raw goods to gobble for growing billions of Men. I did not want to believe this takeover of TNC by energy, mining, logging, and grazing businesses and so I put off believing what I knew until I could no longer shut my eyes to it.

The overthrow of The Nature Conservancy by big business and get-ahead resource managers plays out in ugsome shifts in how TNC cares for its lands and the wild things that dwell therein, and in TNC's thinking—philosophy, ethics, politics, and even in how the new TNC bosses see the science of biology.

There is a load of dirt in The Nature Conservancy's "portfolio" for us to look at here. Again, I'm not alone in my glumness. Some of America's leading biologists are deeply unhappy and cussedly angry over what a few sly ladder-climbers more at home with tycoons than raccoons have done to the once-great Nature Conservancy. They've done this hand-in-hand with donors and board members from big business— foremost from extractive industry and polluters, from mining, logging, energy, agricultural, chemical, development, and other landscalping and befouling multinationals. Grassroots conservationists have grown more and more upset as they see The Nature Conservancy going over to the dark side.

END OF PROTECTED AREAS FOR TNC

In 2007, the executive director of a statewide wilderness club in the West told me what he and many of his fellows in the wilderness shielding network thought, "TNC has totally lost its way. Apparently it is protecting private land so that it can even more scientifically exploit it for human benefits. And TNC donors thought their money was going to preserve habitats for wild species."

The beliefs laid out in McCormick's opening quote to this chapter are much more than a shift in how conservation should work; they are a wholesale spurning of what Nature conservation has been for over one hundred years. They also cast off what had driven The Nature Conservancy from its founding to its slipping away from conservation under John Sawhill in the 1990s.

Protected areas are the hallmark of conservation. It is what we do. It is what we have done since Yellowstone. The Wildlands Project book *Continental Conservation* says bluntly, "Conservation strategies that lack meaningful core areas are naive, arrogant, and dangerous." Resourcism instead calls for resource extraction, sustainable development, and management of whole ecosystems *without* protected areas or with only a few tokens (*ecosystem management*). *Continental Conservation* warns, "Such approaches assume a level of ecological knowledge and understanding—and a level of generosity and goodwill among those who use and manage public lands—that are simply unfounded."[3] The

3   Reed F. Noss, Eric Dinerstein, Barrie Gilbert, Michael Gilpin, Brian J. Miller, John Terborgh, and Steve Trombulak, "Core Areas: Where Nature Reigns," in Michael E. Soulé and John Terborgh, editors, *Continental Conservation: Scientific Foundations of Regional Reserve Networks* (Island Press, Washington, DC, 1999), 105. Noss's co-authors here, by the way,

new honchos of TNC are overbrimming with godlike gall in their belief that they can run wild things better than wild things can run themselves. Their new outlook gives the heave-ho to 1960s-1970s pollution fighter Barry Commoner's teaching that "Nature knows best." The "Nature" TNC now wishes to "conserve" is more garden than wilderness, no longer self-willed but willed by kindly, wise TNC gardeners, who tell beavers, "Dam here, not there." "This high, no higher." "Our neighbors fear some of you are going to come on their land, so we're going to kill half of you, okay?" The Nature Conservancy now sees biodiversity as a natural resource, not as the Tree of Life to be loved and shielded for its own sake.

We can see the harm done by the new TNC in two landscapes— the United States and the world. Here, I'll throw my rotten tomatoes at what TNC is doing in the United States; I'll go after their worldwide misdeeds in the forthcoming *True Wilderness*. Here, I'll take the TNC tale of woe only up to the rise of their chief scientist Peter Kareiva. In *True Wilderness*, I'll deal with his freakish, farfetched rewriting of what conservation is, and how he thinks he should be acknowledged as the leader of worldwide conservation.

Nonetheless, I need to touch on worldwide conservation a bit to lay the grounds for what follows in this chapter. Unlike wilderness and wildlife clubs in the United States that have been mostly grassroots and have only brought biologists on staff lately, scientists have staffed international conservation organizations since their beginnings in the 1960s. Some of these scientists have forgotten their roots and grown bureaucratic with the professional arrogance of resource managers. The shift over into resource conservation groups began thirty years ago as the International Union for the Conservation of Nature (IUCN), now the World Conservation Union (but keeping the IUCN acronym), enclasped so-called "sustainable development" along with or even

---

are among the most highly thought-of field biologists (those who still work outside and not only inside—the so-called lab rats).

instead of protected areas in Africa and elsewhere. John Oates, a leading monkey researcher in West Africa, has laid this shift bare in his unhappy but truthful book, *Myth and Reality in the Rain Forest*.[4] This trend of backing off from highly sheltered National Parks and other wild havens keeps chugging away. The World Bank and other financial overlords spurred this shift, backed by anthropologists, economists, agronomists, and other social and resource scientists. The anthology *Making Parks Work*, edited by John Terborgh and his colleagues, is a trustworthy and crushing answer to this shift to sustainable development.[5] (Terborgh, by the way, is as highly acknowledged by those in his fields of tropical rainforest ecology, top-down role of large carnivores, and conservation biology as any living biologist. Indeed, were there a Nobel Prize for outdoors biology (not the lab-rat kind), John Terborgh would likely have one.)

Although The Nature Conservancy now seems to be following the IUCN-World Bank-Brundtland Report path, there is a key unlikeness. It is not so much the international poverty-alleviation and development crowd that TNC is in bed with, but with multinational resource-extraction big business. This is a big unlikeness. Sustainable development true believers do enough harm, but they are not Plum Creek, Rio Tinto, or BP. In the United States, national TNC and some of its state chapters are heading along this big business/resource extraction bearing, and also with smaller resource businesses such as ranchers, loggers and sawmills, and housing and retail developers. This is what we will look at in the rest of this chapter, while I'll go after the international conservation sell-out in *True Wilderness*.

---

4   John F. Oates, *Myth and Reality in the Rain Forest: How Conservation Strategies Are Failing in West Africa* (University of California Press, Berkeley, 1999).

5   John Terborgh, Carel van Schaik, Lisa Davenport, and Madhu Rao, editors, *Making Parks Work: Strategies for Preserving Tropical Nature* (Island Press, Washington, DC, 2002).

THE RISE AND FALL OF THE NATURE CONSERVANCY

Understanding where The Nature Conservancy came from shows us how out of touch the new leadership is with the lore and soul of TNC. In 1917, early ecologist Victor Shelford led his fellows in the Ecological Society of America's Committee on Preservation of Natural Conditions to find spots holding representative ecological communities where succession and climax conditions were yet unaltered by civilization—in other words, patches of the most untouched forests, wetlands, grasslands, and such left in the United States. Many of these plots were small, unlike the big, sprawling landscapes in the National Forest backcountry for which Aldo Leopold and the early wilderness team were seeking.[6] Then Shelford and fellows worked to bestir government agencies and private landowners to care for them as natural areas. The ecologists knew they had to work swiftly as many of the plant communities native to the US were going fast. Old-growth Eastern Deciduous Forest, canebrakes, Tallgrass Prairie, White Pine Forest, Longleaf Pine-Wire Grass Forest, Coastal Redwood Forest, and Southwest Riparian Forest were some of the embodying North American ecosystems being shoved by settlement and landscalping down the path of the buffalo and passenger pigeon.[7] Such wild neighborhoods were the meaningful landscapes of

---

6   Paul S. Sutter, *Driven Wild* (University of Washington Press, Seattle, 2002); Dave Foreman, *Rewilding North America* (Island Press, Washington, DC, 2004). Sutter's book shows the side-by-side paths of Wilderness Area and Natural Area workers.

7   Reed Noss, Edward T. LaRoe III, and J. Michael Scott, *Endangered Ecosystems of the United States: A Preliminary Assessment of Loss and Degradation Biological Report 28* (U.S. Department of the Interior, National Biological Service, Washington, D.C., February 1995); Reed F. Noss and Robert L. Peters, *Endangered Ecosystems: A Status Report on America's Vanishing Habitat and Wildlife* (Defenders of Wildlife, Washington, D.C., December 1995). In both of these landmark works, Noss and his fellows give the often-heartbreaking loss of acres and falling percentages of what is left of scores of North American ecosystems. Their reports are key references for conservationists and every conservation office should have copies.

America as seen and felt by the grandfathers and great-grandmothers of Shelford and his biology siblings. Shelford and others knew that without swift sheltering of the tag-ends left, such leftovers of how America looked would live only in the recall of old men and women and then only in books. Shelford's Committee looked at public lands for wild neighborhoods but understood that private land held many forgotten nooks of unlogged forest in the East and plant communities throughout the US not found on public lands.

Within ten years, Shelford and other ecologists learned that we needed to keep all wildlife, too. They boldly stood up against the National Park Service's wolf slaughter in Alaska's Denali (then Mt. McKinley) National Park. Shelford wrote in the Ecological Society's 1932 "Nature Sanctuary Plan" that, "Biologists are beginning to realize that it is dangerous to tamper with nature by introducing plants and animals, or by destroying predatory animals or by pampering herbivores."[8]

After World War II, the aim of the Committee on Preservation of Natural Conditions became even more geared to shielding land—too much so for the Ecological Society, which was becoming an above-the-rumble scientific society. So those wanting to shield natural areas broke off to start the Ecologists Union in 1946, which became The Nature Conservancy in 1950. The Conservancy's calling was to find and buy key natural areas outside the public lands, help them regain health and wholeness, and then steward them as private preserves or pass them on to the Forest Service and other land management agencies. As the Conservancy grew, it began to set up state chapters to spread the workload. A chapter for New Mexico started in 1976 and I was asked to come on the fledgling board of trustees (I was the New Mexico representative for The Wilderness Society at the time).

---

8   Victor E. Shelford, "Ecological Society of America: A Nature Sanctuary Plan Unanimously Adopted by the Society, December 28, 1932," *Ecology* 14, no. 2 (April 1933): 240-245. I'll look at this work more fully in *Conservation vs. Conservation*.

But in the early 1990s, The Nature Conservancy shifted from being the leading private caretaker of the tangled Tree of Life (biodiversity) with its squirreled-away "ecological gems," to a nonprofit business boosting so-called "working ranches" and "working forests" where "happy logging" and other resource gobbling became the goal instead of sheltering wild things.[9] TNC still does some good work shielding wildlife and wild neighborhoods here and there. Unwavering conservationists still work for it; but, at the top and as its Weltanschauung, it has steadily gone over to resourcism since 1990. TNC staffers who love wild things keep their heads low or are squeezed out. Or leave in sadness or wrath.

To take TNC along its new path, TNC's leadership knew it needed to get rid of its outstanding science staff. In the 1980s, Bob Jenkins, TNC's Vice-President for Science crafted a sweeping new path to find, map, and then shelter and restore the slipping-away wild things in each state. This work was done through "Natural Heritage programs"; TNC worked with each state's wildlife and park agencies to set them up and run them. Natural Heritage programs were a strong, workable framework and became a hub for national biodiversity conservation.

Then TNC hired a new President from the business world, John Sawhill.

A leading conservation biologist and keen watcher of the natural heritage programs from that time writes me,

> *From my observations, the unraveling of TNC science began in 1990 under then-new TNC president John Sawhill. Sawhill forced the resignation of Bob Jenkins, who originated the heritage programs and their methodology and was TNC's VP for Science. Further unraveling of TNC science followed with the decision (apparently Sawhill's) to jettison the heritage program network. [The natural heritage scientists were dumped from TNC and started a new*

---

9   Tom Butler, then-editor of *Wild Earth* in Vermont, came up with "happy logging" for TNC in the Northeast.

organization, which was later named NatureServe.] *TNC did give NatureServe a sizeable severance payment, which took care of them (barely, as I understand it) until they became self-supporting.*

Erosion of science at TNC increased when Steve McCormick became president in 2001 and fired most of the top science staff and downsized the entire science program. He hired Peter Kareiva as one of his "lead scientists."

TNC did not fill their chief scientist position until recently, when Kareiva transitioned into that role, which may have happened before McCormick resigned in 2007, but probably not until under the new TNC president, Mark Tercek (who in my opinion is their worst president yet!).[10]

The Nature Conservancy's Shameful "Stewardship"

TNC's cocksure garden-path has led to sundry other stumbles that harm the soundness of TNC's biodiversity "reserves" and bigger "working" landscapes, and TNC's fellowship with conservationists.[11] Wildlovers among TNC's members and donors and in other conservation clubs have been aghast at how TNC has cared for some of its lands and for the wildlife living there, and upset at how badly TNC has worked with smaller conservation clubs and teams.

Setting aside small to middling natural areas is what TNC did wonderfully well, but lording over sweeping empires of "working" timberlands in the Northeast and big cattle ranches in Wyoming is a whole other thing. Ten years ago, the *Los Angeles Times* found that "Nearly half of the 7 million acres that the conservancy said it is protecting in the United States is now being grazed, logged, farmed,

---

10   Tercek comes from Wall Street.

11   I first wrote "other conservationists," then recalled that TNC was no longer a true conservation outfit.

drilled or put to work in some fashion."[12] Since then, the "working land" sleazy, sneaky scam and misspeak has become even more the overlord of TNC holdings.[13] I now think of TNC as a business kind of the "multiple-use" United States Forest Service. Under Sawhill and McCormick, TNC's resource management was said to be done with a light touch, with "biodiversity" the "resource," and with ecological restoration the goal. That's the spin—but other things have been seen on the ground. (It's gotten worse, as we'll see, with Peter Kareiva as TNC Chief Scientist; biodiversity is no longer even the stated goal.) For one, the head of the Wyoming TNC office in the 2000s, who wangled cattle-grazing onto TNC lands, had an anti-wolf bumper sticker on his office wall, a scientist who worked there then has told me. In one western state, wildlovers began calling The Nature Conservancy "The Open Space Conservancy" in the early 1990s; in the Northeast, wilderness watchdogs griped unhappily about "The Logging Conservancy."

One of the great little-known leaders of the conservation network in the last half of the twentieth century is Huey Johnson of California. He was The Nature Conservancy's first Western region manager some forty to fifty years ago and then Secretary of Resources for California Governor Jerry Brown. In 2002, he said, "I knew the founders of this organization [The Nature Conservancy] on a first-name basis, and they would be turning over in their graves" about the drilling, grazing, logging, and so on being done by TNC on its lands.[14]

The Nature Conservancy was started and long run by naturalists; ornithologists and birders were much of the backbone of the outfit. For

---

12 Janet Wilson, "The enemy within," *Los Angeles Times,* September 8, 2002.

13   Steve Trombulak, "Wild Forests ARE Working Forests: Some Thoughts on the Language of Despoilment," *Wild Earth* Fall 1998, 73-76. Trombulak, a top conservation biologist and professor at Middlebury College, rips to shreds The Nature Conservancy's "working forest" blather to mean logging.

14   Wilson, "enemy within."

a score of years, though, bird lovers have been harsh chiders of TNC's phony stewardship. What should be one of TNC's most carefully and lovingly stewarded reserves is the Texas City Prairie Preserve, a 2,263-acre home for the highly endangered Attwater's Prairie Chicken, in the oil patch of east Texas. In 2002, there were only forty of the prairie grouse left in the whole world, down from almost one million not long ago. Half of the last birds live on the TNC preserve. The Conservancy also runs a thickly spread natural gas drilling and pumping business on the less than four square miles they own for the prairie chicken. Oh, TNC also grazes the "preserve" with cattle. A TNC spokesman said of the drilling and grazing, "We believe the opportunity we have in Texas City to raise significant sums of money for conservation is one we cannot pass up." He further said TNC was "convinced" the industrialization on the little "reserve" wouldn't hurt the Attwater's Prairie Chickens. But the president of The Wildlife Society and the man who knows prairie chickens best, Clait Braun, said, "There are no data to indicate that the Attwater's prairie chicken can coexist with oil and gas drilling." And "The Nature Conservancy is speaking out both sides of its mouth: 'We can have this wildlife, and we can make money, too.' ... Well, that's not true. They're exploiting the Attwater's prairie chicken to make money."[15] The Wildlife Society, by the way, is not known as an activist or hardcore bunch—it is a professional society for wildlife biologists.

Fishy land deals with big backers thrust The Nature Conservancy into the news spotlight and before Congress in 2005 thanks to a series of deep-digging investigative articles in *The Washington Post*.[16] It seems some rich folks were giving TNC big bucks to buy nature reserves and then getting a slice for a lovely, hideaway holiday home site. As the story was about to break, I got a call from the President of TNC (McCormick) asking me to talk to the *Post* reporters about

15   Wilson, "enemy within."
16   Joe Stephens and David B. Ottaway, "Senators Question Conservancy's Practices: End to 'Insider' and 'Side' Deals by Nonprofit Organizations Is Urged," *The Washington Post*, June 8, 2005.

how much good the Conservancy had done. As a well-known "radical conservationist" but longtime friend of TNC, he hoped I could offset some of the shady dealing harm. Though I had growing qualms about TNC, I thought of doing his bidding—I liked him and, darn it, I still loved The Nature Conservancy. But after calling some better in the know, I couldn't do it. I felt badly.

I was taken aback by this shoddy behavior—I never thought such dirt would get stuck to the boots of TNC. It helped me see what kind of bigwigs were now helping to call the shots in the Conservancy. Was real estate overwhelming wild neighborhoods on TNC's to-do list? As a share of their so-called "portfolio?" (Beware any land-shielding group that calls their reserves a portfolio; you know business has too big a seat at their table.) This shady deal-making said something about the kind of folks coming into TNC as staff, trustees, and donors. Now The Nature Conservancy was full of big players and high rollers, not frumpy-looking folks with binoculars and beat-up old hats.

Some TNC members and donors became wroth when the stewards of a Nature Conservancy ranch in Kansas poisoned hundreds of prairie dogs on the TNC-owned land. Moreover, they put out the worst poison for the job and they failed to get the legally needed permit for poisoning from the right agencies in Kansas. Now, this "reserve" is in a benighted county in Kansas that bans prairie dogs (maybe they will next ban clean air). TNC holds that they did the poisoning so that none of their prairie dogs would slip over to ranches owned by crotchety wildlife-haters. They thought playing whack-the-varmints with such neighbors would lead to the county leaving alone the prairie dogs in the middle of TNC's ranch. This grisly behavior has led some landowners from Atlantic to Pacific to drop out of easement deals with TNC and some donors to write off TNC. Wildlife shielding clubs and some scientists were madder than hell when news of the sin came out (along with TNC's forlorn spinning).[17] We can lay this sad tale side-by-

17   Mike Corn, "Attitudes toward prairie dogs mixed," *Hays Daily News,* September 17, 2006.

side with a gain for prairie dogs in Mora County, New Mexico.

Brian Miller, steward of the Thaw Charitable Trust's Wind River Ranch on the Mora River, sees healthy prairie dog towns as key for rebuilding the former cattle ranch's land health (he did his Ph.D. on black-footed ferrets and is widely acknowledged for knowing prairie dogs, the prey for ferrets). Mora County also had a throwback ordinance against bringing prairie dogs into the county. It had gone through with little thought a few years earlier when these anti-prairie dog ordinances became the thing to do in hinterland counties. Well, everyone loves Brian and he is a great neighbor to the ranchers around Wind River Ranch. The County Commission tossed the ordinance and the neighbors didn't object to starting the prairie dog colony on the Wind River Ranch. Brian has since run some workshops on Wind River to show how prairie dogs are good for grasslands, and takes visiting school groups to the colony.

For at least thirty years, TNC has often dealt with other conservationists in a cheeky and smarter-than-thou way. But only in the last ten years have they worked against land-shielding goals held by other conservationists. Does the leadership of TNC know how disliked TNC is among other conservationists? Or even among some of its own staff? Former members? I'll give just two tales of how TNC has gone against others. Since the 1930s, conservationists have worked to shield the lands of the Colorado Plateau. Nowhere else in the world is there such a landscape: an eye-stretching dryland of sandstone slickrock, weathered by wind and rain and frost into buttes, slot canyons, and arches, with mighty canyons carved by big rivers flowing with the snowmelt-water of high mountains far away. Not only was this the last truly unknown landscape in the Lower 48 states, it held the biggest roadless area until Glen Canyon Dam flooded the heart of it in the 1960s. President Franklin D. Roosevelt's Secretary of the Interior Harold Ickes worked for a four-million-acre National Monument in the 1930s. World War II put aside Ickes's hope that Roosevelt would proclaim it. In the 1960s,

Kennedy's Secretary of the Interior Stewart Udall worked hard for an 800,000-acre Canyonlands National Park, smaller indeed than Ickes' great dream and even smaller after the senators and representatives of Utah and the West wore it down (at 337,570 acres, the Park ended up less than half of what Udall wanted and less than one-tenth of what Ickes wanted). Since then, we've worked to make it bigger and to set up Wilderness Areas on BLM and National Forest lands nearby.[18] As long as he lived, Udall spurred us to make the Park bigger.

In the fall of 2010, Utah conservation clubs met with then-Senator Robert Bennett's staff about filling out Canyonlands National Park with some of the public lands next to it. Clubs and teams from the fairly mellow Grand Canyon Trust to the tough Southern Utah Wilderness Alliance (SUWA) "all had well thought out proposals for park 'completion.' The Nature Conservancy stood out in their opposition to park expansion as it might affect grazing at the Dugout Ranch," wrote Brooke Williams of SUWA. So much for TNC showing how livestock grazing could be done in way that fit with land protection. When an opening to enlarge one of America's greatest National Parks came along, TNC was more worried about a few scrawny cows for which it has a permit on BLM land that would be put in the Park than in the wildland itself. Here TNC behaved like a run-of-the-mill benighted rancher, caring about their commercial grazing and not about a great hope for the land. They tipped their hat on how they saw the Canyonlands in a press release about their "partnering" with the Dugout Ranch, which leases thousands of acres of public land for cattle grazing. The press release began, "The Colorado Plateau is a landscape in crisis. Climate change coupled with increasing human demands are *threatening the region's* natural resources and communities."[19] Whoa. What about the

---

18   Dave Foreman and Howie Wolke, *The Big Outside Revised Edition* (Harmony Books, New York, 2002), 253. In 2002, the whole roadless area with Canyonlands NP at its heart was 875,000 acres.

19   The Nature Conservancy, "A New Resource on the Range: Utah Ranch Becomes a Living Laboratory," October 25, 2010.

local communities scalping the land for over one hundred years? It's the wild things and wilderness of the Colorado Plateau that are threatened, but TNC doesn't talk about that.

In Maine in 2011, a state court turned down a "sprawling resort and residential development in the Moosehead Lake region" by the big logging and land development business Plum Creek, widely thought a thug by wildlovers. Conservationists and sportsmen cheered the ruling that would stop the wrecking of one of Maine's loveliest and most loved landscapes. Plum Creek appealed the ruling. Then The Nature Conservancy jumped into the legal case—by joining Plum Creek in its appeal.[20]

I could keep going with sad tales from my files, but they would only be more of the same.

Big Business Takes Over The Nature Conservancy

Why has this happened? One big thing drove this shift from conservation to resourcism. Staffers at The Nature Conservancy have told me that the clout of corporate donors and the business bigwigs on TNC's board have been the key.

In short, big business has taken over TNC. I don't see this as a conspiracy; it was good, clever, business—seeing an opening and leaping through it. Businesses do this to each other all the time; it's how Mitt Romney got so rich. "What is it that the new leadership of TNC wants most of all? Money. Who has lots of money? We do," thought the sharp businessmen asked to give big bucks or to sit on TNC's board. They also prodded TNC to hire folks who were more businesslike and friendlier to big resource-extraction industry. With TNC, it didn't take long for the fat cats to reshape the outfit and to shift its goals and thinking. Those who would go against the new path were fired—such as the science and natural heritage staff back in the 1990s. Then TNC

20   Associated Press, "Nature Conservancy sides with Plum Creek in Maine," April 27, 2011.

found scientists like Peter Kareiva who would fit in and see it as a way to become a Big Shot.

THE END OF PROTECTED AREAS?

Steve McCormick, the President of TNC in 2005, wrote, "We need to move past the place where we see people as essentially enemies of nature. We need to break down the barriers between urban and rural, between set-asides and sustainable use, between 'us' and 'them.'"[21] These are upset-the-apple-cart words to wilderness and wildlife conservation. They butt heads with what the founders of the Society for Conservation Biology believe. Michael Soule' and Bruce Wilcox wrote in the first chapter of the 1980 landmark book *Conservation Biology* that "nature reserves" are "the little fragments of landscape where Man expects to preserve nonhuman life." Moreover, they wrote, "Nature reserves are the most valuable weapon in our conservation arsenal."[22] The heart and soul of conservation biology is the optimum design of protected areas or wild havens. The bedrock work of the wilderness and wildlife conservation network for well over one hundred years has been setting aside wild havens of sundry kinds. When TNC lost that wisdom, they lost most of their worth for conservation. What Soulé and Wilcox write is wise and free of gall, with a goal of keeping all life and evolution's hope for life tomorrow. On the other hand, McCormick's words about doing away with set-asides highlight how TNC's target shifted in the early 1990s under Sawhill by taking on "working" cattle ranches and "working" sawtimber forests. The shapers of TNC today aim to raise institutional money from and rub shoulders with the movers and shakers of the industrial world.

---

21 Steven J. McCormick, "Beyond 'Man Versus Nature,'" *Nature Conservancy*, Spring 2005, 5.

22 Michael E. Soule and Bruce A. Wilcox, "Conservation Biology: Its Scope and Its Challenge," in Michael E. Soule and Bruce A. Wilcox, editors, *Conservation Biology: An Evolutionary-Ecological Perspective* (Sinauer Associates, Sunderland, MA, 1980), 4.

TNC's new road has long been the way of hard resourcism and Man's overweening gall. It is worrisome what this could mean for the scores of little reserves long owned and cared for by TNC as toughly sheltered wild neighborhoods for threatened wildeors and ecosystems. Members and donors need to know how well TNC is going to care for awesome spots such as Sonoita Creek and Ramsey Canyon in Arizona. What does "breaking down the barrier between set-asides and sustainable use" truly mean? Why, it means nothing less than the end of protected areas. The "barrier," after all, is the barbed-wire fence that keeps hungry cattle, yahoos on ATVs, and firewood-cutters out of the lush, tangled, healthy Sonoita Creek riparian forest where live birds and grow wild blossoms that seldom can be seen elsewhere in the United States. This "breaking down the barrier" whim belittles the whole thought of wild havens. It goes against what we have learned about Man and wildlands. It rings of the way the U.S. Forest Service spoke against Wilderness Areas. It is pissing on the lore and bequest of conservation, public and private, since Yellowstone National Park was withdrawn in 1872. The only way "to move past the place where we see people as essentially enemies of nature" is for people to quit being the enemies of nature. The best way we have found to do that is with "set-asides." And barriers—by wall or law—are the only way to keep landscalping out of the loveliest, most winsome, and wildly tangled "hot spots of biodiversity" in The Nature Conservancy's "portfolio" of land and water riches. Not so long ago, The Nature Conservancy was all about sheltering the "Last Great Places." Not only have they dropped that campaign, they do their best to hide that they ever did it.

Matchless "hot spots" of biological diversity have been bought and set aside by TNC over the years; that work is far and away the most worthwhile thing TNC has done, and for buying and caring for such "hot spots of biodiversity" TNC earns backing—but only for such work. The Nature Conservancy's help in buying bottomland-woods in Arkansas for the Ivory-billed Woodpecker stands out. I don't know now if an Ivorybill was truly seen, but big steps were taken to keep and rebuild the best kind of neighborhood for it. Whether or not any Ivorybills are there, a throng of other Earthlings now have a better home in the White River bottomland big woods.

Within the staff of The Nature Conservancy are conservationists of all kinds working on keeping whole the best homes for wild things. Alack, they are now being wedded to resource managers who want to show how wildlife and their neighborhoods can be healthy without "set-asides" and where gas is drilled, trees are logged, cows eat the grass, and tucked-away plots are sold to high rollers for get-away starter castles. In a way, we see the whole twentieth-century dustup between resource conservationists and Nature conservationists being replayed within the organization and lands of The Nature Conservancy today. Resourcism has won hands down.

PETER KAREIVA AND THE END OF WILDNESS

Peter Kareiva, chief scientist for TNC (who says he's not a "biodiversity guy"), was lead author of worrisome papers in *Science* and in *Scientific American* in 2007. The articles took conservationists and biologists aback. The title alone of one in *Science* is a broadside against the beliefs and work of the "old" Nature Conservancy: "Domesticated Nature: Shaping Landscapes and Ecosystems for Human Welfare." I find it nothing less than a declaration of war against wild things. Kareiva says that shielding wild things for their own sakes is a "failed conservation strategy" and must be set aside for "conservation" for people.[23] What is wrong with this belief is that shielding wild things for themselves is not a strategy but a deep-seated ethic, as I've shown throughout this book. Furthermore, without past conservation work throughout the

23   Peter Kareiva, Sean Watts, Robert McDonald· and Tim Boucher, "Domesticated Nature: Shaping Landscapes and Ecosystems for Human Welfare." *Science* June 29, 2007, Vol. 316, 1866-1869; Peter Kareiva and Michelle Marvier, "Conservation for the People," *Scientific American*, October 2007.

Earth, the Tree of Life would be in far worse shape and we would have lost many more Earthlings in the wild. Kareiva shows no mark that he is one like Aldo Leopold who cannot live without wild things. Indeed, his strategy of conserving only what helps Man, makes the 3.5-billion-year-old Tree of Life wholly a resource for Man and means the end of wildness. Kareiva and coauthors have written that Man shapes or harms in some way the whole Earth, so there are no longer any truly wild or untouched spots. Conservationists have known that since before I was born. But Kareiva and crowd then say therefore we should give up on keeping wilderness and wildeors. Instead we should go with the flow and tame everything with enlightened ecological management. Knowledgeable conservationists and conservation biologists have sadly known for some time how thoroughly we've wounded Earth. But even if there are no wholly untouched wild lands or waters, we should still work our butts off to keep them as wild as they are and to rewild them as much as possible.

I don't have room here to go deeper into why this is a howling bad thought, but it means giving up and ending the fight for wild things. Kareiva's article has upset conservationists and conservation biologists to no end. But it is the path TNC began following even before McCormick wrote about ending "set-asides." Their path is that the needs of Man always lord over the needs of all other Earthlings. I'll take on Kareiva's end-of-wild-things and Man-first thoughts in *True Wilderness*, along with the others riding that bandwagon. As well as I can tell, Kareiva and none of his fellow Earth-tamers have had true time in wilderness or run-ins with wildeors.

Indeed, Kareiva flat-out damns wildlovers who are "insensitive to humans with needs that might supersede biodiversity."[24] This is what Gifford Pinchot and other resourcists would have said about John Muir and friends one hundred and ten years ago, with only the words updated.

---

24   Peter Kareiva, Robert Lalasz, and Michelle Marvier, "Anthropocene Revisited," *Breakthrough Journal*, April 2012.

It is full-on resourcism from The Nature Conservancy. "Superseding" the needs of all other life (biodiversity) for the needs of Man is truly the root of mass extinction and other wounds to Earth. Getting Mankind to self-brake and to put the needs of the Tree of Life ahead of ours at long last is what true conservation is about. With his stand Kareiva has taken himself and The Nature Conservancy off the fence onto the side of the foes of Nature conservation and wild things. Kareiva's beliefs are what the wilderness-wildlife network has been fighting since the days of John Muir. He is no conservation leader; rather he is a leading foe of conservation.

The American news business, with the *New York Times* in the lead, has given Peter Kareiva a soapbox as no true conservationist, scientist or not, has been given. We may ask why the news business builds up Kareiva. It's the same as with the Danish phony environmentalist, Bjorn Lomborg, a few years back—the old "man bites dog is news" deal. Because Kareiva flips long-standing conservation on its head, his blather draws the news like rotten meat draws flies. What the news business doesn't understand is that Kareiva, like Lomborg before him, is not a conservationist. He is a resourcist at home with the old timber beasts of the Forest Service and dam builders of the Bureau of Reclamation. He's nothing new at all; he's a throwback to the beliefs and work that conservationists fought throughout the twentieth century.

What makes someone a conservationist (of the Nature conservationist kind)? Aldo Leopold gave us the key: they do not want to live without wild things. Conservationists are also most often some kind of outdoorsman (woman) and naturalist. Then they stand with David Ehrenfeld and others in chiding Mankind for its overweening gall toward Earth and its Tree of Life.[25] I do not think Kareiva and his crowd meet any of this bill of fare.

25   David Ehrenfeld, *The Arrogance of Humanism* (Oxford University Press, New York, 1978).

Though I have a pretty strong stomach for reading and understanding those who work for Man taking over more of the wild world (knowing your foes is a wisdom from the first stirrings of empire in China), I can only take so much reading of today's overblown blather from TNC. Nonetheless, I've made myself plow through some of TNC's self-tooting from the last few years. I gather from it that they now more or less take these stands:

- Multinational resource-extraction and development corporations are on the whole trustworthy, good world-citizens, who want to protect biodiversity while making Mankind healthier and wealthier.
- Conservationists greatly overstate the harm Man has done and is doing to Earth and wild things.
- "Nature" is "highly resilient" and bounces back once we grub out whatever it is that we want.
- The goal of conservation is to help Mankind; the economic benefits of biodiversity should always be first.
- Moreover, TNC and its fellows such as World Wildlife Fund and Conservation International, hold that they are the leaders of the conservation movement, although they are widely loathed by conservation biologists, grassroots conservationists, and many former members, staff, and donors to TNC, WWF, and CI.

The Nature Conservancy shows its ties to resource-extraction corporations by working with them in ICCF—International Conservation Caucus Foundation, which brags, "Achieving global conservation solutions by uniting Corporate Leaders, NGOs, Policymakers."[26]

See Table 5.1 for how The Nature Conservancy now grounds itself with ICCF.

---

26 http://iccfoundation.us/

It is glaring to me that in nearly every way, The Nature Conservancy is no longer a Nature Conservation organization but a Resource Conservation one; they are far more Pinchot than Muir. Sorry. That is unfair. To Gifford Pinchot.

The great threat from Peter Kareiva and The Nature Conservancy is how their thinking is the hot, new thing for conservation funders in the Consultative Group for Biological Diversity and the Environmental Grantmakers Association. Kareivaism has little sway among grassroots conservationists—most have likely never heard of him. But if the grantmakers wowed by Kareiva's resourcism start to shove it onto the wilderness and wildlife clubs and teams they fund, it could well lead to the Waterloo of enviro-resourcism and conservation. Which could be good or bad hinging on who is Bonaparte and who is Wellington.

Author Mary McCarthy famously said of literary critic and her political foe Lillian Hellman, "Every word she writes is a lie, including 'and' and 'the.'" Well, since I'm sweeter than Mary, I'll say only that I now think that every word in The Nature Conservancy's name is a lie, *except* "The."

So. I've dropped my Nature Conservancy credit card and, along with many others I know, have dropped my TNC membership. After having loved the work of The Nature Conservancy for many years, I am deeply sad.

**Table 5.1. What Conservation Must Look Like
in the 21ˢᵗ Century**

From the ICCF Conservation Update July 11, 2011
Environmental influence has been dwindling ever since
the mid 70s, partially due to the public's association of the
movement with "fortress conservation"—an uncompromising
stance on environmental conservation that ignores
human needs

Leaders in the conservation movement have adopted an
alternative stance that incorporates human resource use into
conservation

The Nature Conservancy promotes a realistic approach to
conservation by collaborating with corporations to leverage
their resources, and emphasizes the economic value of
ecosystem services in a market context

There is a direct connection between international
conservation and ...
- U.S. competitiveness
- U.S. national security
- Sustainable supply chains for U.S. businesses
- Americans' health
- Goodwill toward America around the world

CHAPTER 6

Society for Conservation Biology: Slipping Away from Protected Areas

*There simply is no precedent for what is happening to the
biological fabric of this planet and there are no words to
express the horror of those who love nature.*
—Michael Soulé and Bruce Wilcox, 1980[1]

MY FIRST MEETING WITH CONSERVATION BIOLOGY came from Michael
Soulé and Bruce Wilcox's 1980 anthology, *Conservation Biology: An
Evolutionary-Ecological Perspective,* which was forthright, bold, and
full of heart. Tom Lovejoy, then with the World Wildlife Fund, in the
"Foreword" said bluntly, "This reduction in the biological diversity of
the planet is the most basic issue of our time."[2] Soulé and Wilcox wrote,
"There simply is no precedent for what is happening to the biological
fabric of this planet and there are no words to express the horror of

1   Michael E. Soulé and Bruce A. Wilcox, "Conservation Biology: Its
    Scope And Its Challenge," in Michael E. Soulé and Bruce A. Wilcox, edi-
    tors, *Conservation Biology: An Evolutionary-Ecological Perspective* (Sinauer
    Associates, Inc., Sunderland, MA, 1980), 7-8.
2   Thomas E. Lovejoy, "Foreword," in *Conservation Biology,* ix.

those who love nature."[3] Such words hit me with a flash of insight and understanding—as well as fellowship. This landmark anthology followed the 1978 Conservation Biology Conference called by Soulé in San Diego. The conference and the book were the lift-off for the activist science of conservation biology.

I read *Conservation Biology* shortly after helping to start Earth First! and it gave me my new path, a deeper understanding of what conservation needed to do, and a new thrust for my Earth First! sermons. The anthologies edited by Soulé, *Conservation Biology: An Evolutionary-Ecological Perspective* (1980) (with Wilcox) and *Conservation Biology: The Science of Scarcity and Diversity* (1986), underlined how conservation science could better lead the way protected areas were chosen, designed, and cared for.[4] That is what I did—for ten years I had worked on getting Wilderness Areas designated by Congress. Howie Wolke and I wanted Earth First! to take the lead on shaping Wilderness Areas more as ecological wild havens than recreational ones. Conservation biology was what I needed and—bingo!—here it was.

"Nature reserves," wrote Soulé and Bruce Wilcox in the first anthology, "are the most valuable weapon in our conservation arsenal."[5] (Put that alongside McCormick's puffery about doing away with set-asides.) Likewise, the target for the Society for Conservation Biology

3   Michael E. Soulé and Bruce A. Wilcox, "Conservation Biology: Its Scope And Its Challenge," in *Conservation Biology*, 7-8.

4   Soulé and Wilcox's *Conservation Biology* was one of the first books sold by the *Earth First! Journal*. The publisher told me in the late-1980s that we had sold more copies of it than any other bookseller. One of the best deeds of 1980s Earth First! was how we brought awareness of conservation biology to the wilderness and wildlife conservation network and taught it through book sales and through articles by Reed Noss in *Earth First!*. Back then I said that the two conservation groups to first head down the conservation biology track were Earth First! and The Nature Conservancy. Haw! Neither of the outfits waving those names today are the same as the ones in the 1980s.

5   Soulé and Wilcox, *Conservation Biology*, 4.

and its journal, *Conservation Biology,* from their beginnings in 1985 and 1987, and for another score of years was on protected areas. All of this underscored what wildlovers have long known: *Conservation without tough protected areas is not conservation.*

For nearly ten years, though, there have been worrisome trends in the Society for Conservation Biology (SCB) and more than a few of its scientist members have backed away from the no-time-to-waste, wild-loving, hallowed fight called by Michael Soulé and other founders thirty-five years ago. One former leader tells me, "Major attempts at internationalization and attendant political correctness (which began around 2001) hastened SCB's downfall." There are still good folks in SCB and a snarling catfight about where to go. Overall, the North American section of SCB, which has its own board and president and annual meeting, is yet good. But, in the whole SCB, many of the old-timers are giving up and heading off elsewhere. One former board president I know has dropped his membership. Like TNC's brass, though, some in SCB would go head over heels to resourcism and away from keeping and restoring wild things for their own sakes.

From the early 2000s on, the Society for Conservation Biology has rather remade itself from a kith of scientists with a "mission" to stop wholesale extinction and to bring back species and ecosystems, into one that now bills itself as "The International Organization of Conservation Professionals." This new byword is about as thrilling and farsighted as "The International Organization of Sidewalk Professionals." Portland State political science and law professor David Johns, who has long helped SCB from his leadership perch with The Wildlands Project, writes that "an effort to grow membership doesn't necessarily represent an abandonment of mission"; but he then acknowledges that "maturing organizations tend to be more concerned with organization than mission." He recalls that some SCB presidents in the 1990s were not "staunch conservationists but often concerned with the profession's legitimacy and were quite cautious."

Such shifts have led one hoary, farsighted conservation biologist to grouse about writing an essay called "Whatever Happened to Conservation Biology?" Some former and sitting members of the board of governors of the Society for Conservation Biology have told me that SCB has lost its "mission-zeal," as it truly has become an organization for international professionals in conservation and resource management. One unburdened himself to me, "To the degree SCB emphasizes itself as a professional society rather than a more mission oriented group of people, the magazine gets inundated by people looking to publish, etc. ... Many folks are concerned about this trend inside the organization...." Johns warns that while this is true, it doesn't mean one side has "won." But my other insider says, "As SCB has grown, it has moved toward being a 'professional society,' meaning that it is a venue for publishing and giving papers (both important for careers), and for networking."

The Wildlife Society and Ecological Society of America became such clubs for professionals long ago, it seems to me. The Society for Conservation Biology was started somewhat (maybe unacknowledged or even unwittingly) because The Wildlife Society and Ecological Society of America were no longer mission-oriented and were becoming old-bones-stiff with professionalism. I worry that SCB could go even further down that hallway to become an International Society for Biodiversity Management on the frame of the Society for Range Management. Nowadays, articles in *Conservation Biology* help one on to tenure. David Johns nods his head that "a good deal of what is published is not terribly helpful to conservation." I read fewer and fewer articles in the journal. SCB meetings become job fairs. The Ragnarok of extinction is nudged away by career ladder climbing.

Even more worrisome, however, is that social scientists working with tribes, big-organization boosters of sustainable development (them again), and wilderness and wild-haven deconstructionists have wormed their way in, thereby weakening faithfulness to toughly protected areas. Their articles asking about the worth of wild havens and ripping conservation biology greats such as John Terborgh have led to ongoing brawls in *Conservation Biology.*

John Terborgh writes that, while in North America it is the political right that is against protected areas, in "Latin America it comes from the left in the guise of environmentalism. I refer to the *socioambientalista* movement." They "seek to rectify past injustices and current inequities by keeping the frontier open" for distribution to the poor. They consider conservationists who propose protected areas as "ideological archenemies."[6] Such socioambientalistas now seem to be welcome in the Society for Conservation Biology and their letters and articles questioning and undercutting protected areas and biodiversity conservation in the journal give the wrong feeling that wild havens are being truly questioned as the heart of conservation. In *True Wilderness,* I'll further look at how socioambientalistas wilt wilderness and wildlife conservation.

"I think North America is like South America," says another old-timer after reading Terborgh's letter. "Folks like Kareiva (certainly leftist) are now against protected areas because they are elitist, biased for native species, bad for native Americans because they were supposedly kicked out to make some Parks...." Though Peter Kareiva and those with him work with and praise multinational resource-extraction businesses, they stir their bilge against wild havens with social-justice rhetoric.

Giving room for such babble in *Conservation Biology* seems as wise as acknowledging Republican presidential candidates' cockeyed potshots at the "hoax" of overwhelming climate upset as worthwhile, or slipping "intelligent design" into the curricula of high school science classes to "teach the controversy." From what I have seen, the socioambientalistas

---

6   John Terborgh, "Letters," *Conservation Biology,* Vol. 19, No. 1, February 2005, 5-6. One could translate socioambientalista into English as social-environmentalist.

and some of their social-science friends in the United States, Canada, Australia, and Europe are no more earnest for keeping wild things than are the politicians who tell lies about the Endangered Species Act. Moreover, rightwing members of Congress and other shills for rip-it-out businesses have learned from the socioambientalistas to play their clients as forlorn, penniless victims in an embattled subculture threatened by snooty elites.

The seeming righteous believability of the socioambientalistas leads folks to overlook all the South American conservation biologists who are working their hearts and souls out to set up more wild havens for threatened wildlife, shielded from hunting and landscalping. Indeed, the 2012 big shove to water down the Brazilian Forest Code, which tells landowners to leave much of their land in uncut forest, is being made by the Communist Party of Brazil. Aldo Rebelo, the "charismatic leader" of the Communist Party "says that with the Brazilian population expanding, the country needs to produce more food—and expanding land use is the obvious thing to do."[7]

In the same 2005 issue of *Conservation Biology* as Terborgh's letter, there was a politically correct review knocking a book Terborgh helped edit, *Making Parks Work.*[8] The reviewers, the CenTREAD Working Group, were in Environmental Studies at the University of California Santa Cruz (UCSC). This made their review twofold bad since the Environmental Studies Department at UCSC was begun by the farsighted conservationist Ray Dasmann, and was later chaired by Michael Soulé. Anticonservation social scientists have become a fifth column within SCB and the whole field of Environmental Studies.[9]

7   http://www.bbc.co.uk/news/science-environment-13544000
8   CenTREAD Working Group, "Making Parks Work: a Thought-Provoking Argument, but Not a Guide," *Conservation Biology*, Vol. 19, No. 1, February 2005, 279-281.
9   However, I have met some wonderful teachers, wildlovers, and natural historians in Environmental Studies Departments where I have been brought in to speak.

One steadfast older conservation biologist tells me, "The SCB has been hijacked by the socioambientalistas and *Conservation Biology* is now publishing a lot of soft-headed, sentimental, touchy-feely stuff that is poison for the kind of conservation we advocate. This is completely denaturing *CB* as the voice of our movement and sowing grand confusion in the minds of our colleagues and the public." Since he wrote me, things have gotten much worse at the journal. Another top conservation biologist told me this year, "A few years ago, the board stupidly changed the editorial structure and operations of the journal and are now micromanaging it horribly. Very recently, all three former editors-in-chief—Ehrenfeld, Noss, and Meffe—resigned from the editorial board in protest, along with at least a third of the editorial board."

Conservation Biology ran an article in 2005 by a social scientist carping about how hard it was to work with biologists on an interdisciplinary project about sea turtles.[10] She was upset about how hard she found it to get articles published and unhappy that biologists didn't cite her articles that were published. Her overriding worry was how this would lame her quest for tenure. She also was unhappy that "natural scientists working with a charismatic species are more often than not conservationists." My goodness, these biologists liked the sea turtles they were studying! And they likely wanted to shelter them from poaching! I wonder if a social scientist working on an interdisciplinary research product with medical researchers would be upset if they cared about a woman's health? At least she was truthful enough to write that "the advocacy positions of social and natural scientists may be fundamentally different and can cause conflict." She further wrote that "conservation biologists working in an interdisciplinary context may have to suspend their own advocacy activities for the sake of the

---

10   Lisa Campbell, "Overcoming Obstacles to Interdisciplinary Research," *Conservation Biology*, Vol. 19. No. 2, April 2005, 574-577.

broader project goals."[11] In other words, run-of-the-mill academic research projects that help one get tenure outweigh shielding wildlife from extinction.

Such crap notwithstanding, SCB has among its folks some of the most unafraid, forthright, wild-loving field biologists of all nationalities, working throughout the world in grueling and sometimes deadly settings. They are my lionhearts. And *Conservation Biology* still has some good articles on how to better design protected areas, research on how humans ransack wilderness, and stirring thoughts about the goodness of other beings for their own sakes. Bringing in paltry, Man-worshipping social analysis belittles and waters down conservation biology's mission. (Social analysis in the *service* of this mission is needed and welcome.) The creeping resourcism ideology in *Conservation Biology* comes with Subcommandante-Marcos ski masks instead of red suspenders and checkered wool shirts or boardroom suits.

On the other hand, the Ecological Society of America (ESA) seems to be getting a little more fire in the belly. Recall that the forerunner to The Nature Conservancy was an ESA committee until after World War Two. Three or four years ago, Josh Tewksbury at the University of Washington pulled together a new Natural History Section for the ESA. Both Tom Fleischner and Reed Noss have spoken at its meetings. It will nudge and coax biology undergrads and graduate students into learning about natural history and drawing on it for their research. As SCB loses sight of the big outside, maybe ESA is building a new home for biologists who care about wild things. Sadly, nearly all of those who come to the Natural History symposia at the ESA annual meeting are "in the 45-75 age group." Biology professors need to work to bring natural history into the career track for their students. Indeed, that may be the key chore in university biology departments. In something of a turnaround, The Wildlife Society also seems to be getting feistier. Conservation biologists come in sundry kinds and hues. Some work

11   Campbell, "Overcoming Obstacles," 576.

on an ecosystem as a whole; others work on kinds of wildeors, such as prairie dogs or big cats. I've heard from a few of these "wildlifer" conservation biologists that they were going back to work with The Wildlife Society instead of SCB. Heck, maybe SCB and TWS will switch jobs.

I think there is a quick way to get SCB back on track. That is to go back to the heartfelt beliefs and wild love of the first conservation biologists writing in Soulé and Wilcox's *Conservation Biology*. Take the words of Tom Lovejoy, Soulé and Wilcox, and others, and set them up as the vision statement for SCB. Those who can't stand up for these beliefs should be welcomed to leave. Conservation biology doesn't need fence straddlers, either.

Since 1992, I have seen a shift in resource management agencies as some staffers have learned from conservation biologists and now work to shield Endangered and Threatened Species and other "nongame" wildlife, and to set up wildlands networks. I've spoken at a handful of meetings of state and federal wildlife and land agencies about the vision for a North American Wildlands Network and have gained warm and eager welcomes. The science of conservation biology has upended the thinking of ecology and the work of conservation even in resource agencies and schools. While the Society for Conservation Biology may have gone downhill to meekness and selfish careerism, the wisdom and work of conservation biology as an activist science has opened eyes and given a new, stronger meaning to the work of many. The kind of conservation biology shaped by wild-loving biologists at its beginning is likely the best thing to happen to today's conservation. The key founder and leading sparkplug for the science of conservation biology in the late-1970s and early-1980s, Michael Soulé, is one of those truly few who make a world anew. So not all is bad news.

CHAPTER 7

The Environmentalist Stereotype

[W]e need you to leave this movement.... You are making us weak.[1]

—Adam Werbach, to those
in the conservation or environmental
movements who are not progressives

A WING OF THE PROGRESSIVE MOVEMENT?

Politicians in thrall to both befouling and landscalping industries slam "The Environmental Movement" as a socialist or at least liberal gathering, and as a "special-interest group" in the Democratic Party.[2] This tag began in the Nixon days somewhat as a red herring and, although still slung as a hoped-for slur, it has become truer since the 1970s. "Liberal Democrat and Proud" is the heart of what I

---

1   Adam Werbach, "Is Environmentalism Dead? A Speech Presented to the Commonwealth Club," San Francisco, 2004, 31.

2   In *The Nature Haters,* a forthcoming book in *For the Wild Things,* I'll take a good look at the socialist mudslinging from some of our commie-under-the-bed foes.

call "The Environmentalist Stereotype." Other marks are that the "environmentalist" is urban, politically correct, antihunting, and a vegetarian. Right-wing loudmouths and editorial cartoonists toss in ponytails on the men, hairy legs on the women, Birkenstocks, dope smoking, and other cartoon hallmarks. I name what we have here as the *The Environmentalist Stereotype*, in caps throughout the book and in my other writing.

The Environmentalist Stereotype is a key prop under the Myth of the Environmental Movement. It is another root for why I think that conservationists should be leery of being called environmentalists. The stereotype plays out in two ways: it is a feeling held by those outside the conservation and environmental networks, and by many within both networks. It goes beyond only a stereotype, however, when our foes use it to win over others to be against shielding wildlife or stopping pollution when they might otherwise be open-minded, and when leftist or progressive political activists use it to more tightly tie "The Environmental Movement" to the left or to the Democratic Party (or to its near match in other countries). It also goes beyond the stereotype when it is held up as an underlying need for belonging to either network. It is not the half-truth of The Environmentalist Stereotype that hurts, but the way it is wielded to narrow the breadth and depth of backing for wilderness and wildlife. The right may well be an outside foe, but the left can be an inside threat to the conservation network.

Owing to this threat, conservationists must show the public, news businesses, and "decision makers" that there are lots of conservationists who do not fit The Environmentalist Stereotype and that our stands are not beholden to progressive dogma nor are they wrapped up in political correctness, which I'll go into later in this chapter.

Over the two and a half years I spent on the Sierra Club's National Board of Directors, I often ran into well-meaning folks who took it as a given that I was a leftist or a liberal. For my part, I chided Sierra Club leaders, staff, and volunteers not to heedlessly fasten the Club to the left and liberal wing of the Democratic Party, or to the Democratic Party at all. (I found it wryly funny that the politically most conservative member of the Sierra Club's Board was the best-known founder of Earth First!.) With the takeover of the federal government by the Bush Junior gang, this linkage with progressivism and the Democratic Party became even more widespread—rather understandably, I must say. Carl Pope, then-executive director of the Sierra Club, said in 2004, "Environmentalism is part of a broader progressive movement, which the right has invested enormously in undercutting for the past thirty years."[3] I don't think he would have been quite so forthright in the mid-1990s. Adam Werbach, a former president of the Sierra Club Board of Directors, bade in a 2004 speech that environmentalists "cease being environmentalists and start becoming American progressives." He went so far as to tell those of us who weren't progressives or liberals to "leave this movement. . . . You are making us weak." Moreover, he said, "It's time for us to drop our veil of bi-partisanship and fight to fix the deeply broken Democratic Party."[4]

However, the late Phil Clapp, president of the National Environmental Trust and someone who was older and far wiser than Werbach, warned, "The real problem the environmental community has to address is, how do we get the political center to stand up for strong environmental laws? We have to show blue-state Republicans and red-state Democrats that the environment is not one of those 'liberal' issues—like gay marriage, abortion rights, and gun control—that they have to be afraid of." And Josh Reichart of the Pew Charitable Trust warned, "To insist that one cannot be an environmentalist unless he or she is pro-choice or pro-gun-control, for instance, is likely to further weaken environmental interests rather than strengthening them."[5] What they are warning against is The Environmentalist Stereotype,

---

3   Carl Pope, "Carl Pope Response to 'the Death of Environmentalism,'" letter to environmental grant-makers,

4   Adam Werbach, "Is Environmentalism Dead?" 2004 speech to the Commonwealth Club in San Francisco.

5   Margaret Kriz, "Out of the Loop," *National Journal*, February 5, 2005.

though they don't use those words, and they are putting their fingers on the foremost organizing challenge before conservationists and environmentalists, and a lead thrust of this book. It would be good if both networks could have a little get-together on how to shed our politically correct stereotype and how to find friends in the political middle.

This belief that conservation and environmentalism belong in the left came out in a letter I got in 1998 from an outfit called Economics America offering (for a fee) to list the New Mexico Wilderness Alliance in a reference work called *The Left Guide*. It would show "organizations and publishers that focus on civil rights and liberties, abortion rights, progressive economics, consumer protection, the environment, homosexuals' rights, organized labor, grassroots organizing, and other aspects of social change."

Cognitive scientist Stephen Pinker, sloshing about to understand the right-left split, writes, "[I]f someone is sympathetic to rehabilitating offenders, or to affirmative action, or to generous welfare programs, or to a tolerance of homosexuality, chances are good that he will also be a pacifist, an environmentalist, an activist, an egalitarian, a secularist, and a professor or student."[6] Pinker may be somewhat shallow and overstated here—but there is more than a ring of truth to what he writes. Overall, Democratic office-holders today (and since the 1980s for the most) vote much better than do Republicans (except on immigration). The Republican Party to-do list in whatever layout it is offered is chock-full of anticonservation and anti-environmental bluster and lies. Read it carefully and you will think they dug up someone from a Dark Ages peat bog to write it (or a television comedy writer). All but one of the Republican presidential candidates in the summer of 2011 called for doing away with the Environmental Protection Agency (EPA), which was brought into being by President Richard Nixon, and

---

6   Stephen Pinker, *The Blank Slate: The Modern Denial of Human Nature* (Viking, New York, 2002), 286.

which has likely done more for the health of Americans than any other arm of government in the last two score years. Conservationists and environmentalists are more likely to be Democrats than Republicans. However, the progressive Democratic stereotype weakens both the environmental and conservation webs. Conservationists and environmentalists must make it sharp, as Clapp and Reichart bade, that we do not have to be Democrats or liberals, and, if we are, that we do not shun conservationists and environmentalists who are not.

Thoughtful, more open-minded Republicans may be leaving the party after its takeover by nuts. This makes our welcoming even more worthwhile and needed. Since I first drafted this chapter in the Bush days, Republicans, shoved by the Tea Baggers, have gone off the deep end on many things—being against conservationists and environmentalists is near the top of their hate stack. If it wasn't truly going on now, it would be unbelievable to me that one of the two political parties in the U.S. would have become so backwardly revolutionary in so many bad ways.

AIN'T NECESSARILY SO

Although the authoritarian right has been leading the war against conservation and environmentalism since the beginning of the Reagan Administration, shielding wildlands and wildlife can be grounded in a true conservative outlook. The link comes through in the words *conservation* and *conservatism*. In chapters 9 and 10, I'll offer some ways for making conservation more welcoming to sane conservatives. John Bliese's book, *The Greening of Conservative America,* shows that shielding wilderness, endangered species, and wetlands, and stopping greenhouse gas pollution can be rooted in good conservative thinking. And he sets out a workable path to do such.[7] Bliese also shows that wanting livable cities and clean air and water can come from a conservative outlook. He is not alone. Gordon Durnil, a top staffer in the Bush

---

7   John R. Bliese, *The Greening of Conservative America* (Westview Press, Boulder, Colorado, 2001).

Senior administration, wrote a good book on how stopping pollution is conservative—*The Making of a Conservative Environmentalist*.[8] Moreover, while the Sierra Club, Defenders of Wildlife, the Alaska Wilderness League, and some other mainstream conservation groups were selling out on the Wilderness recommendation for the Arctic National Wildlife Refuge in the fall of 2011, Republicans for Environmental Protection (REP) (now ConservAmerica) was steadfast for the biggest Wilderness recommendation alternative.

I believe that love for wild things and care for our health can come from any political sitting or from somewhere wholly away from politics. The true foe is any belief that cannot see clean air, clean water, and wild things as good. At this time, that narrow outlook holds more sway within the Republican Party than in the Democratic Party.[9] This is no reason, however, for conservationists and environmentalists to tie themselves too tightly to the Democrats. Barack Obama, I hope, has shown conservationists that just because a politician is a Democrat does not necessarily mean they are the friend of conservationists or environmentalists.

(Let me come clean. I think of myself as a rather off-kilter, freethinking, traditionalist conservative since I have the bedrock quirk of the breed: I think ill of Mankind and do not trust in good behavior from most. Therefore, I am seldom let down. I have had this belief as far back as I can recall; yea, even unto childhood. This, by the way, is perhaps the big crack between traditional conservatives and libertarians, who are often handmaidens of big business instead of trustworthy watchdogs for the free market.[10] However, I have not voted for a Republican, other than for a state or local office, for more than a score of years.)

8   Gordon K. Durnil, *The Making of a Conservative Environmentalist* (Indiana University Press, Bloomington, 1995).

9   But in Brazil and some other Latin American countries, it is often the Marxist left that is as strong a foe of conservation as extractive industry and big ranchers.

10   The Tea Party folks, bless their tiny little brains, are so muddled in their unhappy thinking that they truly cannot be put into any political cubbyhole. But they are handy playthings for those of great wealth who wish to keep it.

THE POLITICAL SPECTRUM (OR SPECTRA)

At this spot on our hike through the Myth of the Environmental Movement, we need to step off the trail, sit down, and take in the bigger landscape for a while. Although a little off to the side of our chat here, this overlook is key since it shapes how I see some things and will pop up now and again in *Take Back Conservation*.

Of all the sock-drawer layouts to frame American politics, the most shallow, baffling, and downright wrong is also the most stock: the flat, one-line political spectrum of right to left. We try to cram every likely political belief into this one row of drawers; in doing so, we craft some odd jumbles. This isn't at all amazing; it follows how we mostly think: flat and in a line.

In his book, *The End Of The Republican Era*, political scientist Theodore Lowi offers a more thoughtful and rightly built *chest* of sock drawers by saying that there are three freestanding political spectra in American politics:

1) *Conservatism* from Patrician (secular) to Populist (religious).
2) *Liberalism* from Old Liberalism (Libertarianism) to New Liberalism (New Deal-type Regulatory State).
3) *Left* from Old Left to New Left.[11]

I would nail on a fourth:

4) *AntiEnlightenment* from Postmodern Deconstructionism to Neoconservatism. (I'll pick through this row of drawers more in *True Wilderness* and *The Nature Haters* in the *For the Wild Things* series.)

What comes now is grounded on but does not only follow Lowi; I have drawn on my own offbeat, murky, and sprawled background as well.

---

11   Theodore J. Lowi, *The End of the Republican Era* (University of Oklahoma Press, Norman, 1995).

The Conservative political spectrum grows out of a belief that there are root values (goods) in society, and that the state has a job to set standards and bring them to bear. We can roughly cleave it by class between well-schooled traditional (Burkean) conservatives and mostly poorly schooled religious-right populists. Liberalism is a capitalist spectrum with Old Liberalism or Libertarianism on one side and New Liberalism, which backs capitalism but believes in government regulation of it, on the other. The Left political spectrum comes from Europe and is socialist, or anticapitalist. It takes in Communism, Social Democracy, and the New Left, as well as such oddities as Marxist feminism and left-wing anarchism. (Social Democrats in Europe have lately mellowed their anticapitalist stand.) AntiEnlightenment wants to overthrow the Enlightenment, reason, and science, with postmodern deconstructionists saying truth is unknowable and neoconservatives seeking to go back to theocracy and feudalism; both sneer at science, foremost at Darwinism. Others that have strong antiscience strains (though not always anti-engineering) are much of the Left, Libertarianism, and Religious Populism.[12] These drawers are where many Nature Haters or slightly less hothearted anticonservationists lodge. However, finding a Cannot here and there in these drawers is not wholly farfetched, only unlikely.

What is everyday taken to be conservatism now shakes out of an odd ragbag: the populist conservatives of the religious right; secular conservatives who believe in tradition and lawfulness; libertarians, some of whom have taken the poppy-dream of private property to a cultish holiness blooming in Xanadu and who seem to believe the "free market" has ghostly might[13]; pork-barrel socialists, chanting the mantra of jobs as they work to keep welfare flowing to big businesses who often then send jobs overseas; corporatists who want to hold onto

---

12   The way sundry political cubbies have unlike thoughts on science and engineering is greatly overlooked, but it is meaningful for understanding where clashing bands stand on a sweep of things.

13   Hogwarts should have a professor for free-market economics.

their economic overlordship and keep the commonwealth flowing to their CEOs, directors, and big shareholders; imperial militarists; right-wing authoritarians; and the darkly un-American overtheorized cult of neoconservatives. I no longer think of this creepy, eldritch mishmash as conservative, and will call it the *authoritarian right* (John Dean's 2006 book, *Conservatives Without Conscience,* nabs today's "movement conservatives" and shows that what holds them together is authoritarianism[14]). The Tea Party crowd, or "Tea Baggers" as I call them, is a new take on unlearned but proud right-wing populism and could be a spanner in the works for the whole "conservative" ragbag. I'll look at it along with its forebears in *The Nature Haters.* Today's "conservative" cluster reminds me of the bar scene in *Star Wars,* I've got to say.

Liberalism, now often called progressivism, is also a mishmash: friends of a New Deal kind of regulatory and welfare state; what's left of the once-mighty labor movement; the offspring of the Marxist Left with their kneejerks against capitalism, private property, profit, and corporations; the peace and justice movement; and the politically-correct crowd that sees folks cleaved into two classes—the oppressor class of white, heterosexual males and the oppressed class of everyone else. I swear, I sometimes wonder how any political network with so many smart and caring folks that has such flat-Earthers and out-and-out greedheads for foes and with so much riding on the outcome can be so downright inept and cowering. The true token of today's Democrats is not Andrew Jackson's rough, tough jackass but Robbie Burns's wee, "cowrin" mousy.[15]

Owing to the wackiness of the authoritarian right, what once would have been Rockefeller Republicans have become Independents or

14　John W. Dean, *Conservatives Without Conscience* (Viking, New York, 2006).

15　I know, I know that Andrew Jackson did not give the Democrats the donkey as their token, but I can't help thinking of Jackson as the rough, tough jackass of American political history.

Democrats, and thus loosely tied to Progressivism. I guess so anyway; I truly don't know how or where so many folks have wandered off. The same might be said of upstanding traditional conservatives, though, forsooth, righteous, thoughtful Americans of whatever politics today should find themselves without much of a home. In which political house do you gag the least? I rather like ConservAmerica, but I can't bear thinking of myself as a Republican in any way these days.

Within these right (conservative) and left (progressive) deck parties is a good deal of infighting over how to rejigger the deck chairs as our shadowy captain presses the throttle forward with his invisible hand and gooses engine speed into the brave new iceberg of rising China, Islamo-fascist jihad against the West, the economic crumpling of the civilized world, overpopulation, global weirdness, landscalping, and mass extinction.

THE LEFTIST BID TO TAKE OVER "THE ENVIRONMENTAL MOVEMENT"

With his standout bluntness, George Sessions, a steadfast crafter of Deep Ecology in North America, writes:

> During [the 1960s Marxist/leftist intellectuals and activists] criticized the environmental movement for diverting attention from their anthropocentric preoccupation with social justice issues. However, after Earth Day 1970, as the environmental movement continued to gain strength and public support throughout the 1970s and 80s, leftist intellectuals and activists began to seize upon the public successes and high visibility of the environmental movement to try to coopt it in the service of their social justice agenda.[16]

---

16   George Sessions, "Reinventing Nature, the End of Wilderness? A response to William Cronon's *Uncommon Ground*," *The Trumpeter*, Winter 1996, 35.

Beyond the many good-hearted conservationists and environmentalists who see themselves as political progressives are those who are thoughtfully shoving environmental and conservation clubs further to the left. In the Sierra Club, social-justice workers have risen in the population work of the Club, thereby hobbling work for population stabilization.[17] Adam Werbach, when he was yet someone, bade we all become liberal Democrats. But Mark Dowie and Robert Gottlieb in their books, *Losing Ground* and *Forcing the Spring,* go further left and make sweeping calls for "The Environmental Movement" to be run by cares of class, race, sex, and anticapitalism (the grab bag of today's Marxism). Dowie writes that "justice [is] the critical ingredient of any social movement."[18] He scolds us outdoorsfolk:

Unlike the other new social movements of the 1960s and 1970s (women's, peace, civil rights, and gay liberation), which are essentially radical, the ecology movement was saddled from the start with conservative traditions formed by a bipartisan, mostly white, middle-class, male leadership.... rarely have they challenged the fundamental canons of western civilization or the economic orthodoxy of welfare capitalism....[19]

It was this kind of radical-left takeover of Earth First! in the late 1980s that led Nancy, me, and our conservationist friends (the wicked *foremanistas*) to leave Earth First!, by the way.

In the first draft of this chapter, I gave more than a few pages to the work of the Marxist Left and left-wing anarchism to take over or

17   Foreman, *Man Swarm,* 164-167.

18   Dowie, *Losing Ground,* 3.

19   Dowie, *Losing Ground,* 28. I believe for Dowie the word "radical" means "Marxist." Notwithstanding the overheated fretting of some Cold War anticommunists, Marxists were not and are not always subversives who backed the now-dead Soviet Union and the newly capitalist Red China. I also think that my friend Mark here bears out what I wrote in chapters 1 and 2.

shape the environmental and conservation networks. I've cut most of that since I've come to believe that neither has much weight any longer. The much bigger threat comes from more mainstream progressivism, such as The Environmentalist Stereotype, the rise of enviro-resourcism, wilderness (or Nature) deconstructionism, and running from a straightforward stand on population stabilization. These are the threats to which I give myself in this and other books. The most baleful hold the far left has on more mainstream progressives is political correctness. It spikes all the woes listed above.

Take Back Conservation is about the inside threats to unwavering conservation. Most, but not all, of these come from the progressive pudding. The outside foes of conservation and the leading wreckers of wild things come more from business and the authoritarian right. My forthcoming book, *The Nature Haters,* will go after them with a sharp and sturdy battle-ax.

Let me underscore that I am not against progressive environmentalism. It is sound and needed. The pitfall is when it wishes to wholly flag environmentalism and conservation as a wing of progressivism and to elbow aside any freethinkers.

As in the early 1970s, some folks in "The Environmental Movement" today are driven more by anticapitalist and social-justice cares than by love for wild things. We can see this split in that conservationists fight big business when it threatens wilderness and wildlife; the others fight for wilderness and wildlife (or clean air) owing to how it is big business that threatens them. Anticorporate fighters have done good work in both the environmental and conservation networks, but there are potholes on such a road when business scathers run things. Mind you, I'm not standing up for big business at all; I think corporations wreck the free market. Making them legal persons was one of the greatest mistakes the United States of America ever made. So long as corporations can keep the "legal fiction of personhood," strict construction of the United States Constitution is a harebrained hoot. No other thing has flipped the Constitution over as has making business corporations legal persons in our legal system.

POLITICAL CORRECTNESS

Maybe the worst thing with which the left has saddled liberalism or progressivism is political correctness. I think it is the most harmful lump that progressivism has tossed into the Environmentalist Stereotype. Political correctness is cringe-worthy to many Americans who would otherwise be somewhat friendly to conservation stands and thoughts. I've left a handful of outfits owing to it. So have other conservationists I know. What about folks even more mainstream in their lifeways and less keen to conservation than Nancy and me? The whiff of political correctness alone, I think, keeps thousands of likely friends away from conservation work. In most of the U.S. and Canada, to draw new folks to conservation, we should look to the middle, not to the politically correct left.

At its worst, the hallmarks of political correctness are:

1) Multiculturalism—folks are not taken as selves, but by their group identity; all cultures, but for those grounded in Western Civilization, are sound and good. Cultural relativism and identity politics are other words for this.

2) Victimization—the world is cleaved into an oppressor class (white, heterosexual males and corporate executives) and the oppressed class (everyone else).

3) Progressive Humanism—people (as a whole and as selves) are good and sooner or later perfectible (if one does bad things, it is owing to having been oppressed at some time); institutions and corporations are bad.

4) Guilt—upper-middle-class, well-schooled whites should feel guilty for their "privileged" standing and for the injustices done to the oppressed classes over the last five hundred or so years.

5) Social Justice—at its far edge, resources should be equitably redistributed (from each according to his means, to each according to his needs). This holds for person-to-person sharing of wealth and nation-to-nation sharing of wealth.[20]

6) Entitlement Rights—unlike age-old American rights, such as those in the Bill of Rights, which are fetters on government— new rights are put forward that are in truth entitlements, such as the right to a job with a minimum wage, the right to health care, the right to housing, and so on.[21] (Let's be truthful, unlike some GOP barnburners, things we have paid for such as Social Security and Medicare are owed to us and are in no way handout entitlements. Nor are our public lands socialism.)

I have written about political correctness bluntly; however, even with milder wording, political correctness can be harmful. While each of these shades of political correctness may be grounded in true injustice, in their politically correct hue they are outliers to true life and as such cannot be the grounds for workable answers. Moreover, in today's America, hard political correctness is such an outlier it could never draw enough backing to help throw out the Republicans. I back environmental justice and see it as a good thing for the environmental network. However, in its politically correct utmost, it hurts conservation in a sweep of ways such as backing the "right" of natives to kill threatened whales. Political correctness is woven through the stands of Dowie, Gottlieb, and other leftist scolds of "white man" conservation. (The

---

20   The politically correct seem to think that any gap between people and between nations is due wholly to injustice, exploitation, and dominance, and has nothing to do with talent, energy, and resources on hand. Come on: some folks are poor for being thickheaded or lazy or lacking drive (I have kin who show this). Some nations are poverty-stricken owing to corrupt and incompetent leaders, a lack of a social work ethic, lean land with little fertility and few raw goods, or overpopulation (or all of the above). In messy reality, poverty is rooted in all of the above.

21   These things may be good for a nation to try to make available to all, but they should not be seen as rights.

radical-right can play the victim just as well, however, as I will show later in *The Nature Haters*.) Hallowed multiculturalism is likely the thing most wrong with liberalism, progressivism, and the Democratic Party.

Progressives, some of whom are environmentalists and conservationists, may not fully believe in all the strands of political correctness when they acknowledge them. But many stand up for political correctness out of fear of being snarled at by the PC watchdogs. This is true for backing off on population stabilization, most of all for not acknowledging immigration as the biggest driver of population growth in the U.S.[22] Political correctness is a straightjacket conservationists must wriggle out of and stay out of. It has nothing to do with backing the worthy goal of environmental justice.

Fairness does not have to be politically correct. Dr. Martin Luther King, Jr. said, "I have a dream that my four little children will one day live in a nation where they will not be judged by the color of their skin but by the content of their character." This is at odds with group identity.

GREENS AND CONSERVATION

The "Greens" are wilting as a political force in the United States. However, I need to bring them up since another of the harmful things about The Environmentalist Stereotype is that it lumps the Green-political movement in with conservation and environmentalism. As conservation and environmentalism have their own beginnings, beliefs, followers, and clubs, so do the Greens.

Green political parties were set up in some states and nationally in the 1990s. In New Mexico, the Green Party gathered up to 12 percent of the statewide vote in 1994, thus gaining major party status. Since that time, Green candidates have taken votes away from conservation-friendly Democrats running against anticonservation Republicans. The worst of the Republican honchos in the state have egged on the Greens to run candidates.

---

22   Foreman, *Man Swarm*.

The New Mexico Green Party has also backed cutting old-growth ponderosa pines on the Carson National Forest so long as a local Hispano would do the logging. In answer to a pro-logging opinion column by northern New Mexico political *patrons*, one of the founders of the New Mexico Green Party underlined that the Greens did not back conservationist calls to shield National Forest lands from old-growth logging and overgrazing. In a letter to the *Albuquerque Journal*, he wrote, "The Green Party is much more than an environmental party. Our platform calls for social justice, self-determination, universal health care and many other changes. ... I therefore protest your paper's use of the word 'green' to describe the positions and actions of some environmentalists, some of whom may or may not be registered in the Green Party...."[23] I am of the same mind. We wilderness and wildlife folks should stay away from calling ourselves "green." Green politics is another everyday chunk of The Environmentalist Stereotype. The Green Party seems to be no longer a player in New Mexico, thank goodness.

Had it not been for the Green Party, Ralph Nader likely would not have taken enough votes from Al Gore in 2000 to let the Supreme Court hand the presidency to George Bush Junior. Think of that. Think what things might have been like without the nightmare administration of Bush-Cheney for eight long years.

Green parties in Canada, Europe, and elsewhere may be better on wildlife and wildland work. Some Greens in Canada are good conservationists; others are not.

In the next chapter, I'll look at another harmful slice of The Environmentalist Stereotype: being against guns and hunting.

23 Jack Uhrich, "Party Trademarks Word 'Green,'" Letters to the Journal, *Albuquerque Journal*, Nov. 21, 1997.

CHAPTER 8

Animal Rights, Hunting and Conservation

The question is not, Can they reason?
nor Can they talk? but Can they suffer?

—Jeremy Bentham[1]

WHAT RIFT?

A great harm from both The Myth of the Environmental Movement and The Environmentalist Stereotype is that they lead many to believe environmentalists, and therefore conservationists, are vegetarian and antihunting, want more gun control or even bans on ownership, and have other field marks of foes to the hook and bullet bunch. This widespread belief is one of the more crippling limbs of the Myth and the Stereotype, and conservationists need to put an end to it. The authoritarian right, foremost some leaders of the National Rifle Association (NRA) and Safari Club International, have waved this falsehood about so as to get more hunters to fear and mistrust conservationists such as in the Sierra Club and therefore to be against shielding wilderness and

---

1   Nash, *The Rights of Nature*, 23.

wildlife. Some of why the NRA and Safari Club do this is that they most often want more roads, fewer hardships while out, no hurdles on hunting Endangered Species abroad and bringing polar bear or tiger trophies home, and agricultural production of game and trophy wildlife; they also are in the sack with extractive industry (oftentimes they are extractive industry) so they work to get hunting and fishing folks to be against any "lock-ups." However, the most fevered fanners of this fire are slob hunters, gun nuts, and militia wannabes on their home turf. The believed rift between environmentalists (and therefore conservationists) and hunters and anglers is driven by NRA flimflam and the conspiracy madness of gun nuts, yes, but it is grounded on the misunderstandings and dislikes held by some environmentalists and hunters alike. At its heart is a culture war, with both sides out of touch with wilderness and wildlife conservation.

It's been an odd hike, these last forty-some years. When I started in conservation, no one blinked over outfitters, hunters, and sportfishers being leaders in the conservation network. Their belonging and leadership was a given as it had been for over one hundred years. I am a gun owner, have hunted off and on, and now and then fly-fish. I have always been a steadfast backer of the Second Amendment (as well as the other nine). Throughout my wilderness life, I don't think there has ever been a time when many of my friends have not been keen hunters or sportfishers. The New Mexico Wilderness Study Committee, where I got my feet wet, had been started in 1969 by hunters in the New Mexico Wildlife Federation and rock climbers in the New Mexico Mountain Club. In the 1980s, more than a few Earth First!ers hunted and fished. Hunters and anglers were always key leaders and workers for wilderness and wildlife, even if no one thought we needed to ballyhoo it. But now it is widely thought that environmentalists and conservationists are against gun ownership and hunting, and that most of us are vegetarians. Owing to this myth, conservationists now need to show off the anglers and hunters who work for wild things.

I'm glad that conservationists who are hunters are again standing up, and that conservation clubs are reaching out to welcome the sporting crowd and to tell those taken in by the NRA tall tale it ain't so. But how did we get in this mud bog? What the dickens went wrong? What went wrong was lumping conservation in with environmentalism, environmentalists linking up with progressives who are for tough gun control or outright banning, and the authoritarian right's culture-war con job.

Martha Marks, who started Republicans for Environmental Protection, sees the linkage between Vietnam War protesters and Earth Day environmentalism as the beginning of the split. "If you were proenvironment, you must be a long-haired, commie, pinko liberal. And if you were a liberal, you were against gun rights and for animal rights. That was absolutely not true," she says.[2]

Nonetheless, tying the conservation and environmental movements to the antihunting, antifishing, antigun, antimeat-eating animal rights movement has harmed how folks think of us and thereby our political clout. There is nothing wrong with a conservationist being a vegetarian, disliking hunting, or wanting stronger laws on gun ownership. Conservation *clubs*, however, should never have antihunting or anti-gun ownership stands.

Working out the tangle between conservation, hunting and fishing, and the animal rights and animal welfare movements is much needed. Let's go to the beginning.

ANIMAL MOVEMENT

Roderick Nash writes, "As early as the fifteenth century, and increasingly in the seventeenth and eighteenth, protests sounded over practices such as vivisection, cock-fighting, staged fights with dogs

2   Bob Marshall, "The Conservamentalists: Can the sports and the greens find common ground?" http://www.fieldandstream.com/articles/bob-marshall/2004/10/conservamentalists (This is not *The* Bob Marshall, who died in 1939.)

known as bull- and bear-baiting, fox hunting...."[3] In 1789, English utilitarian philosopher Jeremy Bentham called for an end to cruelty to animals: "The question is not, Can they *reason?* nor Can they *talk?* but Can they *suffer?*"[4] In his book, *The Rights of Nature,* Nash shows that this caring for other beings was a widening of Lockean natural rights. Today's animal welfare/rights movement comes mostly out of this thinking, though Buddhist and other beliefs of compassion as "right attitude" also shade it. I believe compassion and respect for other Earthlings should be at the core of the conservation ethic.

However, in beliefs and work conservationists and much of the animal network come from unlike roots.

The beliefs of the animal network are grounded in a kind of compassion—ending the suffering of *individual* beings. This highlighting of individuals and the goal of ending suffering are the bedrock for understanding why the animal network and conservation are sometimes at odds and why conservationists need to show that we are indeed sometimes at odds.

Today's animal network holds a swath of clubs from the Humane Society of the United States (HSUS) to People for the Ethical Treatment of Animals (PETA) to the Animal Liberation Front (ALF), Earth Liberation Front (ELF), and the English Hunt Saboteurs. The spread is in beliefs, stands, work, style, and behaviors. The Humane Society is a mainstream outfit working for the humane treatment of animals. PETA is a radical vegan club against any abuse or use of animals, and undertakes civil disobedience and stunts such as throwing rocks at sportfishers. ALF, ELF, and the Hunt Saboteurs go well beyond PETA in actions such as burning down animal experimentation laboratories and threatening to beat up hunters (I have to think that would be unwise). In the United States, the FBI has gone after ALF/ELF even

3   Roderick Frazier Nash, *The Rights of Nature: A History of Environmental Ethics* (The University of Wisconsin Press, Madison, 1989), 19.

4   Nash, *The Rights of Nature,* 23.

harder than they went after Earth First!, though in this day, more than twenty years after the end of the old Earth First!, there seems to be much overlap. Undercover work, plea deals, getting folks to testify against their friends, and such have gotten some well-meaning young folks long, harsh time behind bars for arson crimes that didn't do much good for anything. They won't be young when they get out. I am truly sorry for some of them, while others are loathsome for saving their own skins by squealing on others—such as one foul knave who ratted on his wife to get a shorter sentence.

Sundry outfits work on sundry things. Clubs may back vegetarianism and humane treatment of animals, and be against animal experimentation, factory farming, fur trapping, fur farming, hunting and fishing, cock fighting, and animals in circuses and rodeos. There are also wide gaps in ecological knowledge and understanding within the animal movement. I've found that many hardcore animal rightists are indoor folks and have little understanding of the wild and no wish to rough it outside.

Some of the middle-of-the-road clubs do not want to be thought of as being in the animal *rights* network, by the way, and want to be known as the animal welfare or animal protection network. I have little gripe about the animal welfare network and find that they often—but not always—work well with conservationists on wilderness and wildlife. In New Mexico, Animal Protection is a lead player in work to deal with highway barriers, as is the Humane Society throughout the U.S. Conservation and animal welfare clubs work together on shielding and bringing back mountain lions, wolves, and other wild hunters. Animal Protection works with conservation clubs to help the reintroduced Mexican wolf (lobo), as do more than a few hunters. A year-end report from Animal Protection of New Mexico highlighted its fights against animal cruelty, getting dogs off chains, and experimentation on chimpanzees, as well as its campaigns to teach folks about the good of beavers, safe passages for wildlife over roads, and reforming cougar management. I back animal welfare outfits on many things, and I give money to neuter and find homes for litters of kittens and stray cats. I overflow with compassion for lone deors, wild or not—but that feeling comes after my love for native wildlife, wild neighborhoods, and the ongoing wonder of evolution. The animal rights outfits I chide here— and coax conservationists to stay away from—are those who are loudly against all hunting and fishing, taking out exotic species and bringing down overpopulated native wildlife, and who free harmful exotic deors where they don't belong and can do harm.

UNLIKENESSES

Wildlovers and far-out animal rightists stare at each other over a wide gap. On two things we come to loggerheads: hunting and fishing, and dealing with exotic species. The grounds for not seeing eye to eye are in Weltanschauung and beliefs about life itself. Conservation is about the health and wholeness of wild neighborhoods and the swirling hither and yon of the evolutionary flow. The animal rights fellowship is about stopping any suffering of individual animals. Their philosophy can be deeply unecological; indeed it is sometimes even abiological. Paul Shepard called it "a pursuit of an abstract harmony with nature."[5] Pain, suffering, and death are inborn in life, in being. Ecologists and conservationists know this well, whereas, at their far edge, animal rightists naysay it and would like to rid the world of it. That the lion shall lie down with the lamb is a blindly unecological dream (unless the lamb happens to be lunch).

Philosophy

Two leading animal rights philosophers, Peter Singer and Tom Regan, stand out for how abiological their abstract schools of thought, animal liberation and animal rights, truly are. Twenty years ago, the

---

5   Paul Shepard, *Man in the Landscape: A Historic View of the Esthetics of Nature* (University of Georgia Press, Athens, 2002(1967)), 194.

editor of the academic journal *Environmental Ethics,* Eugene Hargrove, wrote, "Singer makes the division between animals and 'vegetables' somewhere between the oyster and the shrimp."[6] In other words, Singer, in his wisdom, says that shrimp are "sentient" and can be hurt and can be happy; oysters are not and cannot. It is okay to eat the dumb oysters, but not the smart shrimp. Regan is even more out to lunch with biology. (Both are well rooted in antiscience Weltanschauungs.) Hargrove wrote, "Regan...argues against any direct moral concern for plants, animals other than mammals, or ecosystems; and he criticizes environmentalists for protecting species and systems instead of individual mammals, an approach he calls *environmental fascism.*"[7] He does not think we should care more about Endangered Species than others. He sees one blackfooted ferret as of no more worth than one black rat. Hargrove warns that Regan comes "close to suggesting the removal of predators from natural systems."[8] Philosopher J. Baird Callicott writes that "both Singerian animal liberation and Reganic animal rights imply the ecological nightmare of a policy of predator extermination."[9] Both Singer and Regan are overweening ivory-tower theorists, as much so as postmodern deconstructionists and libertarian economists—brainy folks utterly lost insofar as the true world.

The chapter "Fellow Creatures" in Paul Shepard's 1967 book, *Man in the Landscape,* mightily rips the anti-ecological thinking behind true-believing animal rights. Shepard wrote, "The condemnation of killing wild animals assumes that death is the worst of natural events, that order in nature is epitomized by living objects rather than the complex flow patterns of which objects are temporary formations. The implication is that carnivorous predation as a whole is evil."[10]

6   Eugene C. Hargrove, "Preface," in Eugene C. Hargrove, ed. *The Animal Rights/Environmental Ethics Debate: The Environmental Perspective* (State University of New York Press, Albany, 1992), x.

7   Hargrove, "Preface," x.

8   Hargrove, "Preface," xi.

9   J. Baird Callicott, "Animal Liberation and Environmental Ethics: Back Together Again," in *The Animal Rights/Environmental Ethics Debate,* 261.

10   Shepard, *Man in the Landscape,* 206.

Canadian naturalist John Livingston wrote that "'animal rights,' if carried to its logical conclusion, is potentially destructive to the quality of wildness—the essence of untrammelled being."[11]

PETA and others twist Man's biological and cultural evolution and the findings of primate researchers to say that we are "naturally" vegetarians, rather than omnivores who have always eaten meat when we could. Fieldwork by primatologists and hominin paleontologists has now smashed this vegetarian misbelief, not that it has gotten any true believers to shift their minds.[12] (I am not slamming those who choose to be vegetarians, however; it is a way to somewhat lower one's ecological footprint. Even so, I could never be one.) Learning the philosophical grounds for animal rights lets us understand why conservationists are often at odds with them over hunting, taking out exotic species, and overall caretaking of wild neighborhoods.

Exotic Species

Exotic species are one of the worst threats to wild neighborhoods and many threatened kinds of wildlife the world over. "Wild" pigs rip up some of the last native tropical big woods in Hawaii; "wild" burros drove bighorn sheep away from water holes in the Grand Canyon before burros were killed off notwithstanding bitter naysaying from animal-rights groups; goats freed in the Galapagos Islands (by sailors long ago for food when sailing by) have harmed the wild plants needed by the giant tortoises. But when biologists, with the backing of conservationists, work to rid lands of harmful exotics to shield wild neighborhoods, animal-rights outfits raise holy hell and bring in their mighty political clout to shield the burros, pigs, or goats. Following Regan, they believe that one burro has as much worth as one bighorn.

11   John A. Livingston, *Rogue Primate: An Exploration of Human Domestication* (Key Porter Books, Toronto, 1994), 175.

12   Craig B. Stanford, *The Hunting Apes: Meat Eating and the Origins of Human Behavior* (Princeton University Press, Princeton, NJ, 1999) convincingly offers the evidence for the importance of meat eating by hominins.

Elsewhere, throngs of Bambi-lovers rise up when land stewards work to bring overgrown herds down to what the land can healthily hold. In the eastern half of the United States, deer herds are too high owing to the killing-off of their hunters, wolves and cougars, and the wholesale shift of habitat to early successional stages that deer like; yet some ecologically blind animal lovers hotheartedly fight any work to lower deer populations, which, by the way, would free deer from starvation and road kill. Even some middle-of-the-road animal welfare groups are against controlling overpopulated deer and exotic species; such as taking out an exotic species of deer in Point Reyes National Seashore in California. Worldwide, Paul Ehrlich writes, "Lunatic fringe animal rights groups...are increasingly a thorn in the side of others who are attempting to conserve biodiversity."[13]

Biologically unlearned vandals of the Animal Liberation Front (ALF) and Earth Liberation Front (ELF) have more than once freed fur-farmed mink from their pens. In 1997 in England, they freed 6,000 American Mink, whereupon the big weasels went into the New Forest. The American Mink are not from England, are eager hunters, and the New Forest is one of the dearest wild neighborhoods on the island. "Forest officer Howard Taylor said the massive release of the mink into the forest was a nightmare."[14] The European Mink, which is another species, is half the size of American Mink and is Endangered and gone from most of its former homeland, including England. Widespread planting of American Mink in Europe is a big thing behind European Mink being Endangered and a heavy threat to the scattered bands of European Mink left; American Mink in England would be a big hurdle to overcome before bringing European Mink home to the island.

Time called it "perhaps the largest illegal animal release in U.S. history" when ALF hit a mink farm in Oregon. Many of the loosed mink

---

13   Paul R. Ehrlich, *A World of Wounds: Ecologists and the Human Dilemma* (Ecology Institute, Oldendorf/Luhe, Germany, 1997), 71.

14   "Mink Menace," *Albuquerque Tribune*, August 15, 1997.

were unweaned pups and quickly died.[15] Starvation is not a good death. I dislike fur farming, but I wonder at the bedrock lack of ecological knowledge of ALF and ELF vandals and at their shortsighted thinking.

Against Hunting

While some Main Street animal welfare groups are not wholly against hunting and fishing, most of the animal rights network wants to ban hunting and fishing and killing bothersome deers. For the latter, conservationists are most often against so-called "animal damage control" killing. Too many federal, state, and local wildlife agents are trigger-happy blockheads. At times, though, killing is called for. Outlawing hunting and fishing is a whole other thing. Some animal rights activists are so angry that, in the mid-1990s, PETA undertook rock-throwing at sportfishers. This was too much even for some Earth First!ers. Mike Roselle lambasted PETA for being such numbskulls and acknowledged the conservation work of many sportfishers and their clubs such as Trout Unlimited. He wrote, "It shocks me how many animal rights activists use the exact tone of voice and the same tactics as Operation Rescue activists often do."[16] However, other Earth First!ers upbraided Roselle for being out of line.[17]

WHAT'S WRONG WITH LINKING ANIMAL RIGHTS AND CONSERVATION

The misunderstanding that conservationists and environmentalists back the animal-rights movement and are against hunting and fishing

15 Christine Gorman, "Blood and Fur," *Time,* June 16, 1997.

16 Mike Roselle, "Fish-fry at the PC Corral," *Earth First!* 3/20/96, 23.

17 The new Earth First! of the 1990s and since should be thought of as a wholly new outfit instead of a going-on from the earliest Earth First! of the 1980s. Eighties Earth First! was a conservation group with many "rednecks for wilderness," who were hunters and fishers. Since the early 1990s, EF!, although it sometimes works on wilderness and wildlife, seems to be made up mostly of urban anarchists, animal-rights radicals, class-struggle Marxists, and politically-correct leftists.

is politically deadly. The mistake of lumping animal rights and conservation together in most minds makes it easier for anticonservation firebrands in the NRA to split hunters away from conservation clubs. Extractive industry also does its utmost to spread the lie so as to break up those who want to keep public lands wild. Although many folks and the news business often see the conservation and animal-rights movements as one and the same, owing to their shallow understanding, conservationists have long scorched animal-rights hardliners. As early as 1982, I outlined the split in a column in the *Earth First! Journal*.[18] In 1992, ecophilosopher Eugene Hargrove edited an anthology, *The Animal Rights/Environmental Ethics Debate*, which spotlighted the environmental (conservation) answer to animal rights. Key was J. Baird Callicott's outstanding 1980 paper, "Animal Liberation: A Triangular Affair," in which he wrote, "There are intractable practical differences between environmental ethics and the animal liberation movement.... animal liberation, if pursued at the practical as well as rhetorical level, would have ruinous consequences on plants, soils, and waters...."[19]

I also see a pitfall with the thought of "rights" for other Earthlings. Some conservationists, even me at one time, have talked about rights for other beings. After mulling it over, I think this may be slippery and sloppy thinking. *Rights* as a legal concept should be kept for Man. When we put rights on other Earthlings, we take them out of wildness, out of self-willed land, out of their self-willed being, and bring them into the political, legalistic world of civilized *Homo sapiens*. We stamp our will, albeit a friendly will, over them, in other words, taming them. A better path is to acknowledge that Man does not have the *right* to spread our will over all of being. However, I don't see much wrong with saying *right* in a nonlegal meaning.

18   Chim Blea (Dave Foreman), "Cat Tracks: The Ethics of Vegetarianism," *Earth First!* September 21, 1982.

19   J. Baird Callicott, "Animal Liberation: A Triangular Affair," in *The Animal Rights/Environmental Debate*, 60.

These gaps notwithstanding, many animal welfare organizations often work with conservationists, as I wrote earlier. Animal-welfare backers and right-minded hunters teamed up in Colorado, California, Oregon, and other states in the 1990s to back ballot steps banning shameful and coarsening kinds of hunting such as shooting bears over bait heaps of garbage and old doughnuts, hunting bears with dogs, or spring hunting of bears when sows are just out of the den with cubs. Conservation groups and animal-welfare groups have worked together against the federal government's slaughter of coyotes, prairie dogs, bears, mountain lions, and other predators or "problem animals" for the welfare of a few ranchers and farmers. When it comes to the long years of work in the West to shield carnivores and bring them back, with wolves and mountain lions foremost, there is no true edge between conservation and animal welfare clubs.

Captain Paul Watson of the Sea Shepherd Conservation Society draws heartfelt backing from both conservationists and animal rightists for his bold, high-seas campaigns against illegal whaling, clubbing of harp seals, and drift-netting (I am on the Sea Shepherd Advisory Board). Animal-welfare groups and conservationists are working well together with highway departments to build wildlife passages over and under deadly roads.[20] And let me not use a strawdog: I don't know any animal-rights activists today who follow the far-out Regan anti-ecosystem/antipredator line.

Nonetheless, the conservation movement and the animal-rights movement are not the same. Conservationists should never let anyone mistakenly call us animal rightists. And folks and groups in the animal-welfare movement should go out of their way to cleave themselves from lamebrained animal-rights hits.

Conservation and Hunting

To understand yesterday, today, and tomorrow between conservation and sport hunting and fishing, we need to look at the

---

20   More on the highway barrier effort is at www.rewilding.org.

depth and breadth of the hook and bullet bunch. First of all, hunting and fishing is not conservation. Like climbing and canoeing, they are kinds of outdoor recreation that can best be done in wildlands. For some, hunting and fishing brings a deep tie to wild things, as does climbing and canoeing for others. Thanks to this tie, some of the best conservationists have been and are hunters and anglers. There are lots of hunters and anglers who are not conservationists, however. I'll cleave the hunting and angling clan into three bands.

First is the hunting and fishing "movement." It takes in outdoor writers, good ol' boys with television shows, sportsmen and -women who follow them, staff and earnest members of clubs from the NRA to Trout Unlimited, keen members of state and local hunting and fishing clubs, firearms and gear manufacturers and dealers, and so on. The second band is those for whom hunting and/or fishing is a big chunk of their lives, but who aren't belongers, other than maybe with small bunches of friends. Then there are those like my wife and me who are once-in-a-while fishers or hunters. Within each of these three bands folks can run from hardcore conservationists to resourcists to landscalpers. Some may follow the toughest code of "fair chase" while others are careless slob hunters or put-and-take fishers. There are also hateful poachers, game hogs, and scum who like to kill things whether they are eaten or not. There are those who hate wolves and cougars, Endangered Species, nongame species, and Wilderness Areas, just as there are leading wild-things-for-their-own-sakes conservationists. Scott Stouder, a well-known leader in the righteous hunting/fishing kinship and in conservation, writes, "Animals have a right to exist for their own sake beyond any use they may be to us."[21]

Hunters and anglers were big in the early conservation uprising (and I do believe it was an *uprising*) and are still key today. John Reiger opened a lot of eyes with his 1975 book *American Sportsmen and the*

---

21   Scott Stouder, "The Power of Story," *Backcountry Journal: The Newsletter of Backcountry Hunters and Anglers,"* Summer 2005.

Origins of Conservation, which showed that sport hunters and anglers in the mid-1800s blazed the trail for both resource conservation and wild conservation as they took on the free-for-all market hunters and game hogs, and set standards for fair chase and high-minded hunting and fishing.[22] Read his book to understand how sport hunters and fishers led in the early conservation rising (though some go overboard in thinking that hunters and anglers were the only ones at the beginning). Many wilderness and wildlife shielders, like Michael Soulé and me, have been hunters and anglers (although some of the best have called me the clumsiest flyfisher they have ever seen). Ortega y Gassett, Paul Shepard, Aldo Leopold, and other great conservationists have written how hunting ties one to the land as nothing else does.[23]

Ending the *widely believed* "rift" between conservationists and hunters is much needed, though in truth it is the *believed* rather than the *rift* that needs to be ended. Moreover, the headache is made worse by the way the news business and others spin the coming-together. For example, the *Baltimore Sun,* in an otherwise good article, used the headline, "Unlikely partners unite on the environment." The reporter, Tom Pelton, writes, "But there is mounting evidence that left-leaning nature lovers can gain significant national political influence by forming an unlikely alliance with conservative middle-class hunters." What a wrap-up of the Environmentalist Stereotype! I'm glad he then let Melanie Griffin of the Sierra Club set him straight: "Oftentimes,

22   John F. Reiger, *American Sportsmen and the Origins of Conservation* Revised Edition (University of Oklahoma Press, Norman, 1986 (1975)).

23   Paul Shepard wrote in all his books about the worth of hunting. The chapter "Fellow Creatures" in Paul Shepard, *Man in the Landscape: A Historic View of the Esthetics of Nature* (University of Georgia Press, Athens, 2002), first published in 1967, is good. Three somewhat newer books also do a good job of backing hunting. See Richard Nelson, *The Island Within* (Vintage Books, New York, 1991); Jim Fergus, *A Hunter's Road* (Henry Holt and Company, New York, 1992); and David Petersen, ed., *A Hunter's Heart: Honest Essays on Blood Sports* (Henry Holt and Company, New York, 1996).

environmentalists and hunters and fishermen are called 'nontraditional allies,' but actually they are traditional allies that are coming back together again after a few decades of separation."[24]

The truth is that the split was between *environmentalists* and hunters, not between *conservationists* and hunters. The split was also between caring, conservationist hunters on one side and slob hunters on the other. The hitch between some wild-loving hunters and anglers and conservationists was owing to sportsmen and women tagging wildlands conservationists with the Environmentalist Stereotype. There is and will always be a split between slob hunters on their ATVs who hate wolves and righteous hunters who are conservationists; slob hunters are a big chunk of the anticonservation network.[25] Conservationists, whether they hunt or not, are against slob hunting (such as shooting bears over bait dumps of doughnuts and "hunting" from saddles of all-terrain vehicles) and today's full-on slaughter of wolves by legal hunting and trapping in Idaho, Montana, and Wyoming. Conservation groups must never give in or lower their standards of sportsmanship when seeking to work with hunters and fishers. We must also acknowledge that runaway hunting and fishing have led to the extinction and near-extinction of many wildeors. Today, unthinking hunting and knee-jerk state agency "management" is stopping mountain lions from the Rocky Mountains from making it across the Great Plains to come home to eastern forests, which offer good habitat and more than enough prey.

Respect is one of the underpinnings of conservation. All outdoor recreation, as well as hunting and fishing, should be grounded in an ethic of respect for wild things. Ethical climbing should not brook the thought of "conquest" when getting to the top of a mountain. Likewise, a boater does not "beat" a rapid. Hunting and fishing regulations must be geared to keep and rebuild the Tree of Life and healthy wild

---

24 Tom Pelton, "Unlikely partners unite on environment," *Baltimore Sun,* June 12, 2005.

25 I'll look at them more in *The Nature Haters.*

neighborhoods. Standards should also be grounded in fair chase and on respect: respect for the lone wildeor, the kind of wildeor, its wild neighborhood, ecological and evolutionary processes, and wild things overall. Shooting prairie dogs for "fun" shows no respect for anything. It's loathsome just as is little boys putting firecrackers in frogs' mouths. Such behavior is coarsening and dirties one's inner being.

Today, in the Northern Rockies of Idaho, Montana, and Wyoming, the worst kind of hunters and trappers have worked themselves up into an almost sexual fever of madness over gray wolves, which have made a breathtaking comeback in the last twenty years. One would think the plains, woods, and mountains had been invaded by Satanic, bloodsucking demons killing everything in sight and that it's only the true American men with their NRA hats riding the trails and roads on their ATVs who can save the rest of us. It's almost unbelievable the evil beliefs slob hunters in the Rockies have heaped onto wolves with their frothing mad berserker mob mood to kill and trap every wolf south of Canada. They fit the "Drooling Hunter Who Shoots At Anything That Moves" Stereotype. Righteous, respectful hunters must make themselves heard over the banshee wails of the lynch mob after wolves. Good hunters were among the leaders in bringing wolves back to Yellowstone National Park and the River of No Return Wilderness Area. I know many who are shaking their heads aghast at the zombie hunters full of bloodlust ransacking the backcountry for wolves. The war over anything-goes wolf hunting in the Northern Rockies is the greatest clash between conservationist hunters and landscalper hunters in many years. And while conservationists must make it bright that righteous hunters and anglers are fully a slice of our clan, we must also stand up and lambaste the wolf-hating yahoos working to slaughter wolves.

The dare for conservationists is to kill the misbelief that conservation clubs and the conservation network are against hunting, meat eating, and gun ownership, whatever some lone conservationists might believe. We must welcome hunters and sportfishers back to high standing in our work to keep wild things (some are yet there— they never left), while also being free to work with the animal-welfare network on wildlife shielding and keeping wild neighborhoods. Even in New Mexico where some hunters and anglers have always worked in the conservation network, we still need to shoot down any lies or misunderstandings about conservation and hunting.

Though the NRA keeps telling the big lie about conservation clubs wanting to take away guns, many conservationists are showing that slice of the Environmental Stereotype is not true. The Sierra Club nationally is doing a good job on this with a committee of staff and volunteers who hunt and fish, headed up by Bart Semcer, who is as good as any conservationist working in Washington, DC. They have brought the Club to hunting and fishing shows and to the Outdoor Writers Association conventions. The fairly new bunch Backcountry Hunters and Anglers is speaking out on conservation. Trout Unlimited has a public lands initiative that works to shield roadless areas, led by well-known outdoor writer David Petersen.[26] The New Mexico Wildlife Federation is a bunch of good ol' boy and gal hunters and anglers and is at the heart of public-land and wildlife shielding in my home state. I back all of these.

The dread of wholesale extinction is the nightmare staring down all of us who love wildeors. Whether we think of ourselves first as hunters and fishers, as in the animal welfare network, as conservationists, or as a blend, we must work together to keep wildeors for their own sakes and as building blocks for tomorrow's wild tangle of life.

26   The Sierra Club Hunter-Angler program is at www.sierraclub. org/huntingfishing; Backcountry Hunters and Anglers is at www. backcountryhunters.org. Petersen's books are in Books of the Big Outside on the Rewilding Institute website www.rewilding.org.

CHAPTER 9

Conservatism
and Conservation

Nothing is more conservative than conservation.
—Russell Kirk, 1970

LET ME MAKE THIS AS SHARP as the crystal wine glass I just dropped on my brick floor and as bright as the puddle of blood from my bare foot. I do not mean for this chapter to make conservationists and environmentalists conservatives. It is only to show that we wildlovers have shared values with traditional conservatism, and thereby have ways to winningly talk to those Middle Americans who have traditional conservative values. The folks in ConservAmerica already know this, but there are many others who might back much of what we want if they knew we had shared values. ConservAmerica has been stronger in asking for more Wilderness Area acreage in Alaska of late than the Sierra Club and Alaska Wilderness League. Moreover, in the vote in the House of Representatives (February 2012) to open the Arctic National Wildlife Refuge to oil and gas drilling, twenty-one Republicans voted "No," while twenty-one Democrats voted "Yes."[1] Illinois GOP Representative Robert Dold wrote an op-ed for *Politico* against opening the Arctic Refuge. He underlined how Illinois birds "migrate there to nest and raise young." He quoted President Eisenhower, who first set aside the Arctic National Wildlife Refuge, and asked, "I hope we as a Congress will live by his conservative words and continue protecting the Arctic Refuge."[2]

I also need to make sharp and bright this: so-called "movement" conservatives and newer Tea Party populists are not true conservatives at all. Indeed, insofar as traditional conservatism goes, it seems to be snoring away in a snow cave with Rip Van Winkle somewhere high up in the Catskills. Those who once may have had leanings to tradition-al conservatism, such as George Will, have shown they have stronger leanings to political power and fitting in with the gruesome Republican establishment of today. Thank goodness for ConservAmerica; there are traditionalist conservatives in it. I call on them to take this chapter to heart and help spread the old wisdom of Russell Kirk, Richard Weaver, and others. I'd like to see them in the lead bearing the standards of the old wisdom—piety, prudence, posterity, antimaterialism, and respon-sibility that I write about here.

CONSERVATIVE/CONSERVATION

One needs only to glimpse the words—conservation and conser-vatism—to see their linkage. Until 1980, few would have seen conser-vation and conservatism wholly at odds. However, since then, it has become widely thought that conservation (environmentalism even more so) is a liberal or progressive care, and that conservatism clashes with conservation and environmentalism. This belief is a thumping big

---

1   Lisa Demer and Richard Mauer, "US House OKs Opening Arctic National Wildlife Refuge to Oil Drilling," *McClatchey Newspapers,* February 18, 2012.

2   Rep. Robert Dold, "Don't sacrifice Arctic refuge," *Politico,* February 16, 2012.

hurdle for conservationists. At the least, we need to show that some of the lofty beliefs of traditional conservatism—prudence, piety, antimaterialism, responsibility, and posterity—are also among the core beliefs of conservation. Yet we are bedeviled with "conservatives" since Bush Junior first became President, doing everything they can think of to unmake America's *bipartisan* conservation bequest and the wilderness and wildlife network. This has been going on since Reagan, but went into a cranked, over-the-top drag race under Cheney-Bush Junior (such conservatives also spurn the above upstanding beliefs of traditional conservatism such as posterity). Like "conservative" politicians in Canada, Australia, and elsewhere are doing the same. I'll look at the ugly, sharp cleaving of conservatism and conservation in *The Nature Haters*. In this chapter I'll show how traditional conservatism and conservation share underlying beliefs in what is good. In the next, I will offer some free-market paths to conservation that could help shield wild things and furthermore show that conservationists do not sneer at market paths, which would help us in the political whirl. In the end chapters I'll show how conservationists can draw folks from Main Street.

Let's first take a quick look at how in the past conservation and conservatism have been at least willing to talk. America's first conservationist president, Teddy Roosevelt, was a Republican and is still a leading light for true conservatives (though not to hard-line libertarians, corporatists, and neoconservatives). His great-grandson, Theodore Roosevelt IV, has sat on the Governing Council of The Wilderness Society. Presidents Calvin Coolidge and Herbert Hoover were keen fly fishermen and friends of the National Parks.[3] Stephen Fox tells a dandy tale of how Will Dilg of the Izaak Walton League (the Ikes) worked with President Coolidge and Commerce Secretary Hoover in the 1920s to gain legislation to buy and set up the Upper Mississippi River National

---

3   Horace M. Albright and Robert Cahn, *The Birth of the National Park Service: The Founding Years, 1913-33* (Howe Brothers, Salt Lake City, Utah, 1985).

Wildlife Refuge. Hoover was even the honorary president of the Ikes.[4]

Throughout the congressional fight for the Wilderness Act from 1956 to 1964, the bulldog for Wilderness Areas in the House of Representatives was John Saylor, a conservative Republican from Pennsylvania and ranking minority member on the House Interior Committee. When he dropped the Wilderness Bill into the hopper on July 12, 1956, he said, "We are a great people because we have been successful in developing and using our marvelous natural resources; but, also, we Americans are the people we are largely because we have had the influence of the wilderness on our lives."[5] The leading foe of the Wilderness Bill was a New Deal Democrat, Wayne Aspinall, representative from western Colorado and chairman of the House Interior Committee. Aspinall proudly worked for the mining, logging, grazing, and irrigation industries and the union workers in those dig and cut businesses; he did everything he could in his mighty seat to put off and weaken the Wilderness Bill (Committee Chairmen were much stronger in those days). The late Stewart Udall, Secretary of the Interior for Presidents Kennedy and Johnson during the 1960s, recalled before he died, "In [the 1960s], partisan lines were never drawn when conservation issues were concerned. Kennedy's Wilderness bill passed the Senate by a vote of 78 to 12, with only six members of each party voting no."[6] The Wilderness Society's *Living Wilderness* magazine kept track of the fight for the Wilderness Bill in great depth. It printed many heartfelt and knowledgeable statements by Republican Senators and Representatives about our need for Congressionally sheltered Wilderness Areas.

---

4   Stephen Fox, *The American Conservation Movement: John Muir and His Legacy* (The University of Wisconsin Press, Madison, 1985), 168-169.

5   Michael Frome, *Battle for the Wilderness Revised Edition* (University of Utah Press, Salt Lake City, 1997), v. Frome dedicated the revised edition of *Battle for the Wilderness* to John Saylor.

6   Stewart L. Udall, "Bush's Dark Pages in Conservation History," *Los Angeles Times,* July 26, 2004.

For more than two score years among the stars of American conservatism were the Buckley brothers—the late William F. Buckley, father of *The National Review,* and James Buckley, now a Senior U.S. District Judge. James Buckley was a Republican/Conservative U.S. Senator from New York in the 1970s. As such, he was one of the leading backers of the Endangered Species Act (1973) and the Eastern Wilderness Areas Act (1975). Indeed, Buckley was the lead sponsor of the Eastern Wilderness Areas Act in the Senate. In his hearing statement on his bill, he read from early free-market economist, John Stuart Mill, "A world from which solitude is extirpated is a very poor ideal... Nor is there much satisfaction in contemplating the world with nothing left of the spontaneous activity of nature."[7] Ahh, "spontaneous activity of nature"—is this not a winsome way to say "self-willed land?"

As Under Secretary of State for Security Assistance, Science, and Technology for President Ronald Reagan, James Buckley said in 1981, "The needless extinction of a single species can be an act of recklessness. By permitting high rates of extinction to continue, we are limiting the potential growth of biological knowledge. In essence, the process is tantamount to book burning; but it is even worse in that it involves books yet to be deciphered and read."[8]

I miss Nixon. He was no tree-hugger, but he banned DDT and "predicide" 1080, signed the National Environmental Policy Act (NEPA) and the Endangered Species Act, set up the Environmental Protection Agency (EPA), stopped the ecological nightmare Cross-Florida Barge Canal, wrote an executive order for federal land management agencies to brake off-road vehicles, and took many other good stands on conservation and bridling pollution. Now, he was behind bad things as

---

7   Hon. James L. Buckley, *Hearing Before the Subcommittee on Public Lands of the Committee on Interior and Insular Affairs United States Senate Ninety-Third Congress First Session on S. 316.* February 21, 1973. (U.S. Government Printing Office, Washington, 1973), 35.

8   Colin Norman, "The Threat to One Million Species," *Science,* Vol. 214, December 4, 1981, 1105.

well, such as the Supersonic Transport plane (SST), Alaska Pipeline, and more logging on the National Forests. Overall though, the good outweighed the bad, and conservationists could work with his administration. Ballyhooing its 100th anniversary in 1998, *Audubon* magazine picked Nixon as one of its 100 Champions of Conservation, quoting him, "What a strange creature is man that he fouls his own nest."[9] His Assistant Secretary of the Interior for Parks and Wildlife, Nathaniel Reed, is the best conservationist ever to hold that key job. I don't want to overstate Nixon as a conservationist; much of what good he did was politically smart given the mood of the time. Nonetheless, he was much better on conservation than Reagan and the two Bushes—and Barack Obama, who is the worst Democrat President on conservation since Woodrow Wilson.

Mr. Conservative, himself, Senator Barry Goldwater of Arizona, hated off-road vehicles on the public lands. In 1973, he wrote the Southwest Regional Forester in Albuquerque, "I hope there is some way we could outlaw all off-road vehicles, including snowmobiles, motorcycles, etc., which are doing more damage to our forests and deserts than anything man has ever created. I don't think the Forest Service should encourage the use of these vehicles by even suggesting areas they can travel in ... I have often felt that these vehicles have been Japan's way of getting even with us."[10]

Upon leaving the Senate in 1986, Goldwater was asked if there were any votes from his long legislative career he would switch. He said that he was sorry for voting to build Glen Canyon Dam. Now, unless you are from the Southwest, you do not understand the strength of those words. Bringing wild water under the hand of Man to do our bidding is the religion above all others here. For *the* Arizonan of the twentieth century to rue Glen Canyon Dam was mind-boggling.

9   *Audubon*, November-December 1998, 128. I'm proud to be on this list
      with Nixon.

10   David Sheridan, *Off-Road Vehicles on Public Land: A Report to the
      Council on Environmental Quality* Draft, August 1978.

Yes, even more liberal and Democratic politicians have been backers of conservation. All I am saying here is that conservation and conservatism have not always been at loggerheads in American political history.

For why bipartisanship on conservation and environmentalism died, see *The Nature Haters* forthcoming in *For the Wild Things*.

RUSSELL KIRK: CONSERVATION AND CONSERVATISM

There is nothing inborn in traditional conservative thinking to make it against loving and respecting wild things, setting aside Wilderness Areas, sheltering Endangered Species, being prudent with raw goods, boosting federal ownership of land, and stopping and cleaning up pollution. Likewise, there is nothing inborn in liberal and leftist thinking that makes them any more friendly to the above than conservatism. Love for wild things and one's work to shield it fit within any of the three political spectrums Lowi outlines for the United States.[11] Conservation is not wholly tied to any one of them. However, the political hurdle for conservationists at the onset of the twenty-first century is that politicians, the news business, Main Street, and many conservationists have come to believe that conservation comes out of regulatory liberalism (or anticapitalist leftism) and is at loggerheads with conservatism.

Dr. John Bliese, formerly Associate Professor of Communication Studies at Texas Tech University in Lubbock, has done more than anyone since the 1970s to show not only that conservatism and conservation can be like-minded, but also that the intellectual leaders of conservatism from the end of World War Two to the Reagan Revolution, most of all Russell Kirk, Richard M. Weaver, and Clinton Rossiter, were foes of landscalping. In 1953, Kirk wrote *The Conservative Mind*, likely the foremost conservative work of the last hundred years.[12] In a 1996 article

11   Theodore J. Lowi, *The End of the Republican Era* (University of Oklahoma Press, Norman, 1995).

12   Russell Kirk, *The Conservative Mind* (Regnery, Chicago, 1986 (7th Edition)).

for *Modern Age,* Bliese writes, "If we go back to the 'Founding Fathers' of American traditionalist conservatism, we will find a solid philosophical basis that would lead conservatives to be environmentalists."[13] Conservatives and conservationists alike should read his book, *The Greening of Conservative America,* which is a thorough, truthful, and insightful handling of the ecological and pollution plights before the world today.[14] Bliese gives a guide to what conservatism is, with its sundry wings and their sometimes far-flung beliefs, and he sets out a path rooted in bedrock conservatism to keep the tangle of life and to clean up pollution. Conservationists need to read his book since it is unmatched for teaching us how to talk to middle-of-the-road and conservative Americans about conservation and environmentalism. However, I think even more than his book, Bliese's 1996 article "Richard M. Weaver, Russell Kirk, and the Environment" in *Modern Age* stands out as the landmark statement of how traditional conservatives should be conservationists.

True conservatism has deep ties to conservation through the following thrusts: Antimaterialism, Piety, Prudence, Posterity, Standards, and Responsibility.

Before we look at these principles, however, let's go to writings by Russell Kirk on conservation and pollution. Most of the work by Kirk (and Weaver) was written before widespread heed was given to how we were wounding Earth. Nonetheless, Kirk did not shun the land in his syndicated newspaper column in the 1960s and early 1970s. In 1962, he wrote about pesticides and how they harmed wildlife. He told his readers to read Rachel Carson's newly published *Silent Spring.*[15] This was a big deal since Carson's book led to a bitter wrangle among the directors of the Sierra Club at the time, with some pooh-poohing any

13   John R. E. Bliese, "Richard M. Weaver, Russell Kirk, and the Environment," *Modern Age,* Winter, 1996, 148.

14   John R. E. Bliese, *The Greening of Conservative America* (Westview Press, Boulder, CO, 2001).

15   Bliese, "Weaver, Kirk, and the Environment," 156.

harm from pesticides.[16] In your wildest dreams, can you see any leading conservative today telling folks to read a book like *Silent Spring*?

Bliese writes:

> *In 1965, [Kirk] deplored the fact that "rare, strange and beautiful animals are shrinking toward extinction in much of the world." He argued that "preservation of the multitudinous animal species has been enjoined by religion since the dawn of human consciousness," with specific reference to the story of Noah. He wrote this piece in South Africa's Kruger National Park, but added that "we Americans have done our despicable share in decimating the animal kingdom."*[17]

So, even before biologists like Hugh Iltis and Norman Myers were warning about wholesale extinction, the foremost conservative intellectual in America was highlighting the doom of many beings in his newspaper column.

In other columns in 1965, Kirk took on polluting industries, the threat of insecticides, the harm done by overfishing, strip-mining, nuclear waste, and wasting energy. By 1970, he "applauded" student protests against runaway logging and pollution, and wrote, "Nothing is more conservative than conservation." Kirk, unlike politicians and pundits calling themselves conservatives today, did not hold progress up as some sacred cow. He wrote that "pollution, exhaustion of natural resources, the transformation of city and countryside for the worse, and various social afflictions are bound up with our swift technological advance."[18] He backed those who worried about "obsessive materialism and total infatuation with technology," and warned that "the rising generation has the prospect of bad air to breathe, poisoned rivers and

16   Michael P Cohen, *The History of the Sierra Club* (Sierra Club Books, San Francisco, 1988), 285-289.
17   Bliese, "Weaver, Kirk, and the Environment," 156.
18   Bliese, "Weaver, Kirk, and the Environment," 156.

lakes, cities devastated by a 'progress' hastened through technology, and a society that may become little better than a sullen and violent producer-consumer equation."[19] It sounds to me that Russell Kirk in 1970 pegged the beginning of the twenty-first century pretty well.

Today there are still a few conservative thinkers like Bliese who take Kirk's path. One is John Gray of England, who believes that "a Green agenda should come as a natural one for Tories, for whom the past is a patrimony not to be wantonly squandered." Furthermore, Gray believes that "far from having a natural home on the Left, concern for the integrity of the common environment, human as well as ecological, is most in harmony with the outlook of traditional conservatism."[20]

Now, let's look at the philosophical grounds for a traditional conservative path to conservation.

ANTIMATERIALISM

Perhaps the big gap between today's phony "conservatives" and conservation/environmentalism comes from thinking that big business is seemingly at odds with shielding the land or stopping pollution. Since business cares are widely said to be conservative cares, then conservatives think they should choose to back business rather than conservation. However, Bliese writes, "The assertion that equates conservatism and business interests is pure philosophical chicanery, which Clinton Rossiter called 'the Great Train Robbery of American intellectual history.'" Russell Kirk "claimed that 'the conservative interest in America...never had much sympathy with industrial aggrandizement.' While he recognized that businessmen have historically been 'a great prop of American conservatism,' he severely criticized them for being 'intent upon getting and spending to the exclusion of almost every cultural and social interest.'"[21] In 1981, Kirk asked, "What else do conser-

---

19   Bliese, "Weaver, Kirk, and the Environment," 157.
20   Bliese, "Weaver, Kirk, and the Environment," 157.
21   Bliese, "Weaver, Kirk, and the Environment," 149.

vatives and libertarians profess in common? The answer to that question is simple: nothing. Nor will they ever have. To talk of forming a league or coalition between these two is like advocating a union of fire and ice."[22] The unbridled lust for political might, though, has led to fire and ice humping madly together today.

Bliese wisely writes, "Traditional conservatism cannot be equated with business interests for the most fundamental of reasons: a conservative is not a materialist; he rejects the modern belief that the highest end of man is to be a consumer. The antimaterialist stand runs through virtually all of the fundamental works of traditionalist conservatism."[23]

Two of today's leading conservative columnists *sometimes* seem to go along with Bliese, when they can shake off knee-jerk partisanship, which is not often any more. George Will, in a column hailing those withstanding takeover by national business chains, wrote in 1997, "The revolt against the untrammeled sovereignty of economics—in part, a conservative revolt—holds that…a democratic polity can form itself with political choices rather than perfect passivity in the face of market results."[24] John Leo, in a column blasting advertising everywhere, wrote also in 1997, "It's time to resist the commercialization of everything..."[25] But these writings are from fifteen years ago. Will, today, seems to march in lockstep with the Republican Party.

Who is the leading bulwark against materialism and "the untrammeled sovereignty of economics" today? Were Will and Leo to take off their partisan blinders, they would see that it is none other than conservationists and environmentalists, foremost the Sierra Club and the International Forum on Globalization. Today's mood seems to be

22 Russell Kirk, "Libertarians: The Chirping Sectaries," *Modern Age*, Fall 1981, 345. Quoted in Theodore J. Lowi, *The End Of The Republican Era* (University of Oklahoma Press, Norman, 1995), 143.

23 Bliese, "Weaver, Kirk, and the Environment," 149.

24 George Will, "What Starbucks, Wal-Mart, EEU have in common," *The Albuquerque Tribune*, June 23, 1997.

25 John Leo, "Hucksters Spread Blight to Erstwhile Sacrosanct Places," *Albuquerque Journal*, December 29, 1997.

one of greed. "Get stuff" our meaning in life. "Make a buck" the social good most eagerly upheld by so-called conservatives in Congress. Were they alive today, Russell Kirk and Richard Weaver would have scathing words for business and its political plug-uglies. Why do not more of today's self-called "traditional conservatives" flay the sellout to materialism and business by today's "conservatives?" David Brooks of *The New York Times* is the only conservative columnist of whom I know who is yet somewhat true to conservatism as a way, not an ideology, and who is not a thane to shifting GOP true-believerism (however, I am in no way widely knowledgeable about today's sundry conservative columnists). A score or more years ago, James Kilpatrick was a syndicated columnist and a true, freethinking conservative who often backed conservation, much like Kirk.

When William F. Buckley midwifed *National Review* to life in 1955, he said his new magazine "stands athwart history, yelling Stop."[26] Is this not in every way what conservationists and environmentalists have been doing? Indeed we now know, thanks to historian Paul Sutter rooting about in dusty files, that the founders of the modern wilderness movement (the founders of The Wilderness Society in 1935) were truly *driven* to wilderness by their worry over how automobiles and modern industrial life were threats to all that was good and clean in the world. Antimaterialism and antimodernism, both key traditionalist conservative feelings, were hot in the hearts of Aldo Leopold, Bob Marshall, Benton MacKaye, Robert Sterling Yard, and other TWS founders. Sutter's topnotch book, *Driven Wild*, must be read by anyone who wants to understand what the drive to set aside Wilderness Areas is about. In many ways, it is standing athwart the road of history yelling "Stop!"[27]

---

26 George Will, "Brooks Brothers still suits a traditionalist," *Seattle Post Intelligencer*, January 18, 1998.

27 Paul S. Sutter, *Driven Wild: How the Fight Against Automobile Launched the Modern Wilderness Movement* (University of Washington Press, Seattle, 2002).

If conservationists would talk in the words of traditional conservative feeling, maybe more conservatives would listen to us. However, more of the guilt for this plight can be put on the partisanship of diehard authoritarian conservatives. This is why ConservAmerica, Trout Unlimited, Backcountry Hunters & Anglers, and such clubs are so key for outreach and bridge building.

Piety

Bliese writes, "Perhaps the most fundamental value or attitude for a conservative is what Weaver called 'piety'. . . . He believed that to bring harmony back into the world, we must regard three things with the spirit of piety: nature, other people, and the past." Weaver believed that "creation or nature is fundamentally good . . . and that acts of defiance such as are daily celebrated by the newspapers are subversive of cosmos. Obviously a degree of humility is required to accept this view."[28]

Moreover, Weaver believed that how we hold Nature "is basic to one's outlook or philosophy of life." He wrote toward the end of his life that "man has a duty of veneration toward nature and the natural. Nature is not something to be fought, conquered and changed according to any human whims." Bliese writes that Weaver "condemned modern industrialism which 'is making war upon nature, disfiguring and violating her.'"[29] Good grief, Weaver was ranting like Ed Abbey before Ed Abbey.

Bliese further writes, "Piety toward nature is, thus, a fundamental attitude of traditionalist conservatism, and this obviously has profound implications when we confront today's environmental disasters."[30] What should piety toward Nature mean? Bliese says:

Surely the subsidized, systematic destruction of our public forests can only be seen as the height of impiety, on top of being sheer stu-

---

28   Bliese, "Weaver, Kirk, and the Environment," 150.
29   Bliese, "Weaver, Kirk, and the Environment," 150.
30   Bliese, "Weaver, Kirk, and the Environment," 151.

pid policy. Likewise, with his respect for nature, no traditionalist
conservative could sympathize with an industry that opposes clean
water regulations simply because it is so much cheaper to dump
its toxic wastes in the river—and if it destroys the life of the river
and pollutes drinking water for those downstream, too bad, but the
profits on the bottom line look great.[31]

Piety at its best is respect for land when it is yet self-willed and for
deors when they are wildeors. How can one have piety toward one's
slave or toward that over which one lords?

I thoroughly lack belief in ghosts of any kind, but I am often overcome with piety as I drink in the big outside as it is. I no longer need
thrills and derring-do; watching a prairie dog, plump as an old town
burgher, stand outside its burrow and take in the world, or being up-
lifted by the bluster of a rufous hummingbird on its sky-loping through
New Mexico in mid-summer, can near bring me to my knees with bliss-
ful piety. Piety before the little ones is a deep piety, maybe the deepest, the truest, and the best for the soul. It's one thing to be awestruck
before the workings of the wild or before a wildeor when they threaten
to cripple or snuff me, but I also find myself awash with piety when a
flock of bushtits or a sea of desert marigolds makes me smile without
thinking.

PRUDENCE

"For traditionalist conservatives the most important virtue in
politics is prudence," writes Bliese, who then quotes Edmund Burke,
Clinton Rossiter, and Kirk for backing.[32] Bliese also believes that good
stewardship of raw goods is prudence; squandering them as we do is
imprudence. He says climate change and wildlife extinctions are areas
"in which we are performing uncontrolled and irreversible experiments

---

31   Bliese, "Weaver, Kirk, and the Environment," 151.
32   Bliese, "Weaver, Kirk, and the Environment," 152-153.

on the entire planet." Prudence is how we should guide ourselves through these plights.[33] "Traditionalist conservative values would have us make major efforts to preserve all the forms of life on earth, as a matter of prudence and good stewardship."[34] We can see such beliefs at work in how Republican senators such as James Buckley and Pete Domenici spoke for the 1973 Endangered Species Act. Prudence is at the heart of the precautionary principle, which, Grand Canyon Wildlands Council director Kim Crumbo (who was a Navy SEAL in Vietnam and is a retired Grand Canyon National Park river ranger) writes, "reverses the burden of proof by requiring proponents of anthropogenic change to prove that the proposed actions will not harm species and habitats, rather than requiring conservationists to prove a high likelihood of ecological damage or species loss before halting an activity."[35]

Where is prudence, or her sister, humility, among today's "conservative" anticonservationists? Among today's Republican Senators and Representatives? Is pooh-poohing global climate change prudent? Is underwriting rip-and-chop business to cut down the last ancient forests prudent? Is no-holds-barred landscalping for ticky-tacky development spreading out desert cities like Phoenix (eight inches of rain a year), Albuquerque (nine inches), and Tucson (twelve inches) prudent?[36] Where, for goodness sake, does prudence dare show herself in the au-

---

33   Bliese, "Weaver, Kirk, and the Environment," 153.

34   Bliese, "Weaver, Kirk, and the Environment," 154.

35   Kim Crumbo, "The Precautionary Approach to Ecosystem Conservation," Nov. 24, 1999, draft in author's files. I likely know no one tougher and steadier than my friend Crumbo; through him, I understand that prudence and piety for the wild is a mark of thoroughgoing strength.

36   Phoenix has 4.5 million water-sucking dwellers and grows on like the mile-high dust storms (*haboobs*) that now hit it more and more often. All forecasts are for less runoff on the already overdrawn Colorado, Salt, Verde, and Gila rivers on which Phoenix depends. How can anyone think Phoenix can grow for another twenty years as it has the last twenty years and have water enough? Such thinking is the height of imprudence, if not madness.

thoritarian right today? If she is there at all, she slips silently about in the shadows in a head-to-toe burkha. For today's rightwing holy warriors, prudence is blasphemy, it seems.

POSTERITY

Two hundred years ago, Edmund Burke saw society as "a partnership not only between those who are now living, but between those who are living, those who are dead, and those who are to be born."[37] Put that conservative thought alongside the fast-buck thinking of many American business-lords and Republican politicians today. Rossiter writes, "The spirit of trusteeship—the sense of receiving a precious heritage and handing it on intact and perhaps even slightly strengthened—pervades Conservatism."[38] This understanding of posterity is key to the National Wilderness Preservation System. In the 1964 Wilderness Act, Congress stated its policy was "to secure for the American people of present and future generations the benefits of an *enduring* resource of wilderness." Knowing that the Wilderness Act would protect Wilderness into far tomorrows after they were gone greatly heartened those who crafted the Act, as it does we who have worked to put new lands into the National Wilderness Preservation System. As Howard Zahniser of The Wilderness Society and main wordsmith of the Wilderness Act wrote, "The wilderness that has come to us from the eternity of the past we have the boldness to project into *the eternity of the future*."[39] (Emphasis added.) Edmund Burke would have thought well of the Wilderness Act as a farsighted bond with posterity, methinks, as he would have with the Endangered Species Act. Had he thought about it, he may well have wished that the English barons had taken a Wilderness Act and Endangered Species Act along with the Magna Carta to Runnymede to talk to King John. I do.

37 Bliese, "Weaver, Kirk, and the Environment," 151.
38 Bliese, "Weaver, Kirk, and the Environment," 151.
39 Douglas W. Scott, *A Wilderness-Forever Future: A Short History of the National Wilderness Preservation System* (Pew Wilderness Center, Washington, D.C., 2001).

Russell Kirk wrote that "the modern spectacle of vanished forests and eroded lands, wasted petroleum, and ruthless mining ... is evidence of what an age without veneration does to itself and its successors."[40]

Bliese writes that T. S. Eliot warned "that our disregard for nature 'is leading both to the deformation of humanity by unregulated industrialism, and to the exhaustion of natural resources, and that a good deal of our material progress is a progress for which succeeding generations may have to pay dearly.'"[41] Asking Republican leaders what they think about that today would fetch up smirks and guffaws.

VALUES AND STANDARDS

Kirk wrote that conservatives believed in a "transcendent moral order."[42] Against that conservative outlook are cultural relativists in anthropology, postmodern deconstructionists in social science and literature, politically correct guilt-trippers, and other liberal/left followers of political correctness who see all lifeways as even in goodness and soundness. I guess this makes me a cultural conservative because I believe some things are better than other things are. Until not long ago I thought I believed in transcendental goodness, though in a freethinking way. E. O. Wilson in his book *Consilience: The Unity of Knowledge*, however, gave me a fuller understanding—which left me unsettled. His weighing of how transcendental and empirical ethics are unalike is eye opening. He shows that the gap is not "between religious believers and secularists" but "between transcendentalists, those who think that moral guidelines exist outside the human mind, and empiricists, who think them contrivances of the mind."[43] He writes, "The empiricist argument, then, is that by exploring the biological roots of moral behav-

---

40   Bliese, "Weaver, Kirk, and the Environment," 152.

41   Bliese, "Weaver, Kirk, and the Environment," 152.

42   Russell Kirk, "Conservatism: A Succinct Description," *National Review*, September 3, 1982, 1080.

43   Edward O. Wilson, *Consilience: The Unity of Knowledge* (Vintage Books, New York, 1999), 260.

ior, and explaining their material origins and biases, we should be able to fashion a wiser and more enduring ethical consensus than has gone before."[44] I think Wilson is far too Panglossian about Mankind's wherewithal for reason (and goodness!), but he does show that grounds for weighing behavior as good or bad can come from a wise understanding of the wild world—or how things are and have evolved—and of the evolution of the *Homo sapiens* mind. The key thing, however, is to have straightforward thinking of what is good and to not eschew standards owing to relativism on what is clean-living and a righteous lifeway. I do think that the good of life and the Tree of Life are outside the mind of Man, so maybe I am a believer in transcendental values. Don't fret— I'm not going to get any more wrapped up in this hair-splitting.

Any work of Beethoven is better music than anything by Britney. A dusty old red Bordeaux is a better drink than a can of Coors Light—no matter how cold. Georgia O'Keefe's painting of a moonflower (datura) is a better work of art than the sickening "Piss Christ" by Serrano. The Anglo-American take on Western Civilization, with a strong clasp for limited government and acknowledgment of self rights, clay-footed though it is, righteously stands above the wretchedly patriarchal *sharia* society of Islam.[45] And Dick Cavett was a much better television host than Bill O'Reilly.

Likewise, I believe that cross-country skiing is a better way through a snowy landscape than is snowmobiling, that canoeing is better than motor boating, that hiking is better than roaring about on a dirt bike. Saying that dirt biking is as good as walking is like saying that "Ebonics" is as good as English—it's all part of cultural relativism tearing down traditional values. If this makes me a cultural elitist or snob, so be it. (If so, I became snooty owing to the tawdriness about me, not because I was born to be stuck-up thanks to great wealth.) Being widely sought-

44 Wilson, *Consilience*, 262.

45 However, this should not let us think that it is right or wise to foist our political philosophy on other lands.

after does not make something good or better. Popularity has nothing to do with *good*.

William F. Buckley wrote, "It is the proper burden of government to maintain the monuments of a society, and this means not only the Lincoln Memorial, but the prothonotary warbler and the sound of Yo Yo Ma."[46] Wilderness Areas, National Parks, and the Endangered Species Act are monuments to the goodness of the American way no less than are The Declaration of Independence and the Bill of Rights.

George Will writes, "Some pleasures are contemptible because they are coarsening. They are not merely private vices, they have public consequences in driving the culture's downward spiral."[47] Don't-give-a-damn snowmobile, dirt-bike, and jet-ski thrill-seeking is coarsening. Shooting prairie dogs for the glee of watching "red mist" is coarsening. It is a swirl in the downward whirlpool of American culture even more so than is the tawdry trash upchucked into his lap from his television that sickens Will.

I think the authoritarian right and overselfed libertarians have sped the breakdown of standards in our society, indeed the unraveling of *citizenship*. Citizenship is belonging and doing in one's neighborhood however big, whereas greedy individualism lifts up the self over the neighborhood. Are community service clubs such as the Lions, Elks, and Shriners slumping owing to how the greed generation is too self-enthralled, too busy in its mad dash after fast bucks? Good citizenship has become so unwonted that we use the word "hero" now for what once was Main-Street good citizenship. To wit: Giving blood.

I can't help but sneer at the carefree and coarsening bloodiness and low lewdness in everyday culture and how it cheapens the whole of our lives and whatever standards we yet have. But it is kid's stuff alongside the mean-souled politics of bullying, lying, and phony character assas-

46 William F. Buckley, "Wean PBS From Its Federal Subsidy," *Albuquerque Journal,* May 3, 1997.

47 George Will, "'Fear Factor' speeding entertainment rot," *The Albuquerque Tribune,* June 21, 2001.

sination and the self-righteous sham played by the superpartisan pit bulls of the authoritarian right, such as Karl Rove—or the Tea Baggers who shock even Karl. Does not their kind of politics lead to an overall breakdown of standards? Going back to nineteenth-century Robber Baron capitalism makes Wall Street bankers think they are doing nothing wrong.

Conservationists must stand up for straightforward, tough standards in land stewardship and to uphold our beliefs: that we owe wild things sheltering from our works for their own sakes, that other Earthlings are good in themselves. If they are also good to Man for ecosystem services, economics, aesthetics, and happiness, well, that is good, but none are needed to make a wild thing good. It is lily-livered moral relativism that shoves conservationists into wheedling and soft-peddling our beliefs so we don't hurt someone's feelings. We will draw more backing and we will fight better against our foes if we proudly stand behind our wild-loving values and stoutly call for a land ethic rooted in love, piety, and respect for wild things.

Responsibility

Once upon a time, Republicans and conservatives believed in responsibility. Today's phony conservatives in the Republican Party talk about responsibility but wouldn't know what it was even if it came up and bit them on the ass. Nonetheless, a true conservative feeling of responsibility underlies true conservation and respect for the land.

To understand responsibility, we need to understand irresponsibility. Let me offer three kinds of irresponsibility from the larger world of Man and then show how they bear on landscalping.

One, there is an irresponsibility rooted in not understanding the upshot of one's behavior on oneself, such as cigarette smoking and not wearing seat belts. Some of this comes from the teenager's feeling of deathlessness, some comes from having a dirt clod for a brain where one just can't put the two and two of doing and outcome together.

Two, there is an irresponsibility where one has no care for others. Driving drunk does not only put oneself in harm's way as does not wearing a seat belt, but it threatens everyone on the road.

Three, there is further irresponsibility where one scrambles to hide from the outcomes of one's irresponsibility. We all hate Big Brother, but love Big Mother. We snarl, "Don't tell me where I can build my house! This is my private property!" But when the hurricane blows away our home on a barrier island, we run to the government begging for a hand—like the two-year-old who doesn't want mommy telling it not to trundle down the sidewalk, but squealing like a stuck pig when it skins its knee. "Mommy! Mommy!" rugged individualists and daring capitalists squall when they fall. Then there is the hiker in a National Park who blows off the warnings that there is a mean bear on the trail and hikes there anyway. After being roughed up by the bear, she sues the Park Service. The bear gets shot.

A conservative take on responsibility should damn all three. With landscalping and pollution we find irresponsibility of all three kinds.

Landowners who shear and plunder their land without understanding or caring about the upshot of their irresponsibility are somewhat like cigarette smokers or seat belt eschewers. However, they are worse, since their irresponsibility also harms others—downstream, downwind, and next door, as well as wild things on their land. It also harms posterity—tomorrow's owners and coming waves of wild things.

Flighty, rash "libertarians" sing-song the holy words *private property rights* when up against government regulation of their behavior. Of course, property rights are near to hallowed among conservatives. Clinton Rossiter warned, however, that "the Conservative defense of private property is most certainly not a defense of its abuse, neglect, or existence in grotesque forms and exaggerated concentrations. Nor is it primarily a defense of industrial capitalism or large scale private enterprise."[48] My! Private property rights bear with them private prop-

---

48   Bliese, "Weaver, Kirk, and the Environment," 154.

erty responsibilities. What an outlandish thought! As Rossiter says, "No right carries with it greater obligations than the possession of property, which is a legacy from the past, a power in the present, and a trust for the future."[49]

Like Rossiter, Weaver sundered individual property and corporate property, a line I think is too often lost in the tussle over property rights and government regulation to keep wetlands or Endangered Species, or to stop pollution. I think it cuts the other way, too. Small landowners and small businessfolk should not be dealt with like big corporations when it comes to pollution-cleanup laws and the Endangered Species Act. We conservationists should acknowledge that small, noncorporate landowners should not have to bear the whole fare of bestowing a social good—like secure habitat for an Endangered Species. The law should see Jim Bob Throckmorton and Global Land Gobbling, Inc. as unlike in how much sole responsibility each should have for stewarding the greater good on their lands. True, Jim Bob should be a responsible caretaker of the Tree of Life on his hundred acres of woodland, but he may need help from all of us, whereas Global should be responsible without all of us footing the bill. John Davis, in his work shielding and rebuilding wildlands in New England and the Adirondacks, finds that most of the big "working landscape conservation" deals touted by The Nature Conservancy are on corporate lands.

Laws that curb one's irresponsible use of property are valid within a traditional conservative framework. Russell Kirk wrote, "Few people are more reluctant than this writer to interfere with private property and free enterprise. Yet no man, and no corporation, has a vested right to make a town and a country ugly and monotonous, or to annihilate the past for immediate profit. *The time has come when governmental powers must be employed to save what remains of our visible heritage.*" (Emphasis added.) Bliese says, "Kirk's reasoning would *a fortiori* apply to saving the earth."[50]

49 Bliese, "Weaver, Kirk, and the Environment," 155.
50 Bliese, "Weaver, Kirk, and the Environment," 156.

By this thinking, laws to stop pollution or scalping of the land are good and needed within a conservative framework. Rash, thoughtless harm to one's land in this way can come as:

- Fouling your own land or doing a bad job of taking out the raw goods (grass, timber, soil, water, minerals, oil, and such) on your land;
- Working your own land in such a way that fouls others' and the public's lands or cheapens the raw goods and other good things on their lands;
- Fouling public land or wrecking the health and wholeness of public land by one's permitted business (timber cutting, grazing, recreation) and then telling us that if we want them to be more responsible then we have to pay them. The recklessness of some public land permittees and visitors is akin to that of a heavy metal band trashing their hotel room and then skipping out on the bill. I like the sign on the wall of Rudy's, a darned good barbeque joint in Albuquerque, "Your Mother Is Not Here. Clean Up Your Own Mess." Nonetheless, greedy businesses whine that being made to act responsibly or as a good citizen is a "taking" if it costs them higher profits and thereby they should be paid by taxpayers for their "loss." The right stirs a hell of a lot of gall into their victimization cocktail.

A conservative way of looking at pollution, whether it harms Man or wildlife or both, would come from the Texas frontier saying, "You don't piss down your neighbor's well." You clean up after yourself and make sure your crap doesn't get on your neighbor's place. Nowadays, we understand groundwater more and know that if you only piss down your own well, it might come up in your neighbor's well, too. Alack, today too many big and little businesses think nothing of pissing down theirs and everyone's wells. Or of howling about "socialism" whenever we the people, as in state or federal government, tell them to clean up their mess. In the new conservatism, "responsibility" means "socialism" or "tyranny."

Every Monday afternoon, I recall the worthiness of being responsible. My dad was a master sergeant in the Air Force. As a kid, I had the job of cleaning up the yard around our base housing.

"David! Go police the yard," my dad would order, and out I would go. If I didn't get it spotless—as in every cigarette butt and gum wrapper that had blown in, I got to do it over and over until it was spotless. I hated policing the yard.

I still do.

But I still police my yard.

Trash pickup in my neighborhood is on Monday morning. My house and yard sit at the end of a wind tunnel. The wind often blows down from the mountains right at my house on Sunday nights and Monday mornings—when my uphill neighbors have their trash out for pickup. A lot of it ends up in my yard.

Monday afternoon is when I police the yard and the only time I ever wish my wife and I had children. I'd love to be able to bark, "Go police the yard!" I've said it a few times to my wife.

"Nancy! Go police the yard!"

The yard doesn't get policed that way. I might as well be talking to the cats.

Sixty-six years old and I'm still policing the yard.

Police your yard. Don't let your trash blow into your neighbor's yard. Don't piss down your neighbor's well. Take care of tomorrow. If that ain't conservative, what the hell is?

THE UPSHOT FOR CONSERVATION

If we wildlovers talk about piety, prudence, posterity, and other values in the way of Burke, Kirk, and other traditional conservatives as the grounds for keeping wild things, we may show more Main Street Americans that they should back wilderness and wildlife conservation.

Whether worldly or heavenly, traditional or populist, conservatives should take a righteous stand against scalping the land and wasting other Earthlings. In the next chapter, we will see if libertarianism can help conservation.

CHAPTER 10

Conservation and the "Free Market"

The constitution does not guarantee that land speculators will win their bets.

—Law professor John Humbach, 1993

WHETHER DEMOCRATS OR REPUBLICANS run the show the next few years, three things are likely: (1) Business, Republican politicians, Tea Baggers, and other "conservatives" will howl themselves hoarse that laws and regulations to make corporations and businessfolks behave responsibly are socialism; (2) The same pack of knaves will keep up their spooky sing-song that cutting taxes for the rich will make lots of jobs and unleash all kinds of other wonders; and (3) Federal and state spending on almost everything that does not help business and the wealthy will be cut so as to lower deficits without raising government income (taxes).[1] Among the many harmful outcomes, two fore-

---

1   There are lots of businessfolks and even some bigger corporate businesses that do their best to be responsible. I'm sorry to wield such a broad brush against business. When I scorch "business," I mean the irresponsible, "movement-conservative" businesses, big and little.

[217]

most should worry conservationists and environmentalists. One is that government spending for what we hold dear (National Parks, clean water, and the like) will be cut. The other is that anything "socialistic" (anything that could harm business profits) will be targeted for fettering or shutdown by right-wingers. Throughout the gutter fight for the Republican Party presidential nomination in 2011-12, we heard the candidates out-yelling one another about killing the Environmental Protection Agency (EPA; signed into law by Richard Nixon, they seem to forget), opening all federal lands for energy leasing and exploitation, and how global warming is a hoax.

So, to deal with this madness, we need to pull some new tools out of our kit. To wit: finding other ways to get needed dollars for conservation and environmental agencies, and using the "free market" against the Nature Haters, right-wing liars, and sham libertarians.

The dare for conservationists is to offer or take true free-market steps where they might help shelter the Tree of Life and wilderness, to shield the public lands, and to clean up or plug smokestacks and drainpipes—without sidelining the belief of wild things as good-in-themselves. In other words, conservationists may take market paths as tools that sometimes work for our goals, but we do not have to fake the belief that the market outweighs the Tree of Life as the bedrock good. Although market thinking (or most often phony libertarian thinking) has been wielded to fight wilderness and wildlife, thoughtful, carefully chosen marketism can strengthen conservation. We do need to listen to free-market conservationists like Karl Hess Jr. and Randal O'Toole. One does not need to think the free market has witchy might or that History meant it to be to see that it is oftentimes a good tool.[2]

I think that conservationists have leaned too much on federal law and regulation at times, thanks somewhat to many conservationists (and even more environmentalists) coming from an activist liberal background. Something's wrong? There ought to be a law! The thor-

2   Like Marxists, free-market true believers are historical determinists.

oughgoing irresponsibility and sometimes out-and-out evil of corporate business, though, has brought the true need. Through their lack of land stewardship and good citizenship, grub-and-cut businesses (logging, mining, grazing, irrigation, and energy), subdividers and developers, and befouling smokestack businesses have built the screaming need for the federal government to step in with a big stick. Teddy Roosevelt understood this over one hundred years ago when he took on the trusts and the "malefactors of great wealth." An uncaring, wicked gang in business and their goons in "movement conservatism" along with their dupes in the Tea Party now want to take the law back to where it was before Roosevelt.

Let me lay out a rough path of where conservation might head with some free-market steps. I underline that this is a rough path and it is not the only path for conservation (and environmentalism). I scratch it down to open some eyes and to get others thinking. These steps fall into three cubbies: Regulatory Reform, Free Market, and Incentives. Keep this in mind: In the last chapter, I went into the key philosophical *goods* of traditional conservatism. Overall, libertarianism does not share these values. Indeed, some wings of libertarianism are at war with these beliefs no less than they are with "socialism." Some years ago at a workshop on "free market environmentalism," I gave a talk drawn from an early draft of Chapter 9. Afterward, an editorial page editor for the *Wall Street Journal* told me that conservatives today did not follow or care about Russell Kirk and other traditionals, that today's movement was wholly libertarian.

REGULATORY REFORM
Banning, Not Regulation

What do you do with truly nasty things? Is the only choice between bureaucratic regulation and the hand of the market? No, there is another choice: flat-out banning. This is what we did with DDT (although "movement conservatives" today howl that was wrong).[3] When a chemical or land use is awful, do not work to regulate it with stacks of nitpicking regulations that give work to scores of lawyers and professional experts; instead utterly outlaw it.

Indeed, this is the path of the Wilderness Act—not to think you can regulate the Forest Service, National Park Service, Bureau of Land Management, and Fish and Wildlife Service's road building and logging, or the motorheads' play with dirt bikes and all-terrain vehicles, but straight-out forbid them in Wilderness Areas set up by the law. The 1968 National Wild and Scenic Rivers Act didn't tell the Corps of Engineers and Bureau of Reclamation when and where and how to build dams; it instead said, "*Don't* build them on *these* rivers."

Like straightforward forbidding needs to be done on other public lands and for a cluster of fast-buck scams and outdoor pastimes. To wit: Motorized vehicles of every kind should be banned from going off signed roads; commercial and recreational trapping should be unlawful; and motorized watercraft of any kind should be banned in Grand Canyon and many other National Parks. In the seas, seabed trawling cannot be regulated so that its wracking and wasting is harmless enough. It is deadly in and of itself and must be outlawed everywhere. Likewise, to Davy Jones's locker with whaling and sink the ne'er-do-well IWC (International Whaling Commission), too. Some things are out-and-out bad and cannot be done right. Conservationists and environmentalists should work to end them and not seek win-win outcomes with stakeholders whether it is mountain-top removal for coal mining or fishing for shark fins.

Set the Goals, Not the Way

Too often government regulations for public lands grazing, building and running ski areas, oil and gas exploration and extraction, rec-

---

3   "Movement conservatives" is insider-speak for those in the ideologically hard conservative movement.

reational and athletic games on public lands, and other doings lay out hundreds of tangled, sometimes baffling steps on how things must be done to reach stewardship goals. (Let's not worry now if these and other business and play should be brooked at all on public lands.) Free-market conservationists say that it is better to set up wanted goals or outcomes and then give leeway on how someone gets there. I think this way better understands how our minds work; it could also get rid of much unneeded red tape and bureaucratic spending—which then could go to on-the-ground work. It would take away some of the "mythical anecdotes" Nature haters sing to cast themselves as picked upon and bullied. However, if a permittee falls short of set goals, such scofflaws should be dealt with harshly, or the work shut down, which—you guessed it—will lead to more weepy "we're-victims" whines. This path would only work for some things, such as maybe for downhill ski areas on National Forests. We at least ought to see if it is workable through a dry run or two.

Seek Steps Other Than Federal Government Regulation

The Tea Baggers are only the latest embodiment of a grassroots uprising against what is seen as heavy-handed regulation by federal bureaucrats. Some are driven by greed or by a crackpot "rugged individualism." Many are crybabies who won't take grown-up responsibility for their plight and find public servants or "environmeddlers" handy to finger. Nonetheless, many well-meaning folks (who may not be thoroughly against shielding Endangered Species or setting aside Wilderness Areas) feel that the federal government is a bully and is everywhere and unbending. Landscalpers have cleverly and often believably cast conservation and environmental outfits as special-interest groups wedded to big government bureaucracy and heavy-handed regulation.

Strong federal laws and regulations are often needed to shield the wild things and wild loveliness of the United States, and the health and happiness of its folks. We should be steadfast in backing those laws and regulations and in working to strengthen them where needed. We also need standing in the courts. Many of our most meaningful wins have come before judges. However, there are other ways, such as voluntary agreements, working of the market, tax incentives, "cap-and-trade," and state and local laws and regulations. Wilderness and wildlife keepers need to be in the forefront of delving into these other paths (but we must not let them be grounds for cutting bad deals or for downplaying the inborn worth of wild things). There are those who want conservationists to cut deals with landscalpers whatever the outcome. For them, the deal is the goal, never mind the upshot. That is wrong—ethically and strategically.

Some environmental and conservation clubs have done well by sidestepping government and working with big businesses to get them to take good steps (often after softening them up with boycotts, demonstrations, and other badgering). Government is mostly out of the way in such deals. The Rainforest Action Network (RAN) opened this path, which sometimes can work well.[4] The threat is that enviro-resourcist groups strike soft deals with big business. Tough outfits should not be shy in watchdogging such deals and naming names when the meek or enviro-resourcists sell out wild things, even when they are hoary outfits that have gone soft or to the other side—the Montana Wilderness Association and The Nature Conservancy come to mind, along with a slew of outfits in Canada where such knuckling under to industry seems to be a national pastime.

While some "unfunded federal mandates" are needed and fair, others are an unfair burden on state and local government. The conservation web must be careful in weighing which are needed and which are not. We should also be careful and thoughtful in weighing the outcomes of what seem to be well-founded rules—do they lead to more bitter-

---

4   Mike Roselle, Nancy Morton, and I started RAN at the kitchen table in Nancy's home in Chico, California. Randy Hayes in San Francisco soon stepped in to lead it with Roselle.

ness and long-time political harm than the good they do? Government regulations and standards should be even-handed, user-friendly, and as free of red tape as can be. The paperwork landslide and bean counting small businesses have to do under some government rules shove overwrought small businessfolks into the forefront of antigovernment feeling. Conservationists should work to keep such paperwork as little as it can be.

We do-gooders need to be more thoughtful and open to thinking about how something looks through the eyes of business and others.

FREE MARKET
No Subsidies

While it is often thought that there is no socialist strength in America and that "welfare as we know it" is dead, a mighty block of U.S. senators, representatives, and state governors shove a lineup of socialism, welfare handouts, and entitlement rights. They fly below the radar screen of folk and news-business awareness because they cowl their Big Mother scam with high-flying ballyhooing of the free market, individual rights, and no governmental butting-in. I am not talking about an undercover cell of Maoists, but about pork-barrel "conservatives." Mike Smith, an assistant secretary of the Department of Energy in the Bush Junior administration, laid out their goal in one talk, "The biggest challenge is going to be how to best utilize tax dollars to the benefit of industry."[5]

Anticonservation attorney Karen Budd-Falen stamps her foot down that federal land agencies must "protect the economic or commu-

---

5   Carl Pope and Paul Rauber, *Strategic Ignorance: Why the Bush Administration Is Recklessly Destroying a Century of Environmental Progress* (Sierra Club Books, San Francisco, 2004), 25-26. Notwithstanding how I have often been at odds with Pope, this was a darned good and helpful book. Someone needs to do a like job on the Obama Administration's reckless undercutting and overthrowing of our bipartisan birthright of conservation and environmental bulwarks and caretaking.

nity stability of those communities and localities surrounding national forests and BLM-managed lands."[6] Then-Senator Frank Murkowski of Alaska (later governor), at a Senate Energy and Natural Resources subcommittee hearing on the Forest Service, January 25, 1996, said, "These people [loggers in southeast Alaska] are great Americans. Blue collar Americans. They work hard and look to us for help. We should be able to help them. ... I have constituents out there who are real people, and they are entitled to a job. ... These people rely on the government to provide them with a sustainable livelihood."[7] It might be fair for Murkowski to call on the federal government to underwrite jobs for his folks. However, he should not call himself a conservative Republican and should come clean that he is a welfare socialist.[8] (Alaska is by far the most socialistic state in the union, its make-believe rugged individualism notwithstanding.) And, by the way, who is not a "real person?" I wonder if those who fling the line about have been watching too many vampire and zombie shows on television. I would say that corporations are not real persons, notwithstanding how they are blessed with personhood by twisted law.

Here's what philosophers call a "thought experiment." Daydream that these lines from Smith, Budd-Falen, and Murkowski came instead from a Democratic member of Congress, say a blaring, burly black woman from East St. Louis. Why, the Republicans would be all over themselves calling her a socialist, even a communist. Some might have

---

6   Karen Budd-Falen, "Protecting Community Stability and Local Economies," in Philip D. Brick and R. McGreggor Cawley, eds., *A Wolf in The Garden: The Land Rights Movement and The New Environmental Debate* (Rowman & Littlefield Publishers, Inc., Lanham, Maryland, 1996), 73-74.

7   "Senate Hearing on GAO Report on Forest Service," email from Bruce Hamilton, Sierra Club, January 28, 1996.

8   Murkowski was defeated for reelection as governor by a Republican primary challenge from a little-known housewife and small-town mayor by the name of Sarah Palin. Murkowski's daughter, Lisa, is one of Alaska's senators and thought of as a "moderate" Republican.

heart attacks, their wrath boiling enough to pop arteries. But, when said by other Republicans, it's good, old, all-American conservatism and free-marketism. Their rugged individualism is a toddler's rugged individualism. You don't have to be a world-weary political scientist with a Ph.D. to be clever enough to understand that all this job talk by right-wingers is a two-fold scam. One, it's raw meat to toss to gullible voters, who, if they were smart enough to vote for what's good for them, would never vote for such Republicans. Two, forsooth, it's meant to get government handouts to big business under the hoax of helping them make jobs for "great Americans, blue-collar Americans."

Not only do these so-called conservatives back government job-making and handouts for resource extraction businesses, the subsidies they back help the worst players stay in business. Without government help, the ecologically most harmful ranchers and loggers on public lands would not make it. At the heart of a free market is business wipe-out.

Jared Diamond, a wide-roaming scientist who lays out eye-burning bright insights in his books, enlightens us on this tangle when he writes that in Australia and the United States, "rural people are considered honest, and city-dwellers are considered dishonest. If a farmer goes bankrupt, it's assumed to be the misfortune of a virtuous person overcome by forces beyond his control....."[9] This Myth of Rural Moral Superiority has been used like a never-dying gunslinger to uphold the wants of the old-timey economic elite in the West (and elsewhere).

One of the best and boldest public servants of our time was the late Mike Synar, a rancher and congressman from Oklahoma. Synar led the fight in Congress to straighten out and make fair public lands grazing. He told David Helvarg,

---

9   Jared Diamond, *Collapse: How Societies Choose to Fail or Succeed* (Viking, New York, 2005), 394. Diamond is dead-on here, but can be amazingly naïve when it comes to extractive industry.

*These are a bunch of whining welfare cowboys and the next sound
you hear is the nipple coming out of their lips.... These are the same
people who come into their congressman's office and say, "I want
the government to run like a business." So I say, "Okay, we're going
to give you a dose of free enterprise. We're going to make you pay
the fair market value of the assets you're using up on our federal
lands, whether it's timber or grazing or minerals."*[10]

A 2005 study by the Government Accountability Office shows
that the Forest Service and Bureau of Land Management together
"lose at least $123 million a year keeping public lands open to livestock
grazing."[11] And this is without the costs of long-time wracking of watersheds, water quality, and wildlife being reckoned into the tally. Even the
pro-business British news magazine, *The Economist,* says the U.S. public
land economic system "tempered rugged individualism with socialist
infrastructure."[12]

Karl Hess Jr., who was fired from the Cato Institute for being a
truthful and righteous libertarian and not a biostitute for landscalpers, writes that resource extraction industries and Western boomers
have "been for over a century... the standard bearer of more, *not less,*
government."[13] They "have been nurtured on a cornucopia of federal

10   David Helvarg, *The War Against the Greens* (Sierra Club Books, San
     Francisco, 1994), 33.
11   Jennifer Talhelm, Associated Press, "Grazing Costs Feds Money,"
     Albuquerque Journal, November 2, 2005.
12   "Last Round-Up for the Old West," *The Economist,* March 6, 1993,
     quoted in Helvarg, *The War Against the Greens,* 63.
13   Karl Hess Jr., "Wising Up to the Wise Use Movement," in *A Wolf in The
     Garden,* 161. Karl's daddy is the Karl Hess who wrote Barry Goldwater's
     acceptance speech at the 1964 Republican Convention—the one that
     goes "Extremism in the pursuit of liberty is no vice ...." Karl Jr. is a true
     conservationist who cares about wild things. He has more faith in the
     goodness and wisdom of communities and the common man than I do,
     though. Nonetheless, we are friends and I've done my best (not good
     enough, I fear) to get other conservationists to give him more heed.

subsidies" and "are the nation's lingering link to socialism."[14] "Basically, whatever the West needed and wanted it got from big government."[15] "By every measure, the American West was built on federal dollars.... hundreds of rural communities across the West would be nothing but ghost towns today were it not for the free flow of government dollars from the Forest Service, the BLM, the Post Office, and dozens of federally run or financed welfare programs."[16] Federal payments "bail out the worst of stockmen and they keep the most marginal—and commonly the most environmentally destructive—of ranches in operation, frustrating the efforts of the best and most dedicated federal-land managers."[17]

But Caren Cowan, head of the New Mexico Cattle Growers, said of federal grazing permittees, "We are almost in a life-and-death situation here. It's getting tough to be a cowboy."[18] There is no gainsaying that it's getting tough to be a cowboy. The land has been scalped for over one hundred years and the economics of the range livestock industry have gone south. What Cowan seems to say, however, is that the taxpayers owe a handful of folks the folkloric cowboy lifeway, that ranchers have an entitlement to herd cattle while sucking away bucks from other Americans thanks to their being a quaint reminder of America's days of yore, even though they are the ones answerable for the downfall of the range livestock industry through their lousy and greedy stewardship.

It's tough running other businesses, too. Owners and staff of small, offbeat bookstores are a bunch of Americans with a quaint lifeway who truly give America something worthwhile. Why have they not asked for taxpayer subsidies? My sister, Roxanne Pacheco, and I had a mail-order bookstore for five or six years. Thanks to market seesawing, our lack of

---

14   Hess, "Wising Up to the Wise Use Movement," 162.
15   Hess, "Wising Up to the Wise Use Movement," 164.
16   Hess, "Wising Up to the Wise Use Movement," 166.
17   Hess, "Wising Up to the Wise Use Movement," 176.
18   Paul Rogers and Jennifer LaFleur, "The Giveaway Of The West," *San Jose Mercury News,* November 7, 1999.

working capital, and our own weaknesses running a business, we found ourselves in a "life-and-death situation." However, we did not dream of taxpayers propping us up so we could have the lifeway of owning our own business and letting her, a single mother, work at home and raise her family. We shut down Books of the Big Outside and found other ways to make our livings.

Other ranchers east of the public-lands states huff about the unfair edge public-lands cowboys get. Scott Dewald of the Oklahoma Cattlemen's Association says of the low federal grazing fees, "We consider it to be an unfair subsidy. The fee should be based on public auctions, high bidder takes it."[19]

Cutting subsidies to resource extraction industries is a big way the free market can better steward the land and the wildlife it holds.

Green Scissors

Beginning in 1995, the Green Scissors Campaign brought together groups as far-flung as Friends of the Earth and the National Taxpayers' Union to fight federal spending programs "that damage the environment and waste taxpayer dollars." So often it is pork-barrel politics and subsidies to extractive industry that scalp public lands, wetlands, and homes for Endangered Species. Now that the ballooning federal budget has become the trumpeting, crazed bull elephant in musth in the room, it is time for wildlovers to rally 'round the Green Scissors Campaign. The 2011 offering from Green Scissors was written by staffers from Taxpayers for Common Sense, The Heartland Institute, Friends of the Earth, and Public Citizen. Yes, The Heartland Institute, a hardcore, rightwing, global-warming-denying outfit.

The "Introduction" to *Green Scissors 2011* says:

Green Scissors strives to make environmental and fiscal responsibility a priority in Washington. For more than 16 years, Green

19   Rogers and LaFleur, "The Giveaway Of The West."

*Scissors has exposed subsidies and programs that both harm the
environment and waste taxpayer dollars. The campaign has built
a strong case that the federal government can protect our natural
resources, reduce the growth of government spending, and make
a significant dent in the national debt. Building on last year's detailed cut lists, Green Scissors 2011 identifies more than $380
billion in wasteful government subsidies that are damaging to the
environment and harming taxpayers.*

*Wasteful government spending comes in many different forms. The
most obvious are direct spending on discretionary programs and
mandatory programs such as commodity crop payments. Slightly
less transparent are tax expenditures, privileges written into the
tax code, or below market giveaways of government resources like
timber and hardrock minerals. Even more opaque is preferential
government financing for harmful projects through bonding loans,
long term contracting authority and loan guarantees, and risk reduction through government insurance and liability caps.*[20]

Let me bring out the bottom line here again: "Green Scissors 2011
identifies more than $380 billion in wasteful government subsidies that
are damaging to the environment and harming taxpayers." When you
need to take some ax swings at a $1 trillion deficit, $380 billion in one
fell swoop is a darn good start. Among the fields with thoughtful, prudent cuts in wasteful federal spending and subsidies offered by Green
Scissors are energy, agriculture, livestock, transportation, hardrock
mining, National Forest logging, public lands grazing, flood insurance,
and Army Corps of Engineers boondoggles.[21] The way Green Scissors
has brought together outfits from far-flung political roots shows the

20   Autumn Hanna, Eli Lehrer, Benjamin Schreiber, and Tyson Slocum,
      Green Scissors 2011 (Friends of the Earth, Washington, DC, 2011).
      Online at www.greenscissors.com
21   Hanna, et al., *Green Scissors 2011.*

worth of conservationists tackling government waste and subsidies for the good of wild things.

No Externalities

Forsooth, I have little understanding of economics, but I know that some costs of doing business are *internalized*. In other words, those outlays have to go into the ledger for making the wares. They are then handed on to the buyer in the price of the gimcrack. If such internal outlays make the price of the wares too high...well, that is where the believed-in shrewdness and cleverness of the market is trusted to come up with an answer. Bad businessfolks lose and go out of business if they cannot meet their outlays of making, overseeing, and selling. However, in our phony free market, many costs are *externalized*. Such costs are not tallied into the cost of making the gimcrack and therefore into its price to the buyer. They are externalized to all of us as a whole. Rather like the old rust-bucket Soviet system it seems to me.

With industries that are given leeway to foul air and water and land with deadly banes, all of us pay the bill in health woes and falling good of life. With resource extraction industries, cut-and-run work leads to water fouling, loss of wildlife neighborhoods, earth washing away, blighting of the loveliness of the landscape, cheapening outdoor play, and so on. Loggers, miners, gas drillers, and ranchers do not shell out for these bills; they externalize them to society as a whole, making out like plunderers with the bucks they have squeezed out of the land and water.

Conservationists should howl that such businesses not be subsidized by all of us and that all costs be internalized. Let's de-Sovietize the American economy. Let's drink a draught of free enterprise. If a rancher can put their ledger in the black from their livestock only by cutting gulches, scalping off the grass, and killing wildlife (such as wolves and mountain lions), then that rancher should not be in business. If no rancher can make a living on this or that federal allotment without externalizing many costs, such grazing allotments should be withdrawn from leasing. If a gold mine cannot make a go of it without fouling and wasting the land that all of us have to pay for, then the market says that gold mine will not work and must be shut down, with the owners coughing up the bucks for that shutdown, clean up, and everything else. If logging cannot be done without blowing out hillsides, silting in streams, wasting wildlife homes, and wrecking the salmon fishing business, then it has borne out that it is a loser dollar-wise.

A no-subsidies path can also be taken for landowners who build where wildfire often happens, on floodplains, in hurricane targets, and the like. The U.S. should shell out no help for *foreseeable* natural catastrophes. If folks are foolish enough to build in spots likely to be wrecked, they—who get the happiness of living in such lovely landscapes—and not all of us, should bear the gamble. They are free to buy unsubsidized private insurance and should be goaded to do so by government. Too often Americans have a two-year-old's take on freedom—thoroughgoing self-seeking with no glimmer of responsibility. They want to be free and have the government off their backs, but come hard times or an upset and they want to be taken care of. One of the best ways to keep and shelter barrier islands, wetlands, river bottoms, and forests would be for government to stop insuring devil-may-care building by not bailing out heedless folks from hurricanes, floods, and forest fires. Such owners are now externalizing the true costs of living in lands of high ecological worth to society as a whole. This path should go two-fold for the shady fast-buck scammers who sold them the lots or condos. Unless they fully laid out the threats to buyers, developers should be answerable for flood, fire, and landslide wipeout. If Trent Lott wants to stouteartedly sneer at hurricanes by rebuilding his small castle in their likely path, then let him be the one who gets hit in the pocketbook by wind and wave, not we taxpayers.

Am I a heartless old sourpuss? No, I just believe in personal responsibility. But maybe in today's whiny world that does seem like being a heartless old sourpuss.

Open Bidding

Among conservation clubs, those most willing to try free-market paths are, oddly, among the toughest. In the Southwest, no-backing-down outfits like Forest Guardians (now WildEarth Guardians) and the Southwest Environmental Center (Las Cruces) have outbid ranchers on state grazing permits, offering to pay more to not graze cattle and to heal wracked streams. Back in August 2005, Forest Guardians had over 3,000 acres of New Mexico State Land, 162 acres of Arizona State Land, and 100 acres of City of Santa Fe land under lease. These leases were along four streams, and none are being grazed by livestock now. Furthermore, WildEarth Guardians has gotten helpers, many high-school students among them, for hands-on ecological restoration, such as willow and cottonwood planting to heal old grazing wounds.[22] As of 2012, WildEarth Guardians had 4,000 acres of state leases in New Mexico and 200 in Arizona. They are also doing stream restoration for beaver habitat and knitting streams back together on National Forests in New Mexico.

In the Northwest, Andy Kerr, the tree hugger most hated by the Oregon logging business, and Mitch Friedman of the Northwest Eco-system Alliance (NWEA—now Conservation Northwest) have given free-market paths a go. NWEA has bid on Forest Service timber sales to keep ancient forests from being cut. These folks and others are saying, "You want fiscal responsibility? You want the free market? We'll outbid those who would damage the land so we can keep the habitat healthy."

In a mind-boggling step in 1999, NWEA offered the Washington State Lands Department the dollar-worth of ancient forests in the state-owned Loomis Forest to keep it from being logged. The tab? Eighteen million dollars. Many conservationists thought Mitch Friedman had gone daft, but Mitch and his friends coaxed some five thousand citi-

22   See www.wildearthguardians.org for updated information

zens into believing that Loomis Forest was worth more standing than cut (it has the best lynx neighborhoods in the lower forty-eight states). The wildlands philanthropists ponied up. NWEA laid down the dollars to the state. Loomis Forest still stands for the lynx and other wildeors needing a wild wooded neighborhood.[23] NWEA's work on Loomis Forest yet stands as the most derring-do play of the free market to keep and set aside an outstanding wild landscape for the wildeors living there.

Cost-Benefit Analyses

If we do not let economics (and narrow business-profit tallies foremost) lord over how lands are cared for and how foul banes are quenched, cost-benefit analyses are sometimes good for wild things. Had fair cost-benefit analysis been done, many dams choking once-freeflowing streams would never have been built. Truthful cost-benefit analysis would block most logging and grazing on public lands. Cost-benefit weighing would scream for overthrowing the 1872 mining law. Thorough cost-benefit analysis would kill much buckraking rape-and-scrape—think of the infrastructure cost to bring another 100,000 folks to live in Albuquerque. How much does more crime, pollution, sprawl, sucking up the Rio Grande, and such from new housing, roads, and strip malls cost today's dwellers? What is the health toll of more fouling of air, water, and ground where we live? How fast does it hasten Albuquerque's overshoot and crash insofar as fresh water? For the big, sprawling, busting out at the seams towns in the dry West, growth will hasten death. For each new subdivision, newcomer, mile of freeway, water pipe—sooner comes the day when tumbleweeds and dust devils race down the lonely parkways instead of Hummers and Lexuses; sooner comes the day when broken windows bedeck the new malls

---

23   Mitch Friedman, "A Checkerboard Conundrum," *Wild Earth*, Summer 2001, 34; Mitch Friedman, "Forest Green: How Private Money Saved Loomis Forest Wildlands," *Wild Earth*, Fall 1999, 25-27. See also Tom Butler, *Wildlands Philanthropy: The Great American Tradition* (Earth Aware, San Rafael, CA, 2008), 210-217.

and business parks; sooner come the *haboobs* and sand dunes to strip the paint and siding of empty houses. Even senator-wheedled subsidies can't keep a ghost town-to-be alive long after its landscape can no longer foster it.

Likewise, and I'm sorry, it is sometimes fair to think about costs before calling for the cleanup of old pollution or toxics hellholes—such as arsenic in groundwater and some Superfund sites. We must truthfully ask whether we can afford it. We *are* in a time of limits. Limits, after all, are a keystone of the conservation Weltanschauung. Dollars for cleaning up old mistakes or for conservation otherwise are not bottomless. Moreover, there may be better conservation and human-health gains from spending the dollars otherwise.

While cost-benefit analysis may sometimes be good, conservationists must be sharp that we cannot weigh the worth of wild things in dollars, and that economics are not the key standard for hard choices. We must not get to where the only Endangered Species we try to keep are those with an economic value. Recall the warning from David Ehrenfeld—"Resource reasons for conservation can be used if honest, but must always be presented together with the non-humanistic reasons, and it should be made clear that the latter are more important in every case."[24]

Wildlands Philanthropy

I will take a back seat to no one in standing up for *public* lands— they are what has put the United States at the forefront of world conservation, but conservationists have too often overlooked the good work private lands can play in conservation. Whether or not I can go on their lands, righteous landowners such as Ted Turner, Drum Hadley, Jim Winder, Joe and Valer Austin, the Thaw Charitable Trust, Alan Weeden,

---

24 David Ehrenfeld, "The Conservation Dilemma," *The Arrogance of Humanism* (Oxford University Press, New York, 1981), 210.

Peter Buckley, Doug and Kris Tompkins, Gil Butler, and Roxane Quimby shelter and often rebuild wild things and their neighborhoods. What they do has come to be called *wildlands philanthropy*—buying land to shield its wild things.[25]

On these private lands, new paths of ecological restoration are being worked out on the ground. Jim Winder brought back riparian areas and reintroduced an Endangered fish, the Rio Grande chub, on the Lake Valley Ranch in New Mexico. Joe and Valer Austin have built some 20,000—that's *twenty thousand*—loose rock *grabens* to heal washed-out stream beds on their El Coronado Ranch in Arizona, and now are doing the same on their ecologically rich lands in northern Mexico. Their healing of the watershed and *arroyos* is nothing short of wondrous. When Drum Hadley bought the Guadalupe Canyon Ranch— home of some of the least-seen birds in the United States—forty years ago, much of it had been grazed down to bare dirt and rocks. Now the sideoats grama waves above Drummy's knees, thanks to his thoughtful, careful, always-asking stewardship.[26]

On Ted Turner's sprawling Vermejo Ranch in northeastern New Mexico, former ranch manager Dave Vacker worked with fire and ecologically framed logging to put tens of thousands of acres of once-rundown ponderosa pine back on the track to old-growth shape. The Turner Endangered Species Fund, under the leadership of wolf biologist Mike Phillips, oversees captive breeding and recovery of Endan-

---

25   John Davis, "Wildlands Philanthropy: Private Wealth Protecting
         Public Values," *Wild Earth,* Summer 1998, 19-22; Doug Tompkins,
         "On Philanthropy, Cultural Decadence, and Wild Nature," *Wild Earth,*
         Summer 1998, 14-18; Daniel Imhoff, *Farming with the Wild: Enhancing
         Biodiversity on Farms and Ranches* (Sierra Club Books, San Francisco,
         2003). Tom Butler and Antonio Vizcaino, *Wildlands Philanthropy: The
         Great American Tradition* (Earth Aware, San Rafael, CA, 2008).
26   Imhoff, *Farming with the Wild.*

gered Species on Turner's two to three million acres of ranches. Among these are black-tailed prairie dogs, black-footed ferrets, gray wolves, Mexican wolves, California condors, aplomado falcons, and desert bighorn sheep—and now the bolson tortoise.[27]

In Chile and Argentina, Doug and Kris Tompkins have bought nearly two million acres of private land as wilderness for wildlife through their Conservation Land Trust. They've worked to heal overgrazed, wildlife-empty *estancias* (ranches). They've gotten wealthy friends such as Peter Buckley to buy hundreds of thousands of acres more. Their flagship Pumalin park in southern Chile is some 800,000 acres of fjords, temperate rainforest, and snow-capped volcanoes. While much of it will stay untrodden but by wildlife, they have built National Park kinds of visitor facilities such as campgrounds, trails, a restaurant, cabins, picnic sites, and two visitor centers where a road and two hamlets touch Pumalin. A boardwalk trail takes sightseers to a soaring stand of Chile's national tree, the *alerce*—the Southern Hemisphere's match for the redwood. Before Tompkins's Pumalin work, Chileans had little hope to ever see alerces, nearly all of which grow in hard-to-reach spots or on timberlands where hikers are forbidden. Kris Tompkins, Doug's wife and the former CEO of Patagonia, has teamed with Yvon and Malinda Chouinard, the owners of Patagonia, to set up the Patagonia Land Trust, which buys new National Parks for Argentina (see www.conservacionpatagonia.org). See Table 10.1.

---

27   The bolson tortoise is a Pleistocene leftover that wandered throughout the Chihuahuan Desert. A tiny clan of this Endangered Species was found in a back-of-beyond spot in northern Mexico. It is by far the biggest tortoise in North America, tipping the scales at over 120 pounds! It is being brought home to Turner ranches in southern New Mexico. See Josh Donlan, Harry W. Greene, Joel Berger, Carl E. Bock, Jane H. Bock, David A. Burney, James A. Estes, Dave Foreman, Paul S. Martin, Gary W. Roemer, Felisa A. Smith, and Michael E. Soulé, "Re-wilding North America," *Nature*, Vol. 436, 18 August 2005, 913-914.

Table 10.1. Patagonia Land Trust Biodiversity Purchased Properties

PROPERTY	COUNTRY	ACREAGE
Estancia El Rincón	Argentina	37,065
Monte León National Park	Argentina	165,063
Hostería Monte Leon	Argentina	815
Estancia Dor-Aike	Argentina	81,543
El Piñalito Provincial Park	Argentina	9,301
Esteros del Iberá	Argentina	341,351
Estancia San Alonso	Argentina	26,652
Estancia Guayabi	Argentina	61,565
Estancia Rincón del Socorro	Argentina	28,612
Estancia San Ignacio	Argentina	10,442
Estancia Yaguareté-Corá	Argentina	37,799
Estancia Monterey	Argentina	11,841
Estancia San Nicolás	Argentina	39,734
SUBTOTAL		851,783
El Cañi Sanctuary	Chile	1,295
Pumalín Park	Chile	711,199
Estero Pangal	Chile	1,458
Corcovado National Park	Chile	726,439
Estancia Yendegaia	Chile	95,751
Fundo Río Blanco	Chile	267
Santo Domingo Norte	Chile	1,890
Fundo La Leona	Chile	2,323
Estancia Cabo León	Chile	65,778
Valle Chacabuco	Chile	195,456
SUBTOTAL		1,801,856
TOTAL ACREAGE CONSERVED		2,653,639

User Pays

A *user-pays* path has long been the way for hunting and fishing. Thanks to hunters and fishers being willing to buy licenses, there have been dollars to buy wildlife habitat, run hatcheries, bring income to state game and fish agencies, and so on. The hook and bullet crowd has therefore taken the crowing high ground. "We have wildlife because of hunting and fishing license fees." Notwithstanding state game and fish agencies' agricultural mindset on game such as white-tailed deer, exotics like pheasants, and put-and-take non-native fish from hatcheries, the good ol' boys and gals have a fair pitch. It is time for hikers, birders, river runners, backpackers, and those who like the thought of wilderness and wolves to learn from their rod-and-gun brothers and sisters. If we want the needed income for National Parks to be well run and shielded from threats, if we want Endangered Species sheltered and brought back into wild neighborhoods, if we want lands to hike without dirt bikes and clear cuts and cow pies, we may need to shell out bucks for it. *I'm not talking about how things should be, I'm talking about how they are with today's feverish cutting of federal programs.* We also need to look long and hard at unneeded outlays and work to get rid of them, and make sure that any user fees we shell out go toward truly helpful work such as stopping erosion from hiking trails, say—*not* building more motor-vehicle trails, as conservationist naysayers of user fees warn could happen.

The Annual Pass (formerly Golden Eagle Passport) sells for $80. It gives you wide-open, free-entrance to all National Park units and Wildlife Refuges, and recreational sites on National Forest, Bureau of Land Management, and Bureau of Reclamation lands for a year (other than campground fees and such). It is the next-to best deal in America. Conservationists and outdoorsfolks should ask that it be raised to at least $150 a year, where it would still be a deal. All dollars from it should go to the National Park Service and the National Wildlife Refuge System for national conservation work. Moreover, entrance fees for each National Park and Refuge also should be raised so that the fees are enough to handle stewardship, shielding, and restoration of the unit. Entrance fees should stay with the Park (those Parks that get few visitors should be otherwise funded anyway). We old farts (over sixty-two) now get a big cut on entrance fees. A year or two ago I bought a Golden Age Passport (now named Senior Pass). It gives the same good deal as the Annual Pass (Golden Eagle), but we oldsters buy it for only $10—not for each year, but $10 for one's lifetime—making it the *best* deal in America. This is unfair since we older folks overall have more disposable income than do others. Senior discounts should be ended, even though I'm now old enough to get them.

Campground fees should be high enough for all that is needed for building and running the campground, federal recreational staff, too, or volunteer Campground Hosts. We need to watchdog recreational site management on federal lands to stop handovers to private campground businesses. Public land recreational facilities should be run only by the federal agency and with federal staff or volunteers—other than outfitters and ski areas.

I have found wild rivers, whether in the National Wild & Scenic Rivers System or not, to be the best-run public lands for unmotorized recreation and for biodiversity. Most wilderness rivers I float bill by the head and sometimes the day. River rangers look over gear, make sure permits are right, and give good behavior and safety talks at the put-in. Some are volunteers. Southeastern Utah rivers under the Bureau of Land Management are standouts for wilderness stewardship—the San Juan River and Desolation and Gray Canyons on the Green River are as well run for wilderness recreation as anywhere I know (other than the Arctic National Wildlife Refuge, which is the flagship for wilderness stewardship). River campsites are cleaner and less hammered than many campsites in Wilderness Areas. These are some of the goods from user fees. I'd even like to see river-use fees upped to keep river rangers on the river and to underwrite more ecological restoration—such as pulling out camelthorn and other invading exotic species (cheatgrass may be the worst)—and cleanup (though not much is needed; no one leaves camps cleaner than do river runners).

Wilderness Areas could bill for backpacking, horsepacking, and such as for wild rivers—for each time. On the other hand, Wilderness Areas could be handled like an Annual Pass—buy your pass and you can go into any Wilderness Area in the country for one year. All fees should go toward wilderness (backcountry) rangers, patrolling against motorized trespass and poaching, and ecological restoration—as well as buying out grazing permits. Owing to the aching lack of law-enforcement rangers, many Wilderness Areas are wide open to unlawful storming by snowmobile and dirt bike outlaws. This is a growing threat from coast to coast and from the Arctic to the desert and Everglades.

There should also be a national sales tax on backpacking and river running gear. What is brought in should go to buy private inholdings in Wilderness Areas and Wild Rivers (and those not yet lawfully set aside), and to buy out grazing permittees in Wilderness Areas, National Parks, Wildlife Refuges, Wild Rivers, and other wild havens. Butting heads with ranchers over grazing in Wilderness Areas, wolf and grizzly homelands, and other key wildlife neighborhoods is bad news for all. The most workable (and fair) way to lower or end livestock grazing in Wilderness and other public lands is to buy 'em out. Likewise, dollars from this sales tax on gear could be for voluntary retirement buy-outs in wolf recovery areas. The Rewilding Institute has called for a buyout of grazing permits in the Gila and Apache National Forests where ranchers are fighting Mexican wolf recovery tooth and nail.

There should also be a national sales tax on birdseed, binoculars, and other wildlife-watching gear and gadgets. The tax should go to Endangered Species work. In Virginia, the state wildlife agency gets the chunk of the state sales tax estimated to have been spent on outdoor recreation gear. One third of the agency's budget ($12.3 million) comes from their share of the sales tax. It is earmarked for nongame programs.

Rupe Cutler, a former Assistant Secretary of Agriculture over the Forest Service, tells me, "Now that these 'nonconsumptive users' help support the game department, they have a vested interest and a voice in its policy decisions. That's good for biodiversity."[28]

Concessionaires in National Parks are getting a cheap ride on the NPS's shoulders. Fees for all businesses in National Parks and for outfitters working on public lands should be raised. Driving motorcars in National Parks should have a higher fee since motorized recreation is more costly and harmful for the Park. Campground fees for RVs should be higher than those for tent campers, again since the costs are higher. Public buses, snow coaches, trams, and the like, on the other hand, should be kept cheap or free so as to foster ridership.

There are good arguments against what I offer. If you have to shell out bucks to get into Wilderness Areas, it may take away the feeling of pioneer freedom to play Dan'l Boone. However, we are no longer a land of few settlers and much wildland. Times have shifted. Far higher in rank than our dreams of the unfettered right to roam is the need to keep the land public and to keep it ecologically whole and hale. By asking to lay down a few greenbacks for wilderness and wildlife, we lift ourselves in the wrangle. We are *responsible*. Anyway, this deal was worked out nearly one hundred years ago. Free hunting and fishing were thought bedrock American birthrights. Hunters and fishers at last came to see that hunting and fishing had to be capped for there were too many Natty Bumpos going after too little wildlife. This is like what we now see with other things to do in the outdoors. There is another need, though—and that is to get young folks into the out-of-doors. Boy Scouts, Girl Scouts, public schools, and other such programs could have fees waived. Maybe fees should be lowered or waived for children and students (K-12).

28 Rupert Cutler, personal communication to author, March 30, 2000. Cutler was President Carter's Assistant Secretary of Agriculture and thought up RARE II on the National Forests. He was later executive director of Defenders of Wildlife and is still a conservation leader and friend of mine.

When asking if user fees are workable, keep in mind that fees for river-running permits are not disliked among boaters. They are not seen as a burden but as a given, as are the lotteries for dealing out river trips to give those who float a feeling of aloneness and wilderness instead of a river-jam with elbowing for campsites. However, lotteries are hotly disliked when commercial outfitters get the lion's share of "user days" over those of us who earn time on rivers by hard-earned know-how and buying our own gear. Grand Canyon National Park is woefully unfair in giving commercial outfitters—no longer Mom and Pop businesses, but little cogs in overfat big recreational businesses—unfairly more of the slots on the Colorado River, widely acknowledged top river trip in the United States, if not the world. Moreover, most commercial outfitters run their sightseers down the river quickly by loud and mighty outboard motors so as to run shorter trips and thereby pack more trips and income into their permit. We rowers and paddlers find the roar and the stink of outboards upsetting to what should be wilderness-song of bird warbling and chirruping and whitewater rumpus and racket.

There is also the fear that if the agencies get their income through recreational fees, they may overdo building up Parks and even Wildernesses for feckless glee and overposh sloth and thereby harm wild things. Although this has not happened with river fees (thanks to tight caps on how many put-ins and boaters a day), screens will have to be built in to stop this threat. Many conservationists are also rightly worried about privatizing campground management to for-profit businesses in National Forests and other public lands. The Bush Junior Administration worked front-door and back-door ways to privatize public lands. Such threats undercut work by me and a few others to get conservationists to open their minds about user fees.

Nonetheless, unless we take more of a user-pays path to public lands and wildlife, we will see a steady drop of income for land management agencies and the Endangered Species Act. Deep cuts have already happened. It will get worse I fear, with today's frenzy over budget cutting. I foresee rumbles over whether short federal dollars go to hungry children or to caring for public lands. Right-wing government haters would love to see guts and blood spilled by Democrats over such tussling. I fear that wild things will get the short end of the stick. Given this political climate, the only way to get needed dollars for conservation may be through fees for outdoor play earmarked for conservation and public lands stewardship. A user-pays path will also undercut some of the harmful chiding against conservation and outdoor roving. Someday the United States may come back to a feeling of pride and caring for our wild wealth, and public lands will be given the income they need from taxes. I'm not willing to wait for that. I want public lands well-sheltered and underwritten now.

However, we must once again be steadfast that Earth is the wellspring of all good—the economy isn't—and wilderness and wildeors must be kept for their own sake. Furthermore, lands for wildlife have worth to each of us and to all of us together, as well as ecological worth. A wise society would willingly underwrite the land's keeping and shielding.

PERC (Property and Environmental Research Center) in Bozeman, Montana, is a so-called "free-market environmentalism" think tank. Like others of its ilk, it is more geared to private property and libertarian economics than it is to wild things. But now and then, it does good things through its magazine and its Policy Series of booklets on this or that topic. The one on "Recreation Fees—Four Philosophical Questions" is rather good, I think, and worthwhile for anyone for or against or baffled or open-minded about recreation fees on public lands.[29]

INCENTIVES

Economic Incentives

---

29   J. Bishop Grewell, "Recreation Fees—Four Philosophical Questions," *PERC Policy Series* (PERC www.perc.org, Issue Number PS-31, June 2004).

Too often we think that if folks don't do the right thing out of the goodness of their hearts, they should be made to do so by law. But believers in the market, like Randal O'Toole of the Thoreau Institute, think that a better way to shift behavior is through economic incentives. I sometimes think that my friend Randal has taken on incentives with the hot heart of a born-again Christian, but I also think that, oftentimes, economic incentives (and disincentives) are a fair and good way to get landowners to shelter Endangered Species, to get the Forest Service to stop shoving timber sales, to get business to stop dumping their banes on America, and to get Americans to drive cars with better gas mileage.

Incentives backers see the inner truth of Man unlike the way most liberals do. They believe that most folks are run by inborn selfishness and self-interest chased rationally. Alack for true believers of such theory, the evidence is showing that this "rational player" is a house built on sand. Neurophysiologists, evolutionary psychologists, and other scientific specialists wielding amazing new tools of brain watching and other wonders have shot the market economists' pet theory of the rational player out of the sky with their research in the last twenty years or so.[30] Nonetheless, playing to economic self-interest bears good apples at times. The deal with incentives is to reward good behavior with lower taxes for taxpayers, trustworthy budgets for bureaucrats, and so on, and play to our odd little minds as well as to our pocketbooks.

Could the Endangered Species Act be more landowner friendly without losing strength? Maybe, but we first need to acknowledge that the awful tales about ESA agents running roughshod over property owners are as true as the tale about the lady who put her poodle in the microwave to dry it off. It is hard to work out a deal when one side's stock in trade is a pack of lies—or argument by "mythical anecdote."[31]

---

30   Among many references, see Dominique J. –F. de Quervain, Urs Fischbacher, Valerie Trayer, Melanie Schellhammer, Ulrich Schnyder, Alfred Buck, and Ernst Fehr, "The Neural Basis of Altruistic Punishment," *Science* Vol. 305, 27 August 2004, 1254-1258.

31   Lawyer Glenn Sugameli came up with the wonderful zinger "argument

However, we need to know the gospel truth about the mythical anecdotes to get others to acknowledge them as untrue. With true believers
like ESA-haters, keep in mind that a freighter-load of truth will not outweigh a teaspoon-full of lies. Nonetheless, slapping the mythical anecdotes down with the gospel of what truly happened will often get news
writers and middle-of-the-road folks to not believe the shoot-'em-up
lies. In *The Nature Haters*, a forthcoming book in the *For the Wild Things*
series, I'll take on some of the mythical anecdotes with rock-bottom
documented truth. I likely will do so even sooner in my "Around the
Campfire" e-column.

Little shifts in ESA regulations and how the Act works in the field
could set the stage for a landowner to be proud that an Endangered
Species lives on his or her land.[32] Income for a landowner-friendly path
could come from a sales tax on birdseed and binoculars. Paul Ehrlich
and his coworkers at Stanford University call for incentives such as
"providing tax credits to landowners for habitat maintenance or im-
provement." They write, "Other incentive strategies would be to reduce
corporate and personal income taxes, or capital gains and estate taxes,
when a landowner maintains essential habitat for imperiled species."[33]
Is this bribery, though? Even so, if it works to get hardy swains and
manly men to stop landscalping *and* to stop bellyaching about the "fas-
cist" Endangered Species Act, then I'm for it. Sadly, many true-blue
government-haters and Nature haters will take the incentives and still

by mythical anecdote." Glenn P. Sugameli, "Environmentalism: The Real
    Movement to Protect Property Rights," in *A Wolf in the Garden*, 68. It
    should be widely wielded.

32   David S. Wilcove, Michael J. Bean, Robert Bonnie, and Margaret
    McMillan, *Rebuilding the Ark: Toward a More Effective Endangered Species
    Act on Private Land*, Environmental Defense Fund, Washington, D.C.,
    1996.

33   Lynn E. Dwyer, Dennis D. Murphy, and Paul R. Ehrlich, "Property
    Rights Case Law and the Challenge to the Endangered Species Act,"
    Conservation Biology, Vol. 9, No. 4, August 1995, 737.

bellyache and spin mythical anecdotes the way Rumpelstiltskin spun straw into gold.

In 1998 Defenders of Wildlife began working with farmers, ranchers, and land agencies to fund projects that would "prevent conflicts between humans and large carnivores." Among these are buying guard dogs, bear-resistant dumpsters, electric fences, and hiring range riders. From 1998 through March 2010, Defenders spent $949,353 on 266 projects in many states.[34] The Defenders' compensation funds for those who have lost livestock to wolves or grizzly bears are good examples of using incentives. From 1997 to December 2011, Defenders paid 338 ranchers $289,627 for verified losses from grizzlies.[35] Between August 1987 and October 2009, Defenders doled out a total of $1,368,043 to 895 ranchers for livestock losses from wolves in Montana, Idaho, Wyoming, Arizona, New Mexico, Oregon, and Washington. Defenders of Wildlife wrote, "Our goal is to shift economic responsibility for wolf recovery away from the individual rancher and toward the millions of people who want to see wolf populations restored. When ranchers alone are forced to bear the cost of wolf recovery, it creates animosity and ill will toward the wolf. Such negative attitudes can result in illegal killing."[36]

Although this depredation fund has not done away with bug-eyed hatred of wolves, it shows that conservationists will help stockmen bear true losses from wolf recovery. The Defenders compensation fund also shows how low many wolf-whiny ranchers are. It shows up wolf haters in the Northern Rockies and Southwest to be crybabies without a shred of righteousness. Some dodgy ranchers who grab dollars from

34　Defenders of Wildlife Proactive Carnivore Conservation Fund Fact Sheet http://www.defenders.org/publications/list_of_proactive_carnivore_compensation_projects.pdf

35　Defenders of Wildlife Fact Sheet. See also www.defenders.org/grizzlycompensation.

36　Defenders of Wildlife Fact Sheet. See also www.defenders.org/wolfcompensation.

Defenders go on to hold that they had outlandish losses from wolves and then cuss Defenders for not fully offsetting these mythical kills. Such ranchers flat-out don't want wolves in their world and will do just about anything they can get away with, fair or unfair, lawful or unlawful, to kneecap wolf recovery programs. Grazing permit buy-outs are the only answer for these hard asses who want the puffery of the 1880s, but not the truth. Wolf lovers, though, need to get tougher. When Western he-men play the victim, show them up for it and laugh at them. Say it loud right out in front of God and everybody that the wolf haters are crybabies and are leaches on handouts. Talk the truth about wolves to the news business, politicians, and more or less rational folks. But don't bother talking facts with the wolf haters, just make fun of their manhood.

Pay for Biodiversity Protection and Restoration on Private Lands

A canny path for getting ranchers, farmers, and other landowners in third world countries such as Costa Rica to not cut down the rainforest on their land and to replant native trees pays them (not that much, in truth) to do so. Such a deal in Costa Rica is named *Payment for Environmental Services* and was started in the 1990s. It has led to a steep drop in deforestation. Another way is to make payments to landowners for the ecological services their wild or restored lands yield (clean water, clean air, pollinators, and so on). Payments come from international conservation organizations or agencies, or from national governments for greenhouse gas reduction credits. Something like this could be done in the United States. Stop all subsidies from federal and state governments for landscalping businesses and landowners and earmark the savings to pay landowners for keeping or restoring their lands for wild things and to yield ecological services.

Voluntary Retirement Option

Commercial livestock grazing has brought untold harm and ever-bleeding wounds to the ecological health and wholeness of public lands in the West for almost 150 years. Struggles over livestock grazing have been among the meanest clashes in conservation. Maybe nothing else would do more to bring back the blooming of ecological heartiness on the public lands than taking off livestock. And maybe nothing else would give wild things a healthier tomorrow.[37] But how to do it in a fair and workable way? Oregon's Andy Kerr is as tough and clever as any conservationist today. In 1998, he offered up the Voluntary Retirement Option. He wrote,

> *It would be easier—and more just—for the federal government to fairly compensate the permit holders as it reduces cattle numbers. Since the government spends substantially more than it receives for grazing, in a few years the savings realized by reducing livestock numbers can pay for the compensation.*
>
> *It would be less expensive—fiscally and politically—for the agency to simply buy out the problematic grazing permit and save extensive planning, monitoring, research, public involvement, appeal,*

---

37   Two strong, truthful books stand out for teaching the history and harm of public lands grazing: Debra L. Donahue, *The Western Range Revisited: Removing Livestock from Public Lands to Conserve Native Biodiversity* (University of Oklahoma Press, Norman, 1999); and George Wuerthner and Mollie Matteson, editors, *Welfare Ranching: The Subsidized Destruction of the American West* (Island Press/Foundation for Deep Ecology, Washington, DC, 2002). Wyoming's woolly bullies (big sheepmen and cowmen, some in the benighted state legislature) proved Donahue right in how they worked to lynch her after her book came out. She is a law professor at the University of Wyoming. First they worked to get her fired for writing the book; when the university said they couldn't do that, they worked to defund and shut down the whole School of Law at the University of Wyoming.

litigation and political costs.[38]

At that time, Kerr started up and headed a legislative campaign to authorize and fund this straightforward path: A public lands permittee would be well paid for each AUM he or she is permitted. For this windfall, the rancher would take off all livestock and the federal agency overseeing the land would forever retire the grazing allotment. An AUM, or Animal Unit Month, is a cow and a calf grazing on federal lands for one month. Congressman Raul Grijalva of Arizona soon introduced a national pilot bill with an appropriation of $100 million to buy out grazing allotments. Other bills targeting this or that acreage were also offered, but nothing came of them.

Notwithstanding the early washout on voluntary retirement legislation, some wildlife and wilderness teams such as WildEarth Guardians kept boosting these buyouts. Big livestock groups, though, gainsay voluntary retirement or buyouts, whether buyout funds come from federal appropriations, state appropriations, or from private groups. However, one on one, many ranchers see it as a good deal for themselves and have lobbied their members of Congress for funding voluntary retirement.

After a legislative lull over the last ten or so years, a new bill has been put up. In November 2011, Representative Adam Smith (WA) introduced the Rural Economic Vitalization Act (REVA) as House Bill 3432, which would let third parties compensate ranchers to permanently retire their federal grazing permits. Under this deal, the Forest Service or Bureau of Land Management would then legally and permanently close the allotment to livestock grazing. Wilderness and wildlife groups of all kinds should get behind this bill and ask their representatives to cosponsor it.

Other Buy-outs

---

38   Andy Kerr, "The Voluntary Retirement Option for Federal Public Land Grazing Permittees," *Wild Earth*, Vol. 8, No. 3, Fall 1998, 63-67.

Often the quickest and most workable deal is for wildlovers to flat-out buy a ranch or base property that holds a federal or state grazing lease. The Grand Canyon Trust "negotiated the retirement of 200,000 acres of grazing allotments around the Grand Staircase/Escalante National Monument. We negotiated buy-outs with ranchers, then worked with the Bureau of Land Management to assure the agency amended its resource management plans, canceling grazing permits."[39] The Conservation Fund worked buy-outs to retire grazing in Canyonlands National Park.[40] Conservation Fund buy-outs also got all the cattle out from Great Basin National Park in Nevada (2,432 cattle were taken out from 70,019 acres for $242,900).[41] Alack, slippery resourcists in the Forest Service and Bureau of Land Management have stabbed some of these well-meaning, trusting nonprofits in the back and now tell them that they have to graze cattle on their permits or lose them. Legislation is needed to give "permanent retirement" of such grazing allotments.

Another kind of buyout is private inholdings in Wilderness Areas. Such inholdings are old mine patents or homesteads made before the land was withdrawn from such so-called *entry*. These inholdings can make a green map of a Wilderness Area look moth-eaten thanks to all the white spots. The Wilderness Land Trust raises dollars to buy such inholdings and then hands over the land to the federal agency that oversees the Wilderness Area. When private land inside and next to a Wilderness Area is given or sold to the government, it straightaway becomes Wilderness under the Wilderness Act.[42] In 2004, the Wilderness Land Trust bought 1,360 acres of private land in California's Trinity Alps and Marble Mountains Wilderness Areas, thereby stopping home

39   Geoffrey S. Barnard, undated membership solicitation letter for Grand Canyon Trust, about 2000.

40   Lisa Church, "Fun hogs to replace cows in a Utah Monument," *High Country News*, February 1, 1999.

41   Conservation Fund, 1999.

42   Sections 5 and 6, Public Law 88-577 (The 1964 Wilderness Act).

building, logging, and a road into the heart of the Wilderness. For more information and later inholding buys see their website: www.wildernesslandtrust.org.

No one, though, can match retired hedge-fund billionaire David Gelbaum in buying up private-land holes in Wilderness Areas, National Parks, and wildways between them. While staying out of sight, he helped set up the Wildlands Conservancy in 1994, which, with over $250 million of his wealth, has bought about one million acres in the California Desert to block up conservation lands. Among the mindboggling buys were one thousand square miles of land owned by the Santa Fe Pacific Railroad that were checkerboarded through Mojave National Preserve, Death Valley, and Joshua Tree National Parks. This was one of the great conservation land buys of all time and Gelbaum sought no thanks for his deed.[43]

Often private land has high worth for threatened or rare wildeors, critical habitat, biodiversity, or is needed for wildlife roving in a wildlands network. There is a strong need to set up a database of such private lands and of likely conservation buyers, much like an online dating service.

Water Markets

In the dry West, many streams dry up over summer owing to all the water being taken out for irrigation. How do we leave enough water in streams to keep fish and other native wildlife? One hopeful path is for conservationists, sportfishers, commercial fishers (for salmon), and river runners to form nonprofit water trusts to pay farmers or ranchers to leave the water to which they have "rights" in the stream. Oregon, Washington, and Nevada are already giving this market path a go. In some Western states, state water law would have to be redone for water trusts to work since "instream flow" is not a "beneficial use" of one's

---

43   Kenneth R. Weiss, "The Man Behind the Lands," *Los Angeles Times*, October 27, 2004.

water rights under the law. In such states if you do not take your share of the water out of the stream and put it on your land, you can have your high-dollar water rights taken away (often an acre-foot of water is of more worth than an acre of land). However, if instream flow is made lawful as a "beneficial use," then you could leave the water in the stream and be paid by a water trust for more than you could make with the water irrigating alfalfa or other cheap yet thirsty crops.[44]

Victimization

Film director Edward Zwick (*Glory, Legends of the Fall*) writes:

In what a friend of mine calls the new American hurt game, if you're not offended by somebody, you're nobody.

These days, it seems, people wake up in the morning not only waiting to be offended, but also hoping to be offended. Central to any multicultural orthodoxy is the notion that, unless you are offended, you have no ontology.[45]

Earlier in *Take Back Conservation*, I picked on the left and politically correct liberals. Some of my carping, such as for group identity and victimization, may seem a little over the top for a book about conservation. There is something behind my crankiness, though. I am not just showing off as a redneck or as an uncaring white man. I am after something else.

I frown on entitlement rights. Unlike old-timey American rights, such as those in the Bill of Rights, which are fetters on government, there is a throng of new "rights," which are entitlements, such as a "right" to a job with a minimum wage, a "right" to health care, a "right"

---

44   Clay J. Landry, "Trusting Water Markets," *PERC Reports*, March 1999, 12-13. An acre-foot is the water that would flood an acre one foot deep.

45   Edward Zwick, "In the Hurt Game, Honesty Loses," *The New York Times*, Nov. 10, 1998.

to housing, a "right" to not having your religion "insulted" in any way whatsoever if you are a Muslim or whatever, and so on. The old thinking about rights was that they were shackles on government's might over one: "government shall establish no law, etc." I fear we let some of these be taken away or watered down with the so-called "War on Terror." Nor do we seem to be getting them back from the Obama presidency.

However, when do-gooders say that folks have a right to health care or to a job with minimum wage, they are forgetting that someone has to work to give that entitlement. If you have a right to health care, that means someone is made to work to give you that health care. Now, I think there are good grounds to say that it leads to domestic tranquility and to a better society if society tries to make health care, housing, jobs, good wages, etc. gettable for all its citizens. But that is not the same as saying that everyone has a *right* to such things.

I've cast multiculturalism as "persons are not taken as individuals, but by their group identity" and victimization as "the world is divided into an oppressor class and the oppressed class." The over-the-top of multiculturalism and victimization are mostly laid at the doors of non-whites, homosexuals, and women—and lately, rightly so, Muslims. In truth, the American bunch that most plays group identity and victimization is white men—upmost manly men. Much—perhaps most—populist-anticonservation rabble-rousing is rooted in group identity and victimization. Whine, whine, whine. Ranchers, loggers, dirt bikers, and even some real estate agents see themselves as "embattled minorities" victimized by government and liberals. Rush Limbaugh has built his fat way of life on being their whine sommelier. Hispano intellectuals puffing about the *reconquista* in Los Angeles, welfare mothers in East St. Louis... why I'll put the New Mexico Cattle Growers Association or New Mexico Farm Bureau up against them anytime in a whine festival. It is not conservative, it is not manly, it is not rugged individualism, and it is not free enterprise to be a crybaby, to say you have a right to win in business or be bailed out by government. It seems you cannot keep from nettling whiny thin-skinned folks blighted with the virus of group identity—whether Muslims mired in the Dark Ages or high-heeled American he-men clinging forlornly to the nineteenth century. I have no kindness whatsoever to offer those who wear their cultural sensitivity on their sleeves, always bug-eyed watching for even the mildest slight.

In 1999, columnist Thomas Sowell wrote, "Few skills are so well rewarded as the ability to convince parasites that they are victims."[46] Sowell should know since he has been well rewarded as a writer convincing right-wing crybabies that they are victims of government bureaucrats or elitist environmentalists.

John Humbach, a law professor at Pace University, in 1993 wisely wrote, "The Constitution does not guarantee that land speculators will win their bets."[47]

---

46   Thomas Sowell, "Left, right and the muddle both have made," *The Albuquerque Tribune*, March 10, 1999.

47   Helvarg, *The War Against the Greens*, p. 302.

CHAPTER 11

Take Back OUR
Conservation Movement

Will the defenders of Nature please rise?
—Arne Naess, 1986

TRAMPING DOWN THE TRAIL OF WRITING dibs and dabs of this book over the last ten years, I've become more and more worried that the conservation network is slipping out of the grasp of wildlovers. Happenings over the last year or two have only worsened my worry. Cramming conservation into a briefcase with environmentalism and resourcism has meant that Man-first goods and cares come out on top all too often. Moreover, putting the dollar chase at the core of their being has flipped Save-Earth clubs into corporate businesses. Such is what has led The Nature Conservancy down the primrose path of working with resource-extraction businesses and pulling in hundreds of millions of dollars from them, while turning their backs on traditional conservation and working to subvert the whole movement into backing a new vision of Earth as Man's garden—"The Domesticated Earth."

Arne Naess asked in the ending chapter of Michael Soulé's 1986 anthology *Conservation Biology,* "Will the defenders of Nature please rise?"[1] Dear old Arne's bid twenty-five years ago is even timelier today. Were Arne yet with us and asked his question to a room full of the leaders of all so-called conservation outfits and leading conservation biologists, many of them could not righteously and truthfully stand. If we are to have any hope of halting the Manmade Great Extinction, lovers of wild things must rise and take back the wilderness and wildlife network—both the folk grassroots web and the scientists' conservation biology network. We must boldly and believably stand up for the inborn worth of other life kinds and for our righteous calling to shield and keep whole and well the tall, wide-spreading Tree of Life for the forever of many tomorrows. We must unmistakably tell the world that the phony, sell-out "conservationists" do not speak for those of us who love wild things and do not speak as the true defenders of Nature that Arne Naess sought.

Wild things need truehearted conservationists to do this, those who *feel* in their bones the crushing loss of life all about us. In taking back conservation, we must have grit, knowing that we will make foes and lose friends. It also may be windmills at which we tilt, but, if nothing else, we can show others who love wild things for their own sakes that they are not alone and that we need to come together to stand up for what is good. Like Bob Marshall seventy-five years ago, we want no fence-straddlers.

In the last two chapters of *Take Back Conservation,* I will offer some steps to breathe new life into conservation and thereby let wildlovers regain it. I will split these steps into two fields: those mostly about organizational reshaping, and those about coming home to the true meaning of wilderness and wildlife shielding: our beliefs, stands, and work.

---

1   Arne Naess, "Intrinsic Value: Will the Defenders of Nature Please Rise?" in Michael Soulé, editor, *Conservation Biology: The Science of Scarcity and Diversity* (Sinauer Associates, Sunderland, Massachusetts, 1986), 504-515.

That is, I am talking about two kinds of things here: (1) our strategies for shielding and rebuilding wild things; and (2) the bedrock of how we see wild things as good (values), along with the bedrock of how we see ourselves as lovers of wild things (our *being* or characteristics). Folks may be one on the bedrock, yet many on sundry strategies and ways. I hope so. Owing to the might of those who see little or no good in the wild, we who need and love wild things should always be weighing how we are doing and looking to see if there are new and better ways to do our craft so long as such new ways stay true to the goodness of wild things. The ladder of these steps is in Table 11.1.

Table 11.1.

ORGANIZATIONAL STEPS

• Know how conservation and environmentalism are unlike, and the same for conservation and resourcism. Understand enviro-resourcism.
• Overcome the "Environmentalist Stereotype."
• Reach out to the political mainstream, such as thoughtful Republicans and middle-of-the-road Democrats in the U.S.
• Reach out to wilderness recreationists and naturalists to get them to become wilderness and wildlife shielders.
• Thoughtfully target conservation funding to build a mighty network for the long haul and to end the warping harm money sometimes does to the conservation network.
• Foster strong thinking and ongoing learning within the wilderness and wildlife network.
• Deal with the threats of overprofessionalism, corporatism, and institutionalism in our clubs.

GOODS, POLICIES, AND WORK STEPS

- Rebuild natural history as craft and science, and bring it back as the keystone of conservation.
- Unashamedly stand up for wild things being good-in-themselves, and therefore for the underlying good of wilderness and wildlife conservation.
- Stand up for strongly warded protected areas as "the most valuable weapon in our conservation arsenal."
- Carefully frame the tale of wilderness and wildlife conservation so it is both winning and true to wild beliefs.
- Acknowledge that the overwhelming plight is the Manmade Sixth Great Extinction, driven by the booming population of Men and further goosed by rising affluence and technology (the Man swarm).
- Set forth and work for a vision that is bold, workable, scientifically believable, and *hopeful.*

These steps rope about each other like wintering snakes in a den, but I'll pull each from the writhing bundle to look at it, staying mindful that they are tied in knots about one another—and that some may bite. The upshot of what I bid is that the conservation network needs to poke about in its lore-attic and find its soul and backbone again. Wildlovers need to bring back and update the good old thoughts of wilderness and wildlife keeping and put them in the forefront again, along with what we have learned from conservation biology.

Again, I'm sorry for my U.S.-grounded path. It was beyond my means to fully bring Canada and Mexico into this work. Canada's top wolf biologist and Rewilding Institute Fellow Paul Paquet emailed me,

It is not enough to speak of Republicans and Democrats, when most of 'wild' North America is now controlled by Canadian Liberals, Conservatives, and New Democrats. This is important to me as the eco-cons (The Nature Conservancy, Greenpeace, Forest Ethics) collaborate with industry and government in destruction of the most pristine and intact temperate rainforest in the world, and as a prelude to the negotiated destruction of the boreal and Arctic.

Paul is dead-on. Keep in mind that what I scorch "The Environmental Movement" for in the United States goes two-fold for Canada. It would have been good if I could have looked at the Canadian enviroresourcist outfits of which Paul writes (Greenpeace, etc.) when I was laying into The Nature Conservancy and Society for Conservation Biology.

CHAPTER 12

Back to the Clubhouse: Organizational Steps to Take Back Conservation

There is a cancer on the body politic: money.
—former Senator Ernest F. Hollings (D-SC)[1]

ORGANIZATIONAL STEPS: BUILDING BETTER TEAMS AND CLUBS

KNOW HOW CONSERVATION AND ENVIRONMENTALISM ARE UNLIKE, AND CONSERVATION AND RESOURCISM. UNDERSTAND ENVIRO-RESOURCISM. BOTH CONSERVATION AND ENVIRONMENTALISM WILL BE STRONGER BY KNOWING THEY AREN'T THE SAME. FOREMOST, CONSERVATION CAN GAIN MORE HEED AND CAN DRAW TO A WIDER CROWD OF BACKERS IF IT IS NOT BURIED IN ENVIRONMENTALISM.

---

1   Ernest F. Hollings, "Stop the Money Chase or Bid Ethics Goodbye," *The Washington Post*, reprinted in *The Albuquerque Journal*, February 26, 2006.

One, let's acknowledge that conservation and environmentalism are each their own network, although their cares often overlap and foes are often the same. Let's also acknowledge that the animal rights and Green political movements are their own networks and are sundered from both the conservation and environmental networks—and are sometimes at loggerheads with them. This understanding needs to be in our own minds and in how we package conservation to the world.

Two, let us acknowledge that resourcism or resource conservation stands away from wilderness and wildlife conservation and that they have often been and still are at war, though they can also team up as well. Sustainable development and ecosystem management as they are now done are kinds of resourcism that are backed mostly *instead* of protected areas, not as co-workers alongside. (In *True Wilderness* I will go after sustainable development and those such as The Nature Conservancy who have signed over their souls to it.) Let us also understand that environmentalists can be either conservationists or resourcists, and that enviro-resourcism is a growing Weltanschauung and path that undermines conservation.

Three, the *environmental* movement once again should be more straightforward that it works for Man's health and wellbeing—body and mind. This is the most winning way for it to be framed.

Four, conservationists should not call our clan or ourselves *environmentalists* or *environmental.* For conservationists to call ourselves environmentalists is sloppy thinking and sloppy writing and speaking, which befuddles one and all. Likewise, conservationists should not call ourselves *greens.*

Five, both conservationists and environmentalists should acknowledge the threat from the politically correct left, gird themselves against takeover, and take steps for both networks to pull in other Americans notwithstanding their politics.[2] *It is one thing if most conservationists lean to political progressivism; it is altogether another thing for conservation to be a wing in the progressive network.*

Six, conservationists, hunters and anglers, environmentalists, and animal-welfare workers should think about out how to work well together on campaigns where they are of the same mind, lay ground for ongoing give and take, and understand that at times they will be at odds, sometimes rather heated. Moreover, hunters and anglers who love wild things need to be outspoken conservationists standing up for wolves, cougars, and other wildeors that slob hunters hate and want to wipe out.

And last, I have come to believe that conservationists should ask some in our clubs and network to leave if they keep undercutting our wild things as good-in-themselves beliefs, or in making-over wilderness and wildlife clubs into corporate pabulum. I am not saying, mind you, that folks have to be hardcore believers in wild things for their own sakes to be in our clubs or to work with us, only that they should not undercut what we are and what we do. Moreover, we wildlovers must never be shy in staking out stronger stands than those of fence-straddling "conservationists" or in being straightforward that we think a conservation club or "leader" is being weak or is giving away too much. At times, we need to name names. It is, however, good behavior to warn such folks beforehand that we plan to come out against them and that we will call a sell-out a sell-out. We can begin by coolly shunning the leadership of The Nature Conservancy and flat-out saying that they have turned their

2   However, in sooth, there are those in the hard social-justice crowd whom we can never draw in, and a landslide of unthinking right-wingers who think we are evil. Then there are the flat-out Nature haters and flat-Earthers. So, any work to stretch our target market can only hope for so much—but we can get some in the middle or slightly to the right to at least think with opened minds about what we say. ConservAmerica (formerly Republicans for Environmental Protection) is a standout mark that thinking Republicans can be tough shielders of wild things.

backs on conserving Nature. Whenever a magazine or science journal runs an article by or about Peter Kareiva and his ilk, wildlovers need to flood it with letters saying he is not a conservationist and does not speak for those of us who are.

Lumping conservation in with environmentalism is how enviro-resourcists have found a way to grab leadership in wilderness and wildlife work. As long as we work as one "Environmental Movement," environmentalists will often overwhelm conservationists. Seeing the shielding and rebuilding of wildlife and wildlands as a stand-alone conservation network will get rid of the murkiness, let wildlovers key in on *our* foremost cares, and make it smoother for wildlovers to take back the conservation movement instead of having to take over "The Environmental Movement." I think this will also lead to friendlier and better teamwork between conservationists and environmentalists, even enviro-resourcists.

OVERCOME THE "ENVIRONMENTALIST STEREOTYPE." THE ENVIRONMENTALIST STEREOTYPE—DEMOCRATIC, PROGRESSIVE, POLITICALLY CORRECT, AGAINST GUN OWNERSHIP, ANTIHUNTING, VEGETARIAN—IS HARMFUL TO HOW CONSERVATIONISTS (AND ENVIRONMENTALISTS) ARE FRAMED AND IT KEEPS LIKELY FRIENDS FROM COMING ONTO OUR TEAM. IT NARROWS OUR NETWORK AND SCARES AWAY MANY WOULD-BE FRIENDS.

There are folks in the United States who deep down are not against keeping wilderness and wildlife nor are against cleaning up industry for our health and welfare, but who think they are against *environmentalists,* believing that environmentalists (as well as conservationists) are left-wing socialists who want to take away their guns. We should not shrug off such folks because they are silly paranoids or because their beliefs are wrong. However off-kilter their sketch of "environmentalists" may be, it is true to them, and it keeps them from backing wildlife-shielding steps they might like. Most times, such folks are not going to be hard-core wildlovers and aren't going to become members of our clubs, but they may back how we want to shield wildlands and keep wildlife from being wasted. At the least, maybe they'll quit thinking of us as "environmeddlers" and won't stand against what we want to do as so many of them do now. Here, we are taking about *allies*, either strong or weak, not the inner core.

Let me underline what follows. *I am not chiding conservationists and environmentalists who happen to be political progressives, players in the Democratic Party, or vegetarian.* Many are. Our networks would not be without such folks. For years I have been in the midst of them. They are my friends! The Fox News Channel loony tunes would brand me a progressive and even politically correct! Many environmentalists and conservationists fit the stereotype a lot or somewhat: that's why it has become a stereotype. Nevertheless, I want to knock down the widespread belief that all conservationists and environmentalists fit into the Environmentalist Stereotype. I squabble with those leftist environmentalists who want to drive away likely friends of wilderness (and pollution cleanup) who may not back affirmative action, gay marriage, gun control, and so on. There is no need to link these to conservation. "Greenie" stereotypes of a like kind hound wildlovers outside the United States.

Conservationists (and environmentalists) need to always be aware that the Environmentalist Stereotype shadows them, and need to be ready to run it off—*even when one may fit into the stereotype oneself.* Do not let reporters and politicians get away with taking the Environmentalist Stereotype as a given. I ask my wild friends who fit the Environmentalist Stereotype wholly or somewhat to tell reporters and others that there are lots of conservationists who do not fit the stereotype. (Likewise, I tell reporters that most conservationists do not agree with some of my beliefs.) If we wish to grow our political might, our dare is to show the sundry lifeways and politics of those who love wilderness and wildlife. We also need to groom folks who do not fit the Environmentalist Stereotype to be out-ahead leaders on wilderness and wildlife. Clubs such as ConservAmerica, Backcountry Hunters and Anglers, Trout Unlimited, *some* state wildlife federations, and the Coalition of National Park Service Retirees need to be more forward in the wilderness and wildlife network. I believe that the New Mexico wilderness and wildlife network is as strong as it is because such folks are leaders in the state. In New Mexico, we have shown overall that wildlovers, whatever their politics and lifeways, can work together, camp together, and lobby together. Do not forget that in 2011, ConservAmerica backed more new Wilderness in the Arctic National Wildlife Refuge than did the Sierra Club, Defenders of Wildlife, and the Alaska Wilderness League.

REACH OUT TO THE POLITICAL MAINSTREAM, SUCH AS THOUGHTFUL REPUBLICANS AND MIDDLE-OF-THE-ROAD DEMOCRATS IN THE U.S. MANY AMERICANS (AS WELL AS FOLKS ELSEWHERE) LOVE WILD THINGS AND WISH TO KEEP THEM. HOWEVER, THEY SHY AWAY FROM WHAT THEY BELIEVE ABOUT "THE ENVIRONMENTAL MOVEMENT."

United States conservationists are held back by two stiff winds that we must work our way through by helping to make wilderness and wildlife shielding bipartisan again and to find backing in small towns and the hinterlands. Shucking the Environmentalist Stereotype is the first step. Highlighting how hunters and anglers truly began conservation after 1850 comes next. When folks hear "wilderness lover" or "Endangered Species backer," they should be no more amazed to see a man or a woman with a gun, fishing rod, or straddling a horse than to see a hiker, birder, or river runner.

Here, framing becomes a key need. Too often, the words and how they are said of conservation (environmentalism even more so) come out as class-struggle, politically correct leftspeak. Never mind the beliefs for now; it is the words being spoken or written that drive away some may-be backers. Conservationists need to mark such words, such as *privilege, people-of-_____, address questions of _____, and hegemonic,* and find others without any leftist freight. One of the ways we could reach middle-of-the-road and wild-loving Republicans would be to wield the values of traditional conservatism, as I did in Chapter 9. They are also the values of conservation: Piety, Prudence, Posterity, Antimaterialism, Responsibility. Conservationists need to bring these words into how we talk about our beliefs. Ditching the buzzwords of the left and sometimes wielding the values of traditional conservatism to sell wilderness and wildlife could be a mighty step in reaching out to the millions of Americans leery of "environmentalists."

By no means do I foresee a big wave of Republican officeholders straightaway voting in line with the League of Conservation voters or even ConservAmerica, nor do I see millions of right-wing Republicans belonging to The Wilderness Society. But a small shift can often give the edge to win. Some Republican members of Congress in California (and elsewhere) back Wilderness Area bills in their districts. This is thanks to good work by conservationists and to the Republicans knowing that more Wilderness is what voters want.

Although Democrats won back both houses of Congress in 2006, in 2010 Republicans got back the House and nearly the Senate. Goodness only knows what may befall America in November 2012. If we look carefully at key conservation votes in the House and Senate before the 2006 election when Republicans were in goose-stepping sway, we often see the conservation side losing by a whisker notwithstanding the stouter leeway by the Republicans—thanks to a small cluster of GOP representatives and senators fairly good on conservation and pollution. Alack, these "moderates" were the Republicans that Democrats knocked off in making gains in 2006. I likely would have voted for some of these GOPers such as Shays of Connecticut and Leach of Iowa. Moreover, the Tea Baggers have now cowed any open-minded Republicans into being more in lockstep with the hate-government crowd.

Which party runs Congress is unforeseeable, so conservationists and environmentalists cannot reckon on only Democrats, but must work to find and build good ties with at least a few Republicans in Congress. For all their blather about freedom, Republicans in Congress are shackled thanes to their leaders in and out of Congress. It has become harder for those who care at all for the out-of-doors to buck the bosses on conservation votes. However, I think an unforeseen good thing about the Tea Baggers in Congress is that many of them are unafraid to go against the bosses. Such boldness may put a crack or two in the leg irons locked by GOP bosses on their meek, biddable backbenchers. We'll see how long this lasts, but it could give the handful of Republicans in Congress who like wilderness and wildlife a little more room to vote with conservationists—if we are clever enough to make it smoother for them to do so by ridding ourselves of the Environmentalist Stereotype and by getting a few "rednecks for wilderness" named and known as our leaders in key fights.

One stumbling block for why Congressional Republicans don't stand with conservationists is that conservationists seldom lobby them. Conservationists need to find more "maybes" among the Republicans in Congress and then get in better with them by setting up meetings for them with ConservAmerica, Trout Unlimited, the Coalition of National Park Service Retirees, and like outfits.

However, I think conservationists should even meet and talk with anticonservation and Tea Bagger Republican office-holders, at least those who are not thoroughgoing Nature haters and with whom a meeting could lead to fisticuffs (Steve Pearce, the congressman from southern New Mexico, comes to mind). Sometimes members of Congress are against a conservation bill or other step in their districts owing to their dislike of local conservationists. When we go out of our way to talk with them and when they hear from Republican conservationists, they may not block a Wilderness Area bill or other offering. Sometimes, they vote wrong because they've never heard the conservation side or met any homefolks who backed conservation. Before writing some off as hopeless, we should organize lots of input from their wildloving constituents and then meet with them. It is key in these dealings to find business folks, retired military, hunters, and the like, along with known Republicans to help in the door opening and softening up. California has some pretty right-wing Republican congressmembers who are willing to sponsor and work for *good* Wilderness Area or Wild River bills in their districts. I love hearing my old pal Steve Evans of Friends of the River telling tales of how they got such folks on board. The January 2012 "State of the Wild" report from the Campaign for America's Wilderness looks at the Wilderness Area bills now in Congress; Republican representatives sponsor good bills in California, Michigan, and Nevada. We do not need to make bad deals or sell out; we only need to get a foot in their door, and to think carefully who on our side might have any kind of "in" with such Congressfolks.

Some enviro-resourcists, too, call for conservationists to reach out to folks in the sticks. Their path, though, is not mine. They seem to think that to talk to hinterlands folks, we need to back down or bite our tongues on our values, soften our stands, and overlook the gnawing wounds that ranchers, loggers, and others have made. I read where one so-called "conservation" outfit said that learning about and taking on the "rural values" of their erstwhile foes was a way to work together and find workable answers to our plights. A far wiser path is set forth by Sara Robinson of Campaign for America's Future: "Yes, building a movement is a sales job—but the sale is closed when they accept our terms, not when we bend to meet theirs."[3]

I fear that folks who think we have to bend to the other side have never had a burning, needful love for wild things, or have such weak knees that they bend backward, or take the cake for social and ecological naïveté. Or all three. By having come from that rural culture, I think

---

3   Sara Robinson, "Learning From the Cultural Conservatives, Part I: Messing With Their Minds," Campaign for America's Future, February 29, 2008. Robinson's three-part essay is full of wisdom and good guidance.

I may have more of an understanding than city kids newly overawed by hayseeds. We do not need to sell out in that way to find friends in the hinterlands. The first behest in reaching out to others is that you go to those in that culture who love wilderness, too. Then you go to the more thoughtful, easy-going, friendly folks you've been steered to by your hinterland friends. Back in 2004, Al From of the Democratic Leadership Council acknowledged that truth. "You're not going to convince the hardcore to turn around, and you shouldn't even try because you would compromise your own values."[4] Paul Krugman, Nobel Laureate in Economics, columnist for the *New York Times,* and the kind of tough, straightforward thinker and fighter progressives need more of, put this frame well in writing about President Obama's weak-kneed dealing with the Republicans in Congress: "Such are the perils of negotiating with yourself."[5] Too often, I fear, conservationists first "negotiate" in their own head and water down what they want before ever talking to others.

Conservationists need to talk to the middle, not to the authoritarian right or the Nature haters. To talk to ranchers about wolves, you stay away from snarling wolf haters, and instead find thoughtful ranchers who at least shrug that wolves are here for good and who want to work something out; such ranchers and farmers are out there even if the screamers drown them out. This cultural overlordship by the meanest landscalpers is one way the "consensus working groups of stakeholders" are bad news. Such "stakeholder" groups are most often under the thumb of the loudest mouths among the dying landscalping industries of the West.

In small towns and the hinterlands, there are true Cannots who may keep their heads down. There are also folks who culturally aren't Sierra Clubbers but who like wild things. We need to find such friends. Often all such folks need to speak out is to know that they won't be

4   Terry M. Neal, "GOP Corporate Donors Cash In on Smut," *Washingtonpost.com,* December 21, 2004.

5   Paul Krugman, "The Destructive Center," *New York Times,* February 9, 2009.

left alone. And then let them work with middling, thoughtful folks in their neighborhoods. Other times, we can play to our erstwhile (or not so erstwhile) foes with deals that help them dollar-wise, such as the voluntary-retirement option for public-lands grazing permittees or buying out grazing permittees in hotbeds of wolf hatred such as Catron County, New Mexico.

So, here are my steps for dealing with the hinterlands near wilderness:

Foremost, ask what kind of friends you need and what you want them to do. If you want folks with hinterland addresses to write letters or talk to a congressman, that's one thing. If you need a county commissioner or a commission majority, that's another.

Find friends in the hinterlands by looking in the right spots. In New Mexico, you can find letter-writers in Catron County but I'll buy you a good bottle of wine if you get a county commissioner to back lobos; for that you need to go for a city councilor in Silver City (maybe).

Make deals with foes that give us wild things and gives them greenbacks—buyouts and such.

When it's no deal asshole, we fight them tooth and nail. If the politics are hopeless, we work on stopping inroads into the wild, throwing every roadblock we can in the landscalpers' path, and bide our time for a better political day to ask for a Wilderness Area or other goals.

Keep in mind that sometimes however hard we work and however righteous our hearts, we won't find friends in a town or county where we need them. They might not be there, or they have been so cowed that they aren't going to go against the big shots—even if they believe in keeping wild things. The main reason wilderness and wildlife conservationists aren't known in some counties is because we haven't looked for them.

Conservation Biology tucked away a dandy article called "Conservation and the Myth of Consensus," in its 2005 volume. It should be read by all wildlovers who are being told by enviro-resourcists to sit down and talk with anticonservation stakeholders. You should not only read it but also bring it into how you see the world and how we should more shrewdly fight our foes over wild things. The authors, wildlife biologists and social theorists, wrote, "Consensus processes are philosophically rooted in social constructionism. From a constructionist perspective, the existence of any 'reality' independent of human values, symbols, and meanings is questioned.... [This] approach...has been used to legitimize existing patterns of environmental degradation." They see the roots of this fad in the 1987 Brundtland Report that made sustainable development gospel for the United Nations. They further warn that the "consensus" path among stakeholders "jeopardizes conservation specifically by legitimizing existing hegemonic configurations of power and precluding resistance against dominant elites."[6] Notwithstanding Oscar-worthy performances as whining victims, irrigators, ranchers, loggers, miners, drillers, boomers, and other "Lords of Yesterday" are still the high-horse elite of the West. This is why wilderness and wild-life lovers who understand the West won't play the consensus game so touted by "existing power structures," such as privatization think tanks, the federal government, and enviro-resourcists.

REACH OUT TO NATURALISTS AND WILDERNESS RECRE-ATIONISTS TO GET THEM TO BECOME WILDERNESS AND WILDLIFE SHIELDERS.

The most needed kind of outreach for conservation organizing is better called *inreach*—for it is truly reaching in to our own folks, members, mailing lists, and such to arouse them to do something: come to a hearing or public meeting, write a letter, carry a sign on a picket line....

6   M. Nils Peterson, Markus J. Peterson, and Tarla Rai Peterson, "Conservation and the Myth of Consensus," *Conservation Biology* Vol. 19, No. 3, June 2005, 762-767. I have to chuckle about what I quote from this article—it is in the language of social analysis that I bid conservationists not to speak or write.

If we could get all those who belong to wilderness and wildlife clubs, from the Sierra Club and National Audubon Society to Adirondack Council and WildEarth Guardians to Friends of the Boundary Waters and Backcountry Hunters and Anglers, to stand up and speak out, we would unleash a deafening roar and roiling of the American body politic that would shake the oligarchy and "decision-makers" to the core. Notwithstanding the might of such a spark, we will never stir all our members to roar. Yet it should always be our goal.

Though our clubs work hard at such inreach (some much better than others), they all can work more skillfully and doggedly. The step that would swiftly bear much weight is to sunder begging for dollars from asking for phone calls, letters, and emails against threats or for sheltering wild things. Of the scores of letters, emails, and phone calls I get from a throng of wilderness and wildlife clubs and teams, nearly all are sent for fundraising—recall from Chapter 4 the warning that "The problem is that eventually many fundraisers come to view the issues as commodities with a monetary value separate and apart from the societal cost of the outcome."[7] Fundraising has too much become the tail that wags the dog of inreach. I believe that conservation outfits would better spur their folks to do something if the rabble rousing was not piggybacking the dollar grubbing.

Think of this: going through your mail you find a letter from a national conservation club. On the front of the envelope are the words in red: "Alert! Save Our Wilderness Areas!" The letter inside is not a call to "Send us your check for $50 so we can fight this threat!" There is nothing like that in the envelope. Instead, you are told that in each state wilderness lovers are gathering outside the district offices of members of Congress to stand against a bill that would gut the Wilderness Act and other conservation laws. You are asked to protest legislation that would give the Border Patrol leeway to drive anywhere on the public lands within 100 miles of coasts or borders with Mexico and Canada to

7   Lawrence Noble, "Dividing Citizens Lucrative for Special Interests," *Albuquerque Journal*, November 14, 2005.

catch drug smugglers and waylay Al Qaeda terrorists. You are given the date, time, directions, and organizer contact for the nearest rally to your zip code. The alert also asks you to call, write, or email your members of Congress. If there is any bid for dollars, it is a quiet little box on a return envelope for you to let the club know you are going to a rally or have sent a letter.

In other words, conservation clubs should shift how they see their members—from check writers first to wildlovers willing to stand up for wild things foremost. Such a shift would make the conservation network mightier by far, and I don't think it would harm income.

While stirring up those who belong to wilderness and wildlife clubs is the core of inreach and comes before any outreach, the next target bunch should be thought of as inreach, too.

The low-hanging fruit for conservation calling up has always been outdoorsfolk—wilderness wayfarers, hunters and anglers, and both scientific and folk naturalists. Moreover, the strongest workers for wild things—whether hired staff or grassroots folks—are those who get outside to be with wild things.

Our dare is this: Most wilderness hikers, backpackers, horsepackers, wild-river runners, canoeists, sea kayakers, scuba divers and snorkelers, mountaineers and rock climbers, cross-country skiers and snowshoers, wilderness hunters and anglers, and trail runners do not work to shield wilderness—they don't help to keep mostly wild landscapes roadless and free of development, to set aside new Wilderness Areas and other wild havens, or to watchdog already set-aside wild havens. Most birders, wildlife trackers, butterfly watchers, wildflower lovers, those who want to name trees, mushrooms, frogs, snakes, and other wild things, those who bliss out on or study the behavior of wild things, and the rest with field guides, binoculars, and cameras do not work to shelter wildlife—they don't help to ward wild neighborhoods and rebuild wounded lands and streams, watchdog wildlife management, get slipping-away lifekinds listed as Threatened or Endangered, fight so-called "predator and pest control," and work against all kinds of slob hunting and fishing that snuff and trample native wildlife. Sadly, most "Nature" photographers and natural history writers do not put their shoulders to the wheel of shielding wild things.[8]

Conservation clubs need to wield their skills and wiles to target outdoorsfolk and naturalists—at trailhead parking lots, outdoor-gear and bird-feeding stores, nature centers, wherever—to coax them into our clan, to give them something to do right away (sign a petition, write a quick letter), and to light a fire under them to stand up for wild things.[9] Not to donate money. Let me say that again. *Not to donate money.* Get folks who seek wild things to first stand up for wild things before trying to grub dollars out of them. I think an awful lot of folks who would help wild things fear conservation clubs as mostly moneygrubbers. I some-times think that. That thought needs to be flipped on its head.

Conservation outfits of all kinds need to renew their steadfast tar-geting of those who go to the big outside and those who seek to know wild things. This "inreach" is where our greater might lies and we need to reach for it before we outreach.

THOUGHTFULLY TARGET CONSERVATION FUNDING TO BUILD A MIGHTY NETWORK FOR THE LONG HAUL AND TO END THE WARPING HARM MONEY SOMETIMES DOES TO THE CONSERVATION NETWORK. CONSERVA-TION FUNDERS NEED TO CAREFULLY LOOK AT HOW

---

8   I am proud to be a founding fellow of the International League of Conservation Writers: http://www.ilcwriters.org/Home.html. Bob Baron of Fulcrum Press is working to get more who write about wild things to do more for wild things through the ILCW.

9   "Tabling" is one of the most needed things conservation clubs do. It is not done enough. Moreover, good tabling is a thoughtful art and conservation clubs need to hone that skill.

WELL RIGHT-WING PHILANTHROPY WORKS. FUNDING SHOULD BE SHIFTED TO LONG-HAUL, GENERAL-SUPPORT OF WILDERNESS AND WILDLIFE CLUBS FOR STEADINESS, BUILDING AND BACKING INDIVIDUAL CONSERVATION LEADERS AND SKILLED SPEAKERS AND WRITERS, AND BACKING OUR OWN THINK TANKS. MOREOVER, CONSERVATION LEADERS NEED TO THINK ABOUT HOW TO SHIFT CONSERVATION FUNDING TO CUT BACK ON THE UNENDING TREADMILL OF DOLLAR GRUBBING.

The *Homo sapiens* mind, for all the self-love we shower upon it, has weaknesses by the score. One of these is the headstrong search for the *one* mainspring making something happen—never mind if we are dealing with the commonest sense or the deepest science. So, shake that salt on what I am about to write:

After much thought and forty years of being in the middle of it all, I think the key thing that is wrong with our work today to shield and rebuild the Tree of Life is the dollar chase. "Money is the root of all evil," is more than a clever saying; it is near to being a truism. Money is both the hand on the whip lashing the conservation network into enviro-resourcism and the Holy Grail after which our outfits run. The mushrooming weight of the dollar in nonprofit conservation clubs and teams lurks behind most (maybe all) of the plights I've dredged up in this book. The dollar chase is one thing that we need to trammel.

When I started working for wilderness in the early 1970s, there was not much of a funding establishment for the wilderness and wildlife network. Bunches like the Sierra Club and The Wilderness Society (TWS) got most of their working income from membership fees or from a few big givers and bequests. It is true that dollars were often short and that this led to all kinds of woes, but tight budgets were not nearly as big of a deal then as now, even though there was much less fat to trim then. There were many fewer state and regional outfits in the 1970s and many of those were unincorporated without bylaws and such, and thus couldn't offer tax deductions for gifts. There were darn few hired wilderness and wildlife workers hither and yon in the U.S. and not many at headquarters for national outfits in Washington, San Francisco, and New York. Folks who had 9 to 5 jobs or retirees did most of the work. Some activists had a special patron who funded his or her work, but this was rare. Nonetheless, the conservation movement got a lot done.

I would bet that if we were to even out the dollars for inflation, the income for New Mexico conservation in the 1970s ran one to five percent of what it is now. In New Mexico in the early 1970s, the key wilderness workers were scientists and engineers at Sandia Labs, small business owners, school teachers, college professors, doctors, students, housewives, retired folks, government employees, bartenders, waitresses, and a few dirt bags like me who did grubby, sweaty work of sundry kinds when we could find it. Folks shared gas fill-ups to go to hearings and meetings in other towns or to go to unknown spots to see if such were likely wilderness study areas or to do boundary work on landscapes we already knew and wanted as Wilderness Areas. Membership fees and small gifts went to print and mail newsletters and fliers, postage, copy fees for maps, and such. Bank accounts seldom had more than a thousand bucks. There was only one true office for conservation in the state. That was Central Clearing House in Santa Fe where Black Mesa Defense and other outfits hung out, as well as folks lobbying the legislature when it was in session. The Sierra Club soon moved in, too. Harvey Mudd, who had family wealth, underwrote Central Clearing House. In January of 1973, I was hired by The Wilderness Society to be their field consultant for New Mexico, Texas, and Arizona at $250 a month with $50 a month for expenses. The Sierra Club hired Don Campbell to work out of Central Clearing House on wilderness, too.

We were it for hired wilderness staff. I miss those days, even with my few dollars.[10]

Since the 1980s, the funding world for wilderness and wildlife keeping has been wholly flipped over, and, owing to that, state and national wilderness and wildlife clubs along with the whole conservation network are not the same. Two score or more foundations now give millions of dollars every year to conservation clubs. Some of the big outfits have budgets of over one hundred million dollars a year and hire hundreds of staffers. Some CEOs are paid more than presidents of big universities. Heck, some of the whole "packages" might be chasing what university football and basketball coaches pull down. There are well over one hundred staffers of conservation groups in the U.S. who get more than $100,000 a year. Thanks to such big-business salaries, club heads have big-business thinking. Member chasing and keeping has become an industry. Seeking foundations and high donors and keeping them happy is one of the most time-eating things a conservation outfit now does. And so, the wilderness and wildlife network has much more money. Even small local conservation clubs are now incorporated with thick by-laws, hired staff, and formal boards of directors. There aren't many of the old-time wild bunches left. It seems that hired staffers almost outnumber volunteers. With this amazing growth, conservation outfits get a lot done.

Thank goodness for the foundations and high donors that bankroll our work. My scolding is meant to be helpful and watchful, not mean-souled or unthankful. Notwithstanding all the good that grantmakers have done, however, I think some have unwittingly bungled the *jizz*, mood, and look of the wilderness and wildlife network, keeping it from being as strong and winning as it could be.[11] I went over this plight in

---

10   See my novel, *Lobo Outback Funeral Home*, for a true-to-life taste of what conservation work was like back then. Dave Foreman, *Lobo Outback Funeral Home* (Johnson Books, Boulder, CO, 2000).

11   *Jizz* is a word some birders wield for the look and behavior you catch from a fleeting glance at a bird that triggers a recall of the name even

Table 12.1. What Foundations Should Fund

General operating support

Infrastructure

People and Leadership

Systemic approaches for abating ecological degradation

Ideas

From Lavigne and Orr

chapters 3 and 4; now I want to offer some answers. The first thing is to acknowledge that more money and the chasing after it is not always good. Then we need to carefully study how authoritarian-right and "free-market" funders have worked over the last thirty years. Bart Semcer, a Sierra Club staffer for hunter/angler outreach and a Rewilding Institute Fellow, writes in an email that "the right-wing political machine has been very good at investing in people.... [and] recognizing the importance of capital investment in technology." He goes on to say, "Based on my experience in the conservation movement I have seen little focus on nurturing talent." George Lakoff writes, "The right wing has spent billions of dollars over decades on a widespread system of think tanks, language experts, training institutes for speakers, grassroots organizing, buying media, computer communications, and the daily booking of speakers in the media across the country."[12] This is a pretty good sketch of where conservation and environmental foundations should go.

Peter Lavigne and David Orr offered a good list and a new path for making conservation philanthropy better in the fall of 2004. Among the steps they put forward were: fund general operating support and in-

without a good look and without carefully weighing field marks. It comes from the Air Force on how to identify airplanes: *GIS*—General Identification and Shape.

12   George Lakoff, "Why Environmental Understanding, or 'Framing,' Matters: An Evaluation of the ecoAmerica Summary Report," *The Huffington Post*, May 19, 2009.

frastructure; support people and leadership; fund systemic approaches for abating ecological degradation; and fund ideas. Many foundations now only give dollars to short-lived, set projects with listed outcomes, and not to general support for clubs. This is bureaucratically dumb, to be harshly straightforward, and needs to flipped over. Many of the best leaders, thinkers, and doers in our clan struggle to find dollars. Big donors and foundations need to understand the matchless worth of these folks and then make sure that they are helped to do whatever they do best—with little paperwork or oversight. Moreover, grantmakers need to better trust the clubs they help by giving more general support. In this way, it is the grassroots, with their better, on-the-ground knowledge of what needs to be done, that will choose how to work. Foundations can still make grants only within the edges of what they want to fund, but free-up their grantees more to work within these lines.

I read both *Science* and *Nature* and see that much of this same kind of thinking is going on for research grants. Some scientists are calling for more "fellowship" kinds of grants, which is what I ask above for key conservationists.

I strongly back what Orr and Lavigne offered above, but I've come to think that our dollar plight goes deeper. Former Senator Ernest F. Hollings (D-South Carolina) was one of the more thoughtful and trustworthy politicians in the U.S. In 2006, he wrote, "There is a cancer on the body politic: money." The truth of his upbraiding is widely acknowledged. However, politics is not the only body to ache from hounding after bucks. There is also a cancer on the body conservation: money. Hollings writes that "almost one-third of a senator's time is spent fund raising."[13] This is roughly true for conservation clubs big and little. The upshot is that the money-cancer eats away at the health and righteousness of conservation institutions and—worse—the whole wilderness

13   Ernest F. Hollings, "Stop the Money Chase or Bid Ethics Goodbye," *The Washington Post,* reprinted in *The Albuquerque Journal,* February 26, 2006.

and wildlife web and the work of keeping wild things. It has thoroughly upset the makeup and outward bearing of citizen conservation in the United States.

Conservation clubs and teams of all kinds and weights are damned to a Sisyphean hell on the fund-raising treadmill. This treadmill is never-ending and unforgiving; it gets faster and steeper as one grabs more bucks. From far away and near at hand, I see conservation clubs—unknowingly for the most—choosing fund-raising as their overweening goal and foremost job. This choice is seen as needed for keeping alive by the staff and board members of clubs. Too often, executive directors are hired not for their greatness as conservationists but for their skill at raising dollars. Board meetings spend more time on fundraising and budget than on what needs to be done fighting threats to wild things. Too much running after dollars warps conservation and is the root for many of the woes I've written about in these pages. Conservationists—donors and grantees—must find ways to stop or at least slow the treadmill. Here I have room only to toss out a few thoughts on how this might be done. It is up to the conservation kinship to hone and put to work such answers.

Donors need to take the steps outlined earlier along with further ones. Foundations should give two-to-five-year, general-support grants to clubs they back. They need to trust their grantees' judgment to do right with the money. Overall, foundations should make it as smooth as can be for clubs by cutting paperwork and organizational demands on them. Foundations also need to make their own inside shifts so their requirements are less time-gobbling on grantees and to free up more money for them. Some, such as the Weeden Foundation, do their work with little staff and overhead. Most, however, are overstaffed and rather bloated in their work. By taking a leaner path, more of their money could go to do the real work of conservation. Likewise, foundations should cut backing for consultants to free up more money for hardworking grassroots on the ground.

Big individual givers should become patrons or matrons for a chosen conservation club or leader, as some thankfully do now (I don't know what I would do without mine). By taking on clubs or lone workers with good, two-to-five-year gifts, angels can cut the time and work clubs and leaders need to spend in fundraising. Such backers should also think about whether their dollars might go further if they gave more to small clubs than to big national outfits.

Conservation groups ("grantees") can do much to cut their need for dollars. Foremost, they need to drop the ideology of organizational growth. Before jumping up budgets, hiring more staff, opening more offices, taking on new campaigns, a club—and not just the staff and board—needs to sharply ask why they need growth. The bigger a club becomes, the bigger the slice of its wherewithal and sparkle goes into administrative overhead. Only when growth is well thought-out and truly needed for getting done the work of the club, should it be taken on. New outfits need to grow, yes, but even they should grow thoughtfully and carefully. Some of the big national and international conservation organizations would be as good or even better with half the income they now have.

Wilderness and wildlife clubs today seem to be thoroughly embodied by their staffs. Once upon a time there were few hired conservation staff, as I showed earlier. Many wilderness and wildlife clubs had no staff at all. Grassroots did all the work. Many of these outfits weren't even incorporated and had little income. My wife Nancy Morton, then an intensive-care hospital nurse in Chico, California, helped start and lead the Northstate Wilderness Committee in the late 1970s when she was still a nursing student at Chico State. Other key players were a struggling professional photographer, a gardener, a recycling center manager, the owner of a print shop, one of his pressmen, college students…and so on. They got the Ishi Wilderness Area and others set aside, bettered stewardship and oversight of Lassen National Park, blocked timber sales, got the Forest Service to shift roadless area lines out to take in more acres, shut lands to snowmobiles and off-road vehicles, and much more. There were scores of such clubs with like deeds back then. Such unhired workers should take (not be given) a much bigger job in local and state wilderness and wildlife groups today—or they should go over to Great Old Broads for Wilderness, which recalls the grassroots bunches of yore. Husbands and wives can work out deals where one is the breadwinner and the other works on keeping wild things. Retirees are a great wealth of conservation workers. Now, when I talk about such grassroots, I'm not thinking of them only stuffing envelopes, making copies, or filing (needed as that is), I'm talking about them taking on staff work. Many such folks are as knowledgeable and good as hired staff—and for some work, better. Such a rebirth of citizen conservationists within wilderness and wildlife clubs will take some mood tweaking among hired staff and directors. Going back to the core work of conservationists who do not make their living from conservation will take some strain off organizations to raise more dollars for hired staff jobs. Not only is this step key for cutting the need for dollars, it is also at the heart of breathing new life into and healing the conservation network. This is a straightforward way that wildlovers can take back conservation. The Rewilding Institute would not be without unhired staff, who all are highly skilled and knowledgeable leaders.

A few small outfits yet pay paltry wages to staff. They have no other choice if they are to survive, and some still believe that one shouldn't get a fat income working for a nonprofit or a wilderness club. Many national groups and well-healed regional groups, however, pay their staffers way too much. I think it's shameful. For all my quibbles with the Sierra Club, when I was on the national board, there was a strong tradition that the Club did not pay top dollar to the executive director or anyone else. I hope it is still that way. That many conservation-group staff make over $80,000 a year is amazing and bothersome. Such outfits are also often overstaffed. For such clubs pay should be slowly lowered to what is fair, and featherbedding by unneeded staff should be cut.

Wilderness and wildlife clubs can go leaner in many other ways as well. The flood of direct mail from conservation outfits is outlandish and shabby. Two or three direct-mail businesses handle work for the big outfits (which is why the junk mail all looks the same). Membership growth for the sake of membership growth betters neither the income of clubs (hard-driven membership campaigns often lose money) or their clout.

Some other ways the always growing need for bucks could be capped would be for some clubs to knit together thereby cutting overhead—though this doesn't always work. Making more on sales should be given a go, although I am finding that things such as T-shirts and bumperstickers are much less wanted today—such sales were the key income for the *Earth First! Journal* when I ran it in the 1980s. Conservation clubs need the will and boldness to say no to restricted grants if they would have the club work outside their core goals or if they would call for too much overhead or other burdens, such as hiring folks not right for the club. Clubs also should say no to consultants and training if there is not a true need for such.

These are a few ways conservationists can get off the money-go-round and spend more time on needed wilderness and wildlife work. I urge folks from both giving and getting sides to come together to work it out.

Running for dollars can beget bad behavior in otherwise good conservation leaders. Since you are arm-wrestling with your fellow conservationists for grants, donations, members, you begin to clash over who gets acknowledgment for a win or step forward. Instead of working hand in hand on shared cares, you work to cheapen the other's hard work, undercut them, jump the gun to roll out an offering built by broad teamwork in your lone name first. This goes from being irksome to being downright wretched behavior. So much for being kin, kith, or neighbors. Too often, though, when you are being shoved by donors to show how your club gets more done than others seeking grants and being shoved by your board to raise more bucks, you can drift into a twisted little mind box where your friends (fellow conservationists working with you on a land or wildlife deal) become your foes because they are going head to head with you for bucks from the same foundations or high donors. This is not theorizing from a political-science academic, but what I have seen too often. I am not the only one to see these nasty little soap operas playing out. In some ways this is the most awful upshot of the dollar merry-go-round.

The root of this trouble is with funders who often don't understand the need for clubs and teams to work together and share the limelight. Back in the early days of The Wildlands Project, I met with a wealthy man who was starting a big foundation. He could not understand what we did. I told him that we worked with many other conservation outfits to help them with conservation biology and to get them working on a big North American Wildlands Network vision. Coordinating other groups didn't cut the mustard; he wanted to know what we did, alone as The Wildlands Project.

Thankfully, some funders ask sundry outfits to work together with a shared grant. We need more of that.

Working for a wilderness and wildlife club should not be thought of as a nine to five job. I was thunderstruck some years back when I heard that the ED of an outfit with which I helped told new staff that they would need to work only thirty-five hours a week. On the other hand, there are yet bunches where folks burn the midnight oil. Were I hiring for an outfit today and a would-be staffer didn't want to work more than forty hours a week or in the evening or on weekends, I'd tell them to hit the road. Folks should not be driven to work double time and maybe burn out (as Bart Koehler and I did with seventy to eighty-hour weeks in the 1970s), but hirelings must know what goes with the job.

The above may hurt the feelings of some hard-working and whole-hearted staffers. I am not chiding or putting down anyone. In working on this plight, we need to not pin it on named folks—it is a system-wide woe. Furthermore, as the executive director of a small conservation outfit, The Rewilding Institute, and a former board member of some others, I know what it is like to try to keep an organization alive and to pay salaries for conservation champions.

FOSTER STRONG THINKING AND ONGOING LEARNING WITHIN THE WILDERNESS AND WILDLIFE NETWORK. THE ANTICONSERVATION WEB IS HELPFULLY BACKED BY WEALTHY RIGHT-WING THINK TANKS. THE WILDERNESS AND WILDLIFE NETWORK HAS NOT BACKED ITS OWN THINK TANKS, EVEN WHEN THEY ARE ALREADY SET UP, AND THEREBY HURTS FOR WANT OF AN INTELLECTUAL GROUNDING AND GOOD LONG-THINKING.

Though I'm long gone from the conservative movement, I still watch it. The authoritarian and "free-market" right has deftly called on its intellectuals to craft clever words, frames, and campaigns to hack away at our public lands and conservation laws (among other things). Think tanks have been one key to the right's skill in picking the field for fights and often winning. The authoritarian-right funding arm has backed think tanks and unyielding, ideological intellectuals well indeed. Paul Krugman writes that Irving Kristol, father of neoconservatism, in 1978 "urged corporations to make 'philanthropic contributions to scholars and institutions who are likely to advocate preservation of a strong private sector.'"[14] They followed his bidding. Cato, Heritage, and others are the outcome.

The Discovery Institute, the Seattle think tank that has so well muddied the waters on evolution with "intelligent design" buncombe, shows what a belief-driven think tank can do. As of 2005, they had

---

14   Paul Krugman, "Design for Confusion," *The New York Times,* August 5, 2005.

pumped "$3.6 million in fellowships of $5,000 to $60,000 per year to 50 researchers since the science center's founding in 1996."[15] Think what the wilderness and wildlife network could do with such underwriting! The authoritarian right is darn good at framing, yes, but their shallow words are backed by deep (but misleading) thoughts from their think tanks.

Charity Navigator, which weighs public charities, finds 222 policy organizations in the United States.[16] That's a lot of think tanks. Nearly every field in America has them, but for the wilderness and wildlife network. There are think tanks for resourcism, alternative energy, environmental justice, urban environmentalism, and so on, but not for wilderness and wildlife conservation. Doug Tompkins's Foundation for Deep Ecology (FDE) had a side that was likely the nearest thing to a think tank for wild things (along with the journal *Wild Earth*, which FDE underwrote), but with his move to southern Chile, that side of FDE waned but for his ongoing big books publishing.

It is high time for the Environmental Grantmakers, other conservation foundations, and wealthy folks to carefully look at how the anti-conservation right has wielded think tanks. Then a team needs to make a long-time oath to underwrite a think tank for wild things. At the least, dedicated funding needs to bring back *Wild Earth* or something like it as a thinking forum for wilderness and wildlife conservation. (*Conservation* magazine is not an adequate substitute since its leitmotif is soft resourcism.) If you are old enough to recall them or if you have poked about dusty shelves in a library, you know that *The Living Wilderness* and *Sierra Club Bulletin* were once upon a time thinking publications where twentieth-century conservation was hammered out. John Davis, Tom Butler, and I wanted *Wild Earth* to fill the hole from their loss, but the money couldn't be found to keep it going.

15   Jodi Wilgoren, "Politicized Scholars Put Evolution on the Defensive," *The New York Times,* August 21, 2005.
16   "The Independent Institute Awarded 4-Star Rating by Charity Navigator," *The Independent,* Vol. XV, No. 2, 2005.

Think tanks do not a network make. But they are a key slice of a skillfully working network. Doing must be the heart of keeping wild things, but we shirk a strong mindful grounding to our woe. Without new thoughts and paths, a network becomes dull and slow like cobwebby old bones going to dust.

Since the early 1990s, working with Michael Soulé and other top conservation biologists and thoughtful conservation leaders such as David Johns and John Davis, I've worked to build a think tank for the wilderness and wildlife network. None of it would have happened without foresight and funding from Doug Tompkins. Through *Wild Earth* magazine, The Wildlands Project (Wildlands Network), and The Rewilding Institute, we have come up with new paths for conservation. In this we've done well, at least in two fields. One, we have spread scientific research showing how big wild hunters are needed for keeping ecological health and wholeness and have well shown that missing native wild hunters need to be put back in wildlands. Two, we have worked to shift to wildlands networks instead of island-like wild havens. Wildlands networks tie core wildernesses together with wildlife linkages—or *Wildways*. Together, these paths are called *rewilding*.[17] In the early 1990s, both were scoffed at. Today they are widely held among conservation biologists, grassroots conservationists, wilderness and wildlife clubs, and scientists and some managers in land-managing agencies. At the 8th World Wilderness Congress in Anchorage, Alaska, in 2005, I heard folks from Europe, Latin America, Australia, Asia, Africa, North America, and elsewhere say the word "rewilding." A highlight of the week was the beginning of a new campaign to *rewild* a landscape in Mexico next to Big Bend National Park on the Rio Bravo (Rio Grande). My book *Rewilding North America* goes into rewilding as does The Rewilding Institute website. *Rewilding North America* is a text

17   Michael Soulé and Reed Noss, "Rewilding and Biodiversity: Complementary Goals for Continental Conservation," *Wild Earth*, Vol. 8, No. 3, Fall 1998, 18-28.

or further reading for courses in nearly a score of colleges.[18] So, even without backing from a wide spread of funders, we shifted conservation thinking on what makes healthy ecosystems and on how to better design protected areas as networks. Nonetheless, *Wild Earth* was dropped when The Wildlands Project could not raise enough money for it. Conservation funders lean way over to pay for the sizzle not the steak.

DEAL WITH THE THREATS OF OVERPROFESSIONAL-ISM, CORPORATISM, AND INSTITUTIONALISM IN OUR CLUBS. THE GROWTH OF HIRED STAFF FOR CLUBS BIG AND LITTLE HAS HELPED THE WILDERNESS AND WILD-LIFE NETWORK TO DO MUCH MORE. IT HAS ALSO, HOW-EVER, HAMPERED THE CONSERVATION MISSION IN SOME WAYS, AMONG THEM WATERING-DOWN HOW WE SEE WILD THINGS AS GOOD-IN-THEMSELVES, CHIPPING AWAY AT OUR BOLDNESS, AND SIDELINING UNHIRED GRASSROOTERS. THE LIFTING OF ORGANIZATIONS OVER THEIR MISSIONS HAS HARMED OUR WORK AND OUR SOUL.

I went through some of the pitfalls of professionalism and corporatism in Chapter 4, drawing from my earlier book, *Confessions of an Eco-Warrior.* Many of these woes are not only harming conservation; they are rife throughout today's institutions of every kind. Heck, they are the being of today's institutions and can't be dodged, as political scientists and sociologists have written. Even so, we need to acknowledge and understand such plights and work to lessen the harm they do. However, the ways some woes play out within the conservation clan are tied to us. Perhaps the worst quandary in our field is that some executive directors of conservation clubs big and little are now careerists who are more in the camp of enviro-resourcism than that of conservation.

---

18   Dave Foreman, *Rewilding North America: A Conservation Vision for the 21st Century* (Island Press, Washington, DC, 2004).

Farsighted, value-grounded, uplifting leaders are sometimes not the most skillful stewards for the business end of any kind of organization in any field. As conservation clubs have grown in budgets, members, staff, and so on, short-thinking board members too often hire executive directors not for being great conservationists but for being managers. A few clubs have cleverly cleaved administrative from leadership jobs. Leaders of wilderness and wildlife outfits big and small, whatever their titles, should be truehearted, knowledgeable, tough wildlovers and should lead on policy, speaking out to the news business and otherwise, and firing up folks. *Conservation leaders* are needed here. Good managers and fundraisers, who are also needed, should have titles other than executive director, and not have the wheel for policy, but should have leadership freedom on nuts and bolts management. It's a given that these two need to work together well. The conservation leader should not have a free hand on policy, though. Boards of directors need to have among them the most knowledgeable, unyielding, and canny grassroots wildlovers in the state, nation, or whatever landscapes the club oversees. Such directors should often speak for the club. I think this path may be the best answer we can cobble together. Boards of directors when they are searching for and selecting executive directors need to be guided by it.

Among the clubs I know well, Great Old Broads for Wilderness is my organizational framework. They are driven by love of wild things, they are rife with wit, whimsy, and waggishness, are tough and bold, are a kinship or kith instead of an institution, and are volunteer-driven. Led by Ronni Egan, wilderness horse packer and an old buddy of mine, the small staff is heart and soul in the Amateur Tradition. I think it would behoove other small clubs to have their staffers intern with Great Old Broads so that their madcap and gritty makeup from the old, feisty, grassroots gang rubs off and soaks in.

More than a few conservation staffers and grassroots workers are pretty much unschooled in conservation lore and would be much better in their work if they had deeper knowledge. This weakness is worse for hired staff—wide knowledge is one professional skill staffers must have. It also seems that the younger folks are, the less knowledge they have. Far too many have not read *A Sand County Almanac, Wilderness and the American Mind, Continental Conservation, The Arrogance of Humanism, The Enduring Wilderness, Rewilding North America, The Idea of Wilderness, Driven Wild,* among the key works for our crowd. Staffers should be schooled not only in the nuts and bolts of lobbying and organizing, but also in the history, philosophy, and science of conservation. They need to know the 1964 Wilderness Act and other root laws and programs and how things work inside and out. Such schooling will build the mind of the wilderness network. This is another field, by the way, in which radical-right think tanks have done well. Every year they steep scores of young folks in the thinking side of the radical right and churn out knowledgeable activists and tomorrow's leaders. A key goal of my books, *Rewilding North America* and those in the *For the Wild Things* series, is to gather the knowledge, background, and wisdom from key conservation books, along with my wide, hands-on know-how, and get it out in readable packages.[19]

Were I young enough and healthy enough to be the ED of a wilderness outfit, I would not interview anyone for a job who had not read Doug Scott's *The Enduring Wilderness* and The Wilderness Society's annotated booklet on the Wilderness Act, and who had not done week-long backpack trips into the biggest wildernesses, designated or not, in our working landscape. Nor would I let anyone come on to the job until they had also read Rod Nash's *Wilderness and the American Mind,* and a few other key books. Furthermore, I would quiz them on their knowledge. Bart Koehler and I (along with other TWS field staff)

---

19   The Rewilding Website, www.rewilding.org, has a resource, "The Books of the Big Outside," wherein I give short reviews of over two hundred conservation books, and list the top ones. *Take Back Conservation* and the earlier *Man Swarm* are the first two books in the five-book *For the Wild Things* series.

pretty much had the Wilderness Act memorized thanks to drilling from our fatherly boss Clif Merritt. Our thorough knowledge helped us time and time again whether talking to a member of Congress, arguing with a Forest Supervisor, or debating antiwilderness zealots. In that way, at least, Clif would be my model for running a wilderness outfit.

Patagonia, Piragis, Four Corners Riversports, and Northwest River Supply have trust with their shoppers since their owners and workers spend many days a year screening their clothes and gear in wilderness and on wild rivers in gruesome weather and tough going. Eric Diner-stein of the U.S. World Wildlife Fund and George Schaller, Alan Rabi-nowitz, and other staffers of Panthera have believability since they know the wildeor in the wildeor's home—and have scars and harrow-ing tales to prove it.[20] Staffers of conservation clubs should spend at least two weeks a year in wilderness—and not as time off or as a choice. No ifs, ands, or buts; they will do it. I first talked this up twenty-some years ago and a few clubs do it today. I am thunderstruck when I hear of conservation clubs that hire policy and other core staff who have never been camping before! However well meaning and skilled they may be, I can't trust their sharp-wittedness and toughness if they don't know wild things from being there. Can one weigh the worth of something if they don't know it? Can they fight to the last for it if they don't love it? Have they the right to trade off a wild thing if they haven't wept for it?

Great Old Broads for Wilderness does a topnotch job of get-ting their folks together in the big outside—*Broadwalks*. Other small clubs bring out folks to do ecological restoration such as ripping out exotic plants, making off-road vehicle trails undriveable, and replant-ing grazed-off streams. The New Mexico Wilderness Alliance puts to-gether the *Wild Guide* every year. It is a 150 to 200-page book in full

20   Yvon Chouinard, *Let My People Go Surfing* (The Penguin Press, New York, 2005); Eric Dinerstein, *Tigerland And Other Unintended Destinations* (Island Press, Washington, DC, 2005); and Alan Rabinowitz, *Chasing The Dragon's Tail: The Struggle to Save Thailand's Wild Cats* (Doubleday, New York, 1994).

color, chock full of wilderness outings, outdoor service projects, and a mindboggling sweep of short articles about whatever has to do with wilderness. Thanks to the *Wild Guide*, NMWA gets hundreds of folks outside to learn about key wilderness campaigns, pull up exotic weeds, take out old cattle fence, and restore streams. It shows that NMWA is not a bunch of folks in an office but is staff, volunteers, and friends doing good things in the big outside.[21] Outdoor gatherings should be bedrock for all wilderness and wildlife outfits. This side of "organizational effectiveness" is more needed than any other. Round River Rendezvous up until the late 1980s are a great framework for getting together in the big outside.

Everyone in the conservation clan needs to renew their backing for the leadership of the grassroots. In the history of our calling, grassroots folks have often been at the top in thinking and in work, and as guiding lights. I can tick off names of such folks from all over until dawn comes. Most members of boards of directors should be folk conservationists, not hired staff of other conservation clubs. Again, Great Old Broads for Wilderness sets the mark of grassroots leading a conservation club. ConservAmerica is another. The Sierra Club's great strength is how members work at all rungs within the Club. If 90 percent of the Sierra Club's hired staff left, the Club might be shortly staggered by the blow, but would go on with its grassroots.

Most of the time, big national outfits should be in the background and let local folks have the limelight in news releases and news coverage. Too often, the nationals jump in and elbow locals out of the way. Likewise, staff for local and regional clubs should back off a bit and let their grassroots leaders be quoted in news releases and news coverage. Following these guidelines will undercut the harmful belief that the conservation network is mostly outsiders and hired guns. There are times when it is okay for national groups and hired staffers to be spokesfolks, but the time in the limelight needs to be thoughtfully shared. News outreach is for selling what we believe and want, not for pimping one's club

---

21   New Mexico Wilderness Alliance www.nmwild.org

over others for fundraising. My old boss Clif Merritt in The Wilderness Society taught this path to me forty years ago. Without blaming Clif for too much, an awful lot of how I think the conservation clan should be, I got from Clif—and from his assistant Susan Morgan. I also learned from Clif, though, that there are times when more knowledgeable, wise, and wild national staff need to come down on grassroots who don't know what they are talking about, are making bad deals, or setting bad precedents.

We wildlovers who are lucky enough to be hired by a conservation outfit need to acknowledge that our loyalty should nonetheless be first to wild things, not to our job, not to our career, not to the conservation club for which we work, and not to a "pet" politician. While clinging to our mind-health, we need to be steadfast about the life-or-death dread before us from the scalping of wild things. We need to keep from burnout, but we must work hard and not be laid back.

All this is tough to talk about owing to how it leaves a whiff of cutting down good folks who work for conservation clubs. This is not what I want to do. I think highly of many folks who work for conservation clubs, even many who happen to fit some of the behaviors and beliefs I chide. I'm not giving them the back of my hand; I'm trying to show how they and the conservation kinship can do better. I don't want to put down hired staff; I want to build them up, and to bring back unhired grassroots, too.

Wilderness and wildlife lovers need to shift the way we think about our network: we are a neighborhood of wildlovers, not a congress of institutions.

CHAPTER 13

Goods, Policies, and Work Reforms

*Surprisingly, biocentric values
—valuing nature for its own sake—
are also important for many.*
—Willis Kempton and co-authors on
the finding of their deep opinion survey[1]

BEYOND WHAT WE NEED TO DO to heal our wilderness and wildlife keeping clubs and their network are steadfast steps to be true and bold in what we believe, what we work for, and how we fight. Indeed, the steps I offer in this chapter stand higher than those in the last.

GOODS, POLICIES, AND WORK STEPS:
STAYING TRUE TO THE CONSERVATION MIND AND SOUL

REBUILD NATURAL HISTORY AS CRAFT AND SCIENCE, AND BRING IT BACK AS THE KEYSTONE OF CONSERVATION.

---

1   Kempton, Boster, and Hartley, *Environmental Values,* 214.

I keep going back to Leopold's insight about those who cannot live without wild things for how it grabs so well and thoroughly the inner being of wilderness and wildlife conservationists. It's why I name those who shield wildlife and wilderness *Cannots* and *wildlovers*. Overall, wildlovers want to know something about the wild things they hold so dear. We learn about wild things through the craft of natural history, either as folk naturalists or as scientific authorities. Once upon a time, most grassroots conservationists knew something or a lot about the birds, wild blossoms, trees, and such in their neck of the out-of-doors. Once upon a time, biology was mostly natural history—botany, ornithology, mammalogy, herpetology, ecology, and so on. Nowadays, many leaders and staffers of conservation clubs and teams are more knowledgeable about and enthralled with political things than wild things. Knowing political things is good, too, but their natural history skills and feeling of *wonder* in the big outside is often lightweight.

Nowadays, it seems most biologists are "lab rats" who seldom if ever go outside for their science. Even some conservation biologists are lightweights when it comes to natural history. Peter Kareiva, head scientist for The Nature Conservancy, says, "I'm not a biodiversity guy." As for me, I feel naked without my binoculars.[2] Once upon a time, college biology departments offered a slew of natural history courses and many were field courses. Among the most-wanted college classes, even for nonbiology majors, were natural history field courses. To wit: the only elective Nancy took while working on her master's degree in nursing at the University of Arizona was a field course on the natural history of the Sonoran Desert taught by the legendary Paul Martin. Natural history courses are fading from biology departments today, somewhat owing to how few biology faculty can teach such classes now.

---

2   I was once asked in a radio interview what book I would want with me if I were stranded alone on an island. "The bird field guide for the area," said I.

Reed Noss, at the University of Central Florida and one of the world's top conservation biologists (and unmatched in bringing conservation biology to the conservation network), believes that the root of what is wrong with conservation biology today is the fading of natural history. Tom Fleischner, at Prescott College in Arizona, worries about the overall loss of natural history and has started a campaign to build up natural history as the core of biology and as a love for conservationists. He has edited a book, *The Way of Natural History*, with a wide sweep of authors underlining why natural history is so key.[3] Conservation clubs need to get on what I hope becomes a bandwagon to bring back natural history. All who work on wildlife and wilderness conservation should set goals for themselves to know scads of wild things in the lands where they work. The toughest, most dogged conservationists are those who love wild things and who *know* the wild things living in the wild neighborhoods they haunt—and shield.

UNASHAMEDLY STAND UP FOR WILD THINGS BEING GOOD-IN-THEMSELVES, AND THEREFORE FOR THE UNDERLYING GOOD OF WILDERNESS AND WILDLIFE CONSERVATION. SHIELD OTHER BEINGS FOR THEIR OWN SAKES FROM HARM BY MAN. MAKING ANOTHER EARTHLING EXTINCT IS THE WORST SIN.

For some years bits and slabs of the conservation network have been slowly drifting away from its deepest values. This drift has two streams ferrying it. One, some wildlovers are afraid that straight talk about the inborn good of wild things will scare off most other folks, that it is not a good way to sell others on what we want. Indeed, we are being hammered by enviro-resourcists and resourcists that con-

---

3   Thomas Lowe Fleischner, editor, *The Way of Natural History* (Trinity University Press, San Antonio, 2011).

servation is failing owing to our talking about wild things being good-in-themselves.[4] Two, more and more conservation club leaders do not themselves believe in wild things for their own sakes or in the kind of work such belief bids we do (to wit: the national/international leadership of The Nature Conservancy). Our clubs are filled with workers who seldom get out in wilderness or who can't name even a score of birds. This loss of natural history greatly weakens conservation.[5] David Johns writes in an email that "some conservationists seem to be not just using anthropocentric arguments to advance rewilding goals, but are, in fact, backing off of rewilding goals in favor of sustainable development nonsense." In this way, the soul of conservation is being snuffed. The shift to resourcism, as so-called "sustainable development," is often soft and low-key and thus many don't see it happening. For some enviro-resourcists, the upshot of what they are doing may well be unwitting. When we don't talk about wild things or *be* with them, they wane from our minds—and our news releases.

This drift to talking mostly about the dollar worth of wild things and of conservation work is the mark of a weakness in our hearts. It is also shaky ground on which to walk.

David Ehrenfeld warned in 1978, "Resource reasons for conservation can be used if honest, but must always be presented together with the non-humanistic reasons, and it should be made clear that the latter are more important in every case."[6] He wrote that "there is simply no way to tell whether one arbitrarily chosen part of Nature has more

---

4   Think of "moderates" telling Rev. Martin Luther King, Jr. not to talk about the equality of all Mankind because it might scare some civil rights backers off. I see no difference—none whatsoever—with wildlovers being told not to talk about the self-goodness of all Earthlings because it might scare some conservation backers off.

5   Thomas Lowe Fleischner, editor, *The Way of Natural History* (Trinity University Press, San Antonio, 2011).

6   David Ehrenfeld, *The Arrogance of Humanism* (Oxford University Press, NY, 1978), 210.

'value' than another part, so like Noah we do not bother to make the effort."[7] He went on, "I have tried to show…the devilish intricacy and cunning of the humanists' trap. 'Do you love Nature?' they ask. 'Do you want to save it? Then tell us what it is good for.' The only way out of this kind of trap, if there is a way, is to smash it, to reject it utterly."[8] Years earlier, Aldo Leopold warned that "most members of the land community have no economic value." He bade us not to make up "subterfuges to give it economic importance."[9] I can offer no better words of wisdom to young conservationists than what these two wise men give. Beings and other wild things on Earth are good-in-themselves. That is the bottom line. Insofar as what they are worth in dollars, do not overplay. When someone asks you about a wildeor or wort, "Well, what good is it?" there is only one good answer, "Well, what good are you?" Leopold said the what-good-is-it question was the last word in ignorance.[10]

We should not be shy about saying, "I love wilderness and big cats! And little bats. Bushtits are the soul of winsomeness!" *Merriment over the inborn worth of all life kinds and the slow, unfathomable waltz that has brought the Tree of Life into being is the bedrock of the conservation soul, while the belief itself is the bedrock of the conservation mind.* We conservationists need to underline our Tree of Life righteousness even if we worry that it may be a hard sell to Main Street, which, as I will show shortly, may not be so. If we do not stand up for wild things for their own sakes, no one will. If not us, who will lead Man into a new neighborliness with other Earthlings? Moreover, by forsaking what we hold

---

7   Ehrenfeld, *The Arrogance of Humanism*, 208. Yes, yes, I quoted Ehrenfeld on this before, and I know a writer sins when they plop down the same quote more than once in a book, but what Ehrenfeld writes here is of the utmost worth and it is needed in this spot as it was in the earlier spot.

8   Ehrenfeld, *The Arrogance of Humanism*, 210.

9   Aldo Leopold, *A Sand County Almanac and Sketches Here and There* (Oxford University Press, New York, 1949), 210.

10   Luna Leopold, editor, *Round River: From the Journals of Aldo Leopold* (Oxford University Press, New York, 1953), 146.

dear to ourselves and by hiding such love from others, we will do untold harm to our own minds and souls. As in the old tale of Peter forswearing Christ thrice before the cock crew, we will become woebegone, feeble wretches.

I acknowledge that oft we have not heard it boldly said that wild things are good for their own sakes, and that we have heard for scores of years a sweep of other goods offered as answers for the why of conservation—aesthetic, spiritual, experiential, ecological, economic, utilitarian. Leopold himself gave us many. However, I believe that aesthetic and other such grounds, for most folks offering them, stand for the "big good"—that wild things *are* and therefore are good-in-themselves, and that we Men have no right to carelessly wreck or hobble wild things.

Biologist Campbell Webb, who works in the tropical forests of Indonesia, wrote in *Conservation Biology*, "Finally, perhaps the healthiest thing we can do for our peace of mind is to speak our mind.... we value [natural places and species] just for being. And yet many of us have been acculturated to present only utilitarian arguments for their preservation.... Perhaps the time has come to stand up and speak our minds clearly, especially because most anthropocentric, utilitarian approaches have failed to slow the destruction...."[11]

I am proud to see more and more field biologists standing up like Campbell for the inborn good of other Earthlings. Mike Parr, secretary of the Alliance for Zero Extinction, a new team working to hold onto the wildlife near to "imminent extinction," says, "This is a one-shot deal for the human race. We have a moral obligation to act. The science is in, and we are almost out of time."[12] Many of those who work for zoos and who are backed by zoos for field research are daring shielders of wild things for their own sakes. You don't put your life on the line in a ruthless, Man-eating war of band against band unless you care about the inborn goodness of the gorillas you are sheltering.

11   Campbell O. Webb, "Engineering Hope," *Conservation Biology*, Vol. 19, No. 1, February 2005, 277.

12   Ed Stoddard, Reuters, "Study Pinpoints Species Facing Extinction Threat," December 13, 2005.

For the last twenty years I've been going hither and yon in North America calling for shielding and bringing back big wild hunters owing to how they are "top-down regulators" of prey for the great good of wild neighborhoods.[13] This is what rewilding is all about, after all. However, even this is a utilitarian reason of a kind. The true bedrock for keeping and bringing home big flesh-eaters is for their own sakes. In 2005, scientists at the Wildlife Conservation Society edited a book that carefully weighs how well sundry carnivores from all over the world work for the health of their wild neighborhoods. Nonetheless, Justina Ray and her coauthors wrote, "We suggest that it is important to distinguish between value-based and science-based reasons for carnivore conservation—understanding that the two can be integrated. Too often scientifically grounded principles to justify carnivore conservation have obscured the more fundamental aesthetic and ethical values that lie at the root of many who argue for their conservation."[14] Top-down flesh-eaters have both inborn and instrumental worth. The inborn values are the bedrock upon which the others stand.

We may fear that most Americans, Mexicans, and Canadians (and other *Homo sapiens*) are not believers that other Earthlings have a "right" to be for their own sakes. At least, most are not hard believers in a wild things-first ethic. Nonetheless, Jack Humphrey, the (for-free) webmaster for The Rewilding Institute and former executive director of the Sky Island Alliance, writes in an email, "These days I am more of an outsider than the insider I used to be in the conservation community and I can tell you with 100% confidence, the conservation movement has NOTHING to lose by being bold, outspoken, and unmovable on

13   Dave Foreman, *Rewilding North America* (Island Press, Washington, DC, 2004).

14   Justina C. Ray, Kent H. Redford, Joel Berger, and Robert Steneck, "Conclusion: Is Large Carnivore Conservation Equivalent to Biodiversity Conservation and How Can We Achieve Both?" in Justina C. Ray, Kent H. Redford, Robert S. Steneck, and Joel Berger, eds., *Large Carnivores and the Conservation of Biodiversity* (Island Press, Washington, DC, 2005), 424.

our issues. Why? Because the movement isn't even on the radar of the average people in this country."

From talking with hundreds of folks and from my careful reading of public opinion polls and focus groups, however, I believe that many are swayed by own-sake arguments or at least by the feeling that wild things are *good*. (The lovely, matchless slogan of the Center for Biological Diversity is "Because life is good.") I also believe that heartfelt pleas to keep wildeors and wildernesses grab folks of all kinds. The other day, I ran into a Main-Street Jose on the wilderness-edge trail near my home. He knew little about conservation work, but let me know that he loved seeing snakes on the trail and thought they had a right to live their own lives without being harmed by us. Not many days thereafter I saw a middle-aged man on a side trail poking at the ground with a stick. I sidled over to make sure he wasn't killing a snake and found that he was only trying to get a four-foot-long bull snake out of the trail so it wouldn't be run over by a swift mountain bike. I knew this snake and the other hiker and I had a friendly talk about snakes and lizards and how they might be threatened in the open space owing to too-fast mountain bikers. I often have such trailside meetings with folks from all walks of life. I am friendly when I want to be and skilled (crafty, shrewd) in getting hikers to unclothe their true feelings about wild things to me. I think that getting someone to stand up for wild things to a friendly stranger strengthens the ethic in their own mind and doings. Give it a shot. But be crafty about getting them to talk about their liking for flowers, birds, coyotes, and snakes. Go slow and soft. Nod and smile.

At my talks before all kinds of crowds, such as zoo members, biologists' conventions, universities, conservation conferences, agency workshops, and the general public, I offer the words from Leopold's heart, "There are some who can live without wild things and some who cannot." Then I ask, "How many Cannots are here?" After letting my question soak in for a few breaths, I say, "Raise your hand if you are a Cannot." Nearly all hands are raised, with much chuckling.

Folks have calendars on their walls and photo books on their coffee tables with wildeors living in their wild neighborhoods; folks watch wildlife shows on television. They are gripped by wildlife; their souls glow in the shine of the wildeor; they like wild things! Keep in mind that most public art of the wild (such as in calendars) does not show men, women, or children.

In 2007, I gave a talk at the yearly meeting of the Southwest Chapter of The Wildlife Society (TWS).[15] Most who belong to TWS work for federal and state wildlife agencies, or at universities. And most would think of themselves as in the resource conservation camp (resourcism) and would more or less think of my kind as "preservationists." Bringing home the Mexican wolf then and now is an overwrought clash in the Southwest. Instead of my stock slide talk on the North American Wildlands Network, I spoke about the need to keep wilderness and wildlife for their own sakes, since they are the building blocks of evolution, and underlined the need to get tough about shielding the lobo. Much of what is written above I blended into it.

At the beginning, I asked who was a Cannot. After two or three seconds of antsy looking back and forth with grins, nearly everyone raised their hands. Afterwards two good ol' boy wildlifers asked me if I had some "Cannot and Proud" bumper stickers and said they'd put them on their agency pick-ups. A woman who worked for the U.S. Fish & Wildlife Service and who had given a wishy-washy talk before mine thanked me for reminding her what her job truly was about. I got an email the next day from a tribal wildlife manager for a southwestern reservation thanking me, and telling me how good it was for him and his crew to hear my kind of what-is-good challenge, the oftener, the better. I also heard that a saddle-hardened, world-weary old-timer with one of the state game agencies had told a friend of mine that he had gotten choked up by my talk.

15   The Wilderness Society also calls itself TWS; this could be a muddle, but that TWS (The Wildlife Society) is a "professional" society and TWS (The Wilderness Society) is a non-profit, membership conservation activist group.

Now, I don't pass on these takes on my talk to be cock of the walk like George Bush in high heels, but to show how we have our utmost clout when we talk about our love for wild things and how we must shield wildlife and wilderness for their own sakes. In doing so, we make others think—and those who already care for other Earthlings for their own sakes know they are not alone and will thereby have the derring-do to talk about their beliefs to others. You don't know whom you will reach and what they might do later. This is highly meaningful with folks whom we think are weary and dulled, or whom we think are resourcists, maybe only for not having asked themselves what they truly think about wild things.

Ken Brower, Dave's son, tells me that I am the only one other than his dad whom he has heard preach to conservationists. The answer to this puzzle lies in a sadly overlooked book. "Powerful evangelists for the environmental gospel also include David Brower (raised Baptist), past president of the Sierra Club (sic) and founder of the Friends of the Earth, and Dave Foreman (raised Churches of Christ), co-founder of Earth First!," writes Mark Stoll in his cleverly insightful and eye-opening book *Protestantism, Capitalism, and NATURE in America*. Stoll, who was an assistant professor at St. Edward's University in Austin, Texas, when he wrote his book in 1997, sees the Calvinism which Brower and I were fed when boys as a great swelling wave behind American conservation (as well as other things).[16] I got much of my speaking style from Church of Christ preachers, and Calvinism only strengthened my seeing Man as flawed and sinful at the core and fostered my inborn dislike of hierarchical organizations.[17] I never got to talk to Brower about this and wish I had.

16   Mark Stoll, *Protestantism, Capitalism, and NATURE in America* (University of New Mexico Press, Albuquerque, 1997), 176.

17   Susan Zakin, *Coyotes and Town Dogs: Earth First! and the Environmental Movement* (Viking, New York, 1993) shrewdly looks at how my Church of Christ upbringing came through in how I thought out Earth First!.

Table 13.1. Summary of Wilderness Area Designation Polls in Western United States

REGION / STATE	DATE	WILDERNESS PROPOSAL	FOR %	OPP %	DETAILS	POLLING FIRM
Hispanic voters in CA, AZ, NM	5/2002	Increased Wilderness in all three states			Favor increasing Wilderness areas in own states CA: 81%, AZ: 75%, NM: 72%	Bendixen & Associates
Deschutes Co, OR	2/2005	Badlands, Central OR Wilderness designation	69	19	Support from: GOP 62%, frequent ORV users 35%, all ORV users 56%	American Viewpoint
Curry County, OR	8/2006	Copper Salmon Wilderness	52	37	Conserve 12,000 acres to Wilderness; add N & S forks of Elk River to existing wild & scenic river	American Viewpoint
Colorado -3rd Congressional District	5/2007	Greater Dominguez/ Lower Gunnison NCA/Wilderness	57	27	Support for preserving additional Wilderness in Western CO: 71% overall, GOP 59%, sportsmen 67%, ORV users 61%, hikers/campers 75%	Anzalone Liszt Research
Idaho	11/2007	Boulder White Cloud Wilderness	66	28		Moore Information
Doña Ana Co, NM	5/2009	Wilderness & NCA	79	18	Support from: ORV users 57%, hunters 63%	Hamilton Campaigns
California – 26th Congressional District	8/2009	Additions to San Gabriel, Sheep Mtn. and Cucamunga Wilderness	75	15	Support from: GOP 42%, cyclists 73%, ORV users 57%, sportsmen 76%	Public Opinion Strategies

Colorado - 2nd Congressional District	3/2010	Hidden Gems Wilderness	65	24	Support from: GOP 50%, fishermen 62%, mountain bikers 63%, ORV users 51%, hunters 48%, snowmobilers 40%	RBI Strategies and Research
Washington 6th Congressional District	1/2010	Wild Olympics – Wilderness, Wild & scenic rivers	58	35	66% support additional Wilderness designation in WA	Don McDonough Associates
South Dakota – West River	1/2010	Buffalo Gap National Grasslands - Wilderness	58	31	Support from: GOP women 55%, hunters 60% snowmobilers 58%, ORV users 52%, rockhounds 66%	Moore Information
NE Washington	3/2011	Colville National Forest – increased Wilderness	57	24	Support from: GOP 56%	The Mellman Group & Moore Information
Nevada – Clark County	5/2008	Gold Butte NCA/ Wilderness	66	27		Public Opinion Strategies
Nevada - 3rd Congressional District	4/2012	Gold Butte NCA/ Wilderness	69	20	Support from: GOP 61%, hikers/campers 77%, mountain and road cyclists 71%, sportsmen 67%, ORV users 65%	Moore Information
NM - Taos & Rio Arriba Counties	4/2012	Rio Grande del Norte National Monument	76	19	Support from: ranching/agricultural 71%, hunters 68%, fishermen 77%; 70% overall say "good for the economy"	Anzalone Liszt Research

Thanks to Mike Matz, Director of The Campaign for America's Wilderness and Ken Rait, Director of the Western Lands Initiative; Pew Environment Group, Washington, DC for providing polling documentation and reports.

Leopold's line, "There are some who can live without wild things, and some who cannot," followed by asking, "How many of you are Cannots?" is the best icebreaker I have yet found. Be bold. Find other Cannots. Talk to them about wild things and how we must keep them for their own sakes.

Public Opinion Polling Eye-Openers

Too often conservationists are cowed by the bigwigs, bullies, and blowhards in little towns and the hinterlands and thus gather that these loudmouths give words to the feelings of others thereabouts. Polls in believed hotbeds of the anticonservation angst—the West Slope of Colorado, northern Arizona, even southwestern New Mexico—show more folks for bringing back wolves than against. Polls in western states on setting aside more Wilderness Areas show strong backing and they show that most folks back Wilderness on high-minded grounds: keeping ecosystems unmarred, shielding habitat for "sensitive" wildlife, and other wild-thing goods. A 2005 poll in Arizona showed overwhelming backing for setting aside the Tumacacori Wilderness Area in southern Arizona. Overall, 87 percent of folks backed the Wilderness, with 79 percent of Republicans and 95 percent of Hispanos.[18] See Table 13.1 for a summary of public opinion polls on Wilderness Area designations.

A 2001 poll found that 68 percent of Coloradoans were for wolf homecoming in that state.[19] The Northern Arizona Wolf Recovery poll not only found well more than half for wolves coming home to northern Arizona (81 percent!), but folks gave own-sake grounds for why they were for a wolf comeback. Asked to say why they wanted wolves back, over and over again, men and women offered their thoughts that wolves

18　"New Poll Shows Broad Bipartisan and Cross-Cultural Support for Wilderness in the Tumacacori Highlands," press release from Friends of the Tumacacori Highlands, Sky Island Alliance, and National Hispanic Environmental Council, April 28, 2005.

19　Gary Gerhardt, "Wolf advocates pressing for animals' return," *Rocky Mountain News*, September 10, 2005.

had a right to come home and live in their old homelands. Eighty-six percent said wolves bring a "natural balance" to the Southwest.[20] This is ecosystem thinking. Such backing for wild things cuts through all lines: ethnic, political, rural or urban, income, education, sex....

Willis Kempton and his fellow workers have done perhaps the soundest study of Americans' feelings about Nature. They read this statement to their subjects, "If there is no economic, aesthetic, or other human use for a species, for example, some lichen out in the desert, then there is no reason to worry much about it becoming extinct." Only 13 percent of folks were of that mind (oddly, 15 percent of Sierra Club members were.) Fifty-two percent of sawmill workers were of that mind, but think about it: almost half of sawmill workers took a good-in-itself stand for lichen.[21] For the statement, "Other species have as much right to be on this earth as we do. Just because we are smarter than other animals doesn't make us better," an amazing 83 percent of folks went along, 78 percent of Sierra Club members said yes, and even 56 percent of sawmill workers said yes.[22] In going over the meaning of their findings, Kempton and his coworkers wrote, "Surprisingly, biocentric values—valuing nature for its own sake—are also important for many."[23]

This study is, I think, Earth-shaking for flipping over the beliefs of even many wilderness and wildlife lovers. We think and are told over and over by our friends and even more strongly by our consultants that we will lose folks by talking about wild things being good in themselves. Here, though, we find the truth works. I think being truthful about our values is the strongest way to reach others. There are tattoo shops all over today; find one that can tattoo Kempton's findings inside your

20   "Grand Canyon State Poll—Spring 2005: Grand Canyon Wolf Restoration Project," Northern Arizona University Social Research Laboratory, March 2005.

21   Willis Kempton, James S. Boster, and Jennifer A. Hartley, *Environmental Values in American Culture* (The MIT Press, Cambridge, Massachusetts, 1996), 111.

22   Kempton, Boster, and Hartley, *Environmental Values*, 113.

23   Kempton, Boster, and Hartley, *Environmental Values*, 214.

head. I can't overstate how key his findings are and how we need to let them guide our outreach.

Given this, why are many conservation leaders so afraid of standing up for wild things for their own sakes? Why do our media consultants water down what we believe and love? Although beliefs that wild things are good in themselves may run shallow in America, they run wide, and they do so even without forthright leadership from the wilderness and wildlife network. Folks are ripe to hear all kinds of believable, likable wildlovers talk about keeping wildlife for its own sake, to talk about our job to keep Earth whole. Folks need leadership, they need guiding lights, and they need to be called on to have an ethic that sees wild things as good in themselves. Moreover, I think they see through conservation spokesfolks who talk only about the dollar worth of wild havens or who say that some seldom-seen Earthling may have an answer for cancer. When this happens, they lose trust and think we are run-of-the-mill political spinmeisters. I ask my listeners, "Do we have the generosity of spirit, the greatness of heart, to share Earth with other beings, even wolves?" This righteous, heartfelt dare strikes them in their deepest being.[24]

I am not saying here that love of wild things is behind the way most folks think and behave. I am only saying that conservationists do not drive others away when we talk about wild things being good-in-themselves. And that, my friends, is a big deal. It is such a big deal, that I will write it again: *Conservationists do not drive others away when we talk about wild things being good-in-themselves.*

Without being straightforward about what we believe is good, we are suckers for further watering down of how we talk to others through

---

24   I build on this wild-things-for-their-own-sakes ethic in my chapters in two new anthologies: Dave Foreman, "Wild Things for Their Own Sakes," in Kathleen Dean Moore and Michael P. Nelson, editors, *Moral Ground: Ethical Action for a Planet in Peril* (Trinity University Press, San Antonio, TX, 2010), 100-102; and Dave Foreman, "Five Feathers for the Cannot Club," in Patricia Hasbach, Peter Kahn, and Jolina Ruckert, editors, *The Rediscovery of the Wild* (MIT Press, Boston, in press).

badgering from resourcists. And this is key: by standing up for the in-born, deep-rooted good of wild things, we bulwark our clubs and our network from enviro-resourcists slipping in and taking over. And we strengthen the inborn fuzzy feelings of many folks that other Earthlings are good-in-themselves and that we have no right to dwindle and wilt them away into the shadows of no-more.

STAND UP FOR STRONGLY WARDED PROTECTED AR-EAS AS "THE MOST VALUABLE WEAPON IN OUR CON-SERVATION ARSENAL."[25] GRASSROOTS CONSERVATION-ISTS AND CONSERVATION BIOLOGISTS HAVE LONG SEEN PROTECTED AREAS (WILD HAVENS), THE MORE STRONGLY WARDED THE BETTER, AS THE HEART OF CONSERVATION.

The core job of conservation is to set up, rebuild, care for, and shel-ter protected areas (wild havens) such as National Parks, Wilderness Areas, wildlife refuges, Biosphere Reserves, marine reserves, and so on. We must endlessly and steadily stand up against the foes of both the *thought* of wild havens and the *reality* of protected areas on the ground. In my forthcoming books, *The Nature Haters* and *True Wilderness*, I look at the foes of wild havens and knock down what they say against them. Those against wild havens come from all over the political, geographic, economic, and cultural map. We must not let ourselves be cowed by their economic or intellectual might, or by their self-righteous bullying victimhood. We must always be ready to hit back at falsehoods about wild havens and to show how so-called "alternatives to protected ar-eas" are open doors for plundering. We must also acknowledge that armed wardens keep wild havens of all kinds wild. Without strong, on-

---

25 Michael E. Soulé and Bruce A. Wilcox, "Conservation Biology: Its Scope and Its Challenge," in Michael E. Soulé and Bruce A. Wilcox, edi-tors, *Conservation Biology: An Evolutionary-Ecological Perspective* (Sinauer Associates, Inc., Sunderland, MA, 1980), 4.

the-ground enforcement, wild havens quickly become "paper parks," whether they are rainforest reserves in the third world or Wilderness Areas in "I'll ride my snowmobile wherever I want to" Montana. All conservation clubs must boldly renew their bond to setting aside new Wilderness Areas, National Parks, Biosphere Reserves, natural areas, and other wild havens all over the world.

Some international former conservation groups such as The Nature Conservancy and Conservation International lately have saddled up with the lynch mob after protected areas, as I showed in Chapter 5. A new book, *Rambunctious Garden*—outstanding for its lack of knowledge, understanding, and *being there,* has drawn heed from *New York Times* pundits and their ilk for its lambasting of the idea of wilderness and its naysaying to protected areas.[26] *Rambunctious Garden* mists out of the intellectual culture ripped by Harvard biologist E. O. Wilson:

> *Yet, astonishingly, the high culture of Western civilization exists largely apart from the natural sciences.... [Intellectuals'] reflections are devoid of the idioms of chemistry and biology, as though humankind were still in some sense a numinous spectator of physical reality. In the pages of* The New York Review of Books, Commentary, The New Republic, Daedalus, National Review, Saturday Review, *and other literary journals articles dominate that read as if most basic science had halted during the nineteenth century.*[27]

---

26 Emma Marris, *Rambunctious Garden: Saving Nature in a Post-Wild World* (Bloomsbury, New York, 2011). George Wuerthner takes it to the woodshed in "The Earth as Cookie Jar," counterpunch, June 12, 2012. Pundit, by the way, is Hindu for a learned man (or woman?) or scholar. The chattering class is another name for pundit in the United States. Public blowhard would fit many of our pundits. I have to wonder if those writers and broadcasters on public issues who call themselves pundits do so knowing what the word means and, if so, if they do so with tongue in cheek or for wanting to be truly a public intellectual.

27 Edward O. Wilson, *On Human Nature* (Harvard University Press, Cambridge, MA, 1978), 203.

Groups that have backed off on protected areas such as The Nature Conservancy, IUCN, World Wildlife Fund, Conservation International, and even the Wildlife Conservation Society need to hear from members and donors why we will not renew memberships or contribute to them any more.[28] Newspapers, magazines, and other outlets that run thumbs-up reviews of *Rambunctious Garden* or other unlearned and half-baked (or wild-loathing) writings against protected areas and wilderness, or who clap for the Man-first path of The Nature Conservancy also need to be taken to the woodshed by readers.

All of us who love wild things must renew our steadfast backing for setting aside more *strongly* protected areas and for watchdogging those we already have. Conservation biologists need to come out loudly and with unbridled gumption that protected areas are still the best tool for keeping biodiversity. And conservation outfits of all kinds need to stand tall and unwaveringly behind protected areas—that are well protected. Let us speak without any fog coming from our mouths that protected areas are the main work of conservation and that no other tool or path can do the bedrock job that wild havens do. And let us be as hard and blunt as a Neandertal's oak-burl cudgel to the forehead in warning that the Tree of Life will greatly wither without more protected areas. Last but not least, we must be straightforward that protected areas are only paper parks without on-the-ground wardens and rangers who are better armed than the poachers and others who would cheapen or wound the land or sea behind the boundary.

A core of conservation leaders and thinkers should start working together soon to draft a hard-hitting statement on protected areas for wildlovers and conservation clubs to sign. At the 50th Anniversary Celebration of the 1964 Wilderness Act in Albuquerque in 2014 this

28 The best staffers of WCS such as George Schaller and Alan Rabinowitz bailed from the once-great outfit when they saw it going to mush and started a new, tough, team of wildlife biologists—Panthera: www.panthera.org. Upon birth, it became the best international conservation team in the world.

renewed commitment to Wilderness Areas and other protected areas worldwide on land and sea needs to be highlighted.

CAREFULLY FRAME THE TALE OF WILDERNESS AND WILDLIFE CONSERVATION SO IT IS BOTH WINNING AND TRUE TO WILD BELIEFS. FRAMING IS NOTHING MORE THAN SELLING SODA POP UNLESS YOU HAVE STRONG VALUES, STANDARDS, AND STRATEGIES, AS WELL AS BIG DREAMS. BEFORE YOU CAN FRAME YOUR THOUGHTS AND VISION, YOU MUST HAVE THEM. CONSERVATION-ISTS MUST KNOW WHAT THEY STAND FOR AND TO WHOM THEY WANT TO TALK BEFORE FRAMING THEIR TALE.

A few years ago, some Democratic Party leaders, progressives, and leaders of "The Environmental Movement" clutched onto college professor George Lakoff and his work on "framing" as onto a life raft on a stormy sea. Although framing one's words is a needed step on a winning path, too many have made a shallow mush of Lakoff's teaching.[29] Jim Wallis, editor of *Sojourners* magazine, worries about the Democrats' take on framing, "How to tell the story has become more important than the story itself." He offers a sound, wise path: "Find the vision first, and the language will follow."[30] It would be shameful if environmentalists and conservationists made the same mistake of downplaying what is good with gooey words run before focus groups and then spun by media "experts." We cannot let our network become a 2004 John Kerry, shackled and buffaloed by spinning media whizzes.

I do think some leaders of "The Environmental Movement" have botched framing who we are and what we want. Conservationists now need to be very thoughtful about how we set forth our wants and

29   Matt Bai, "The Framing Wars," *The New York Times Magazine,* July 17, 2005.

30   Jim Wallis, "The Message Thing," *The New York Times,* August 4, 2005.

stands—and it's not by softening our beliefs. I've long bade conservationists to watch their words.

I've also called for an eyes-wide-open way for how we see our fellow Men. Let me call this "conservation as if Man's evolution mattered." A deep insight from Lakoff backs this: Men are not "rational actors who make their decisions based on facts."[31] The authoritarian right has drawn from the cleverness of commercial advertisers (who may understand better than anyone else how Man thinks) in spinning their scams. Notwithstanding all their blather about the good "common sense" of Everyman, these right-wingers reckon that folks are mostly dunderheads. Progressives, who want to believe in the goodness and steady betterment of Man, are unwilling to open their minds to the truth about Man. Not only do folks often behave as dunderheads, they make choices on *feeling*—often half-wittedly. Moreover, Americans—even college graduates—are amazingly illiterate. Though they can more or less read, they cannot truly understand what they read. The National Assessment of Adult Literacy has found that only 13 percent of American adults are at the "proficient" step of literacy—*able to compare "viewpoints in two different editorials."*[32] Think about what that means! How do you have a back-and-forth, thoughtful talk? It doesn't say much for boring folks with facts.

In a kindred field, outdoorsfolks are woefully unlearned about the public lands. Scott Stouder, the western field coordinator for Trout Unlimited (TU), writes that a TU poll showed "35 percent of anglers didn't realize they could fish in wilderness areas, and 34 percent of hunters didn't realize they could hunt in them."[33] We need to school outdoorsfolk from the bottom up about Wilderness Areas, the Endangered Species Act, and other conservation meat-and-potatoes.

31   Bai, "The Framing Wars."

32   Ben Feller, Associated Press, "Study: 1 in 20 U.S. Adults Can't Read English," *Albuquerque Journal*, December 16, 2005.

33   John O'Connell, "Social issues may trump science in debate over roadless areas," *Idaho State Journal*, August 17, 2005.

Bart Semcer writes, "The messages that win people over to the idea that species should be conserved are not the rational ones, they're the emotional. This is true for people with opinions across the political spectrum." David Johns writes me that environmentalists and conservationists:

> [B]elieve that language, reason, and the mental are overwhelmingly determinative. Meanwhile our conservative opponents are successfully manipulating powerful emotions. Why do conservationists and so many of our allies have this block about operating on emotion and deep psychic structure? Madison Avenue is developing messaging using MRI machines. They want ads that go right to the limbic system—never mind all this higher cortical bullshit. As a movement that claims to understand Darwin, I still see enormous resistance to grasping the reality that we are animals, that we are more than our reason and opposable thumbs.

Any kind of framing of the conservation message has to deal with these bothersome gnats if it is to work. Susan Morgan tells me about a hard-hitting team for which she once worked that believed "We will show you the truth through endless details and you will see the light." "Sure," she says.

Let me now take on a few of my pet peeves in language to show how framing is more than clever sloganeering. At the 2005 Sierra Club Summit in San Francisco, the woman who introduced George Lakoff for his talk said that we needed to "reframe how we talk about the environment." That's good, but I believe that the first step in doing so is to stop talking about "the environment" and to start talking about Nature or, better yet, wild things.

Environment is one of those god-awful abstract words belonging to bureaucrats or assistant professors of sociology.[34] How do you love an

---

34   I'm sorry for badmouthing some likely good folks.

environment? Can you even see an *environment?* Can you get lost in an *environment?*

I can see, feel, and love a mountain, a river, a swamp, a sea, a deep wood, a desert, a grassland. But not an environment.

Environment to land is like *relationship* to *love.*

My haggle with the word *environment* is not only one of liking Anglo-Saxon words over French and Latin ones, or how I mostly follow *Strunk & White* in my writing. Words have might, and when we tag the wild world with an abstract and murky word like *environment,* the word itself holds wild things away at arm's length or even more; what it names becomes a resource, an *abstraction*—not something with its own being. Folks can deftly wreck it, then. There is a wealth of strong, straightforward words that do better than this weak, wimpy word. Before letting *environment* dribble out over your lips, say *Nature, land, ecosystem,* or *wild things.* You might even go for *creation.* Instead of *environmentally,* try *ecologically.* Chew over how I've written this book (and *Man Swarm*) without needing *environment* to sketch the wild or otherwise world (other than when I'm quoting someone). *Nature* is a fuzzy and overworked word, too. It lacks a sharp meaning, so I've been seeking words that are more on the mark. This is why you'll read Anglo-Saxon words such as wild things, wild neighborhood, wildlands, wildeors, and so forth from me (see the Glossary).

But overall it might be best to write or say *land* instead of *environment.* By doing so, we link our network tightly to Aldo Leopold's Land Ethic:

> *The land ethic simply enlarges the boundaries of the community to include soils, waters, plants, and animals, or collectively: the land.... In short, a land ethic changes the role of* Homo sapiens *from conqueror of the land-community to plain member and citizen of it. It implies respect for his fellow-members, and also respect*

for the community as such.[35]

A thing is right when it tends to preserve the integrity, stability, and beauty of the biotic community. It is wrong when it tends otherwise.[36]

"A Land Ethic" has a heck of a lot more bite to it than does "An Environmental Ethic." Or even a "Nature Ethic."

Let these words swish about on your tongue; let them whirl and twirl in your heart. Go outside, in the wind, in the storm, far from the maddening town. Ask the griz. Ask a saguaro. Are they in an *environment*? Or are they in *the land*? Do they want their home in an *environment* or in a *wild neighborhood*?

The most sickening take on *environment* is *enviro* as a moniker for conservationists and environmentalists. This slimy slight is even said by thoughtless conservationists, who should know better than to brand themselves thusly. Never, never, never call yourself an "enviro." And don't dare call me an enviro.

Some other widely said words and acronyms are as ugsome as environment.

Green. "Greenies," "green groups," and other spins on the hue are written to mean "The Environmental Movement." This way of talking unhappily links conservation and environmentalism to the so-called Green political movement and Green parties. As we've seen, Green parties in the United States, at least, have little to do with sheltering wild things.

ANWR. The Arctic National Wildlife Refuge is often called "Anwahr." This hurts our work to shield the Arctic since it takes the life out of the name of the landscape and out of the landscape itself—America's flagship wilderness. Arctic. National. Wildlife. Refuge. Each of these

---

35   Aldo Leopold, *A Sand County Almanac* (Oxford University Press, New York, 1987), 204. (Originally published in 1949.)

36   Leopold, *A Sand County Almanac,* 224-225.

four words has wonder, might, and meaning. Anwahr is soulless. It has no meaning. In the mind, heart, and soul of anyone, it is harder to industrialize the Arctic National Wildlife Refuge than to do the same to ANWR, and the oil industry knows it. If we must shorten, say Arctic, as we say Bosque for the Bosque del Apache National Wildlife Refuge instead of "Banwahr." We write the "_nwahr" acronym for no other National Wildlife Refuge. Why do we write it for the flagship refuge? There are many other times when conservationists fall into sloppy shorthand wordage without thinking about what they are giving up in might and wonder. Too many acronyms hurt our work.

Another pet peeve of mine is "developing nations." This framing of forlorn, hungry, overpopulated countries shows the underlying Weltanschauung of cornucopian gall: the belief that the "developed" lifeway in which wealthy nations in North America, Europe, and Far East Asia now bask is the historically determined state of Mankind and that all will someday gain it. This belief is heartless tommyrot. Darn few if any of the wretched lands will better their lot, and "developed" nations will likely see their lot worsen.

Likewise, the word "production" for extracting oil and other energy resources is phony. We do not *produce* such resources; we *extract* them. Millions of years of geology have done the producing.

We need to watch our words.

To Lakoff, framing goes much deeper than word or thought picking for clever advertising. He goes at it down in the brain's physiology. Rewilding Fellow and retired physician Bob Howard, who has been a matchless friend for sparking new thoughts and paths for me, says that a frame is a web of neural circuits and chemistry and that a new thought is made there. If the thought is right, then words will come smoothly. This underlying biology of the mind is why we need to reframe our thoughts and how we offer them to the bigger world of others.

ACKNOWLEDGE THAT THE OVERWHELMING PLIGHT IS THE MANMADE SIXTH GREAT EXTINCTION, DRIVEN

BY THE BOOMING POPULATION OF MEN AND FURTHER GOOSED BY RISING AFFLUENCE AND TECHNOLOGY (THE MAN SWARM).[37] GREENHOUSE GAS POLLUTION FROM THE SAME ROOTS WILL ADD A MIGHTY SHOVE TO THE SPEED AND THOROUGHNESS OF EXTINCTION. BEING STRAIGHTFORWARD ABOUT THE HULKING PLIGHTS BLOCKING OUR WAY DOES NOT CLASH WITH OFFERING A HOPEFUL VISION AND HEARTENING CALL TO WORK EVEN HARDER. IN TRUTH, THIS MASS EXTINCTION IS THE FIRST MASS MURDER OF LIFE. AND WE— *HOMO SAPIENS*—ARE THE KILLERS.

Although many wildlovers have been and still are forthright in warning about the loss of wildlife and the scalping of wilderness, it seems that many leaders of "The Environmental Movement" now are falling over each other in the dash to soothingly say that they are not doom-and-gloomers. This began some nine years ago when two staffers of big international conservation outfits beseeched in *Conservation Biology* that it was time to put Cassandra in the old folks home.[38] (I think some of their ilk would dearly like to put me and a few other old gunslingers for the wild into an old folks' home without Internet or telephone.) One needs to be hopeful, yes. Some folks shut their ears to bad news, yes, but they likely don't listen to anything that has to do with the health of Earth no mind how it is prettied up. I will soon look at the good of a hopeful vision. But this mad dash to slap smiley faces on conservation is at its core underhanded and namby-pamby. Say that we want to sell homes in New Orleans so we don't tell buyers about hurricanes or the likelihood that levees will be overtopped and washed away.

---

37   This is the I=PAT formula (Impact equals Population times Affluence times Technology) as crafted by Paul and Anne Ehrlich and John Holdren. See *Man Swarm*.

38   Kent Redford and M. A. Sanjayan, "Editorial: Retiring Cassandra," *Conservation Biology*, Vol. 17. No. 6, December 2003, 1473-1474. This essay was even worse since both authors have often been stouthearted.

How is this unlike wanting to draw new members to our happy-go-lucky conservation club so we don't tell them about wholesale extinction and we happen to overlook the population explosion, with population growth in the United States coming mostly from immigration?[39]

Dreadful, ghastly threats and woes loom before us. Flashing our whitened teeth will not make them go away. A worrywart can be a tiresome neighbor, yes, but an optimist leads to the flooding of New Orleans. Optimists have let greenhouse gas buildup worsen to where we can no longer head off gruesome climate shifts of some kind. What we need to understand in Greek mythology is that Cassandra was *right* and the Trojans would not believe her. The Cassandra myth was not so much about Cassandra; it was instead an insight that Man is shortsighted and pathologically optimistic. It is the tough, thankless job of true leaders to tell hurting truths, to get ready for the worst. Tough old Hugh Iltis of the University of Wisconsin herbarium is the kind of craggy truth-teller wildlovers still need. As was Senator Gaylord Nelson. And as was Garrett Hardin, who quoted Dan Luten that "the optimists hope their forecasts are self-fulfilling. The pessimists hope their forecasts are self-defeating."[40] (Cutting-edge brain research shows that we may well be hardwired to be optimists.) We conservationists must hammer home that we want to be wrong when we talk about gloomy truths. We are laying out likely ugsome outcomes in the hope that folks will shift their path.[41] *We want to be wrong!* Steadily and sharply saying this is the best

---

39 In fairness, one of the retire-Cassandra editorialists, my friend Sanjayan, who is Sri Lankan, has been a tough truth-speaker on the threat of immigration.

40 Garrett Hardin, "Cassandra's Role in the Population Wrangle," in Paul R. Ehrlich and John P. Holdren, editors, *The Cassandra Conference: Resources and the Human Predicament* (Texas A&M University Press, College Station, 1988), 6.

41 Too often overlooked is that Paul Ehrlich in *The Population Bomb* wanted to be wrong. Why some of his scenarios did not come true is that his book woke some folks up and therefore many of his steps were somewhat carried out, putting off the worst for a few more years.

answer to chiding from the skipping, singing Pollyannas in their polka-dotted pajamas that we are doom-and-gloomers.

We must be clever in how we warn about doom ahead. Eileen Crist has done a great job showing how limits-to-growth warnings have not been clever. Her essay "Limits-to-Growth and the Biodiversity Crisis" shows the way whatever the threat with which we are dealing. She writes that we need "to be as clear and precise as possible about the consequences of the humanized order under construction: in this emerging reality it is not our survival and well-being that are primarily on the line, but *everybody else's*.[42]

In *Rewilding North America* I laid out in harrowing truthfulness the way the growing swarm of Man is driving wholesale extinction and warned that many, many more Earthlings will be doomed unless we act boldly and quickly. My warning was nothing new. Hugh Iltis said the same on the first Earth Day in 1970: We are "pushing, prematurely, tens of thousands of species of plants and animals toward the abysmal finality of *extinction*...."[43] On October 20, 1979, Tom Lovejoy of the World Wildlife Fund said, "The reduction in the biological diversity of the planet is the most basic issue of our time."[44] For over twenty years, E. O. Wilson, today's most-read biologist, has been saying the same thing, as has Richard Leakey, the best-known fossil hunter ever. But even among wildlife clubs that warn about this or that Endangered Species, most do not say forthrightly that we are in a mass extinction and it is the leading plight today. Worldwide economic woes are but a flyspeck next to the overflowing awfulness of what we are doing to the Tree of Life. Were a poll taken of those belonging to the Sierra Club, The Wilder-

---

42   Eileen Crist, "Limits-to-Growth and the Biodiversity Crisis," *Wild Earth*, Spring 2003.

43   The talk was later reprinted in Hugh H. Iltis, "Technology Versus Wild Nature: What Are Man's Biological Needs?" *Northwest Conifer* (Pacific Northwest Chapter of the Sierra Club newsletter), May 22, 1971.

44   Thomas E. Lovejoy, "Foreword" in Michael E. Soulé and Bruce A. Wilcox, editors, *Conservation Biology: An Evolutionary-Ecological Perspective* (Sinauer Associates, Sunderland, Massachusetts, 1980), ix.

ness Society, National Audubon Society, and the other big conservation outfits, how many would say the Sixth Great Extinction was the top threat? How many even know we are in a mass extinction? I'm not talking about Main Street, or the "opinion-makers," or the "deciders," I'm talking about our wildloving kith and kin. How many staffers of wilderness and wildlife clubs would pick mass extinction as the underlying threat? How many are driven by the burning here and now of this ghastly tomorrow?[45]

Some who run big outfits are afraid to be forthright about mass extinction since it might scare off members, would-be members, and donors. In America today, optimism has become a moral virtue, while pessimism is sneered at as if it were some kind of ugly skin ailment or even a nasty kind of sin. Many leaders of "The Environmental Movement" are cowed by this burly, surly Pollyannaism. It seems that being shown as a Cassandra is as shameful as getting caught surfing toddler-porno sites on the web.

Mind you, I do not want every conservationist and every conservation club to drop their must-do, day-to-day work to deal only with wholesale extinction driven by Man's population explosion, nor do I want them to harp on the dread. What we do every day filing lawsuits to shield Endangered Species, getting Wilderness Areas set up by law, bringing wolves home, stopping timber sales ... all this and more is how we keep wild things. But our network must be steadfast in highlighting the truth, and all of us must be aware of what is going on and why it is going on without politically correct, or economically selfish, or patriotically correct blinders. The Big Extinction driven by the Man swarm is the background for all of our other work.[46]

---

45 Looking the dread of mass extinction in the eye can make one stone, as did looking at Medusa. I know that very well. While it is not healthy to dwell on bad news, we conservationists need to acknowledge the bigness of the coming doom.

46 The Rewilding Institute website (www.rewilding.org) names the clubs who are forthright on mass extinction and gives links to their websites.

SET FORTH AND WORK FOR A VISION THAT IS BOLD, WORKABLE, SCIENTIFICALLY BELIEVABLE, AND HOPE- FUL. REWILDING WITH THE NORTH AMERICAN WILD- LANDS NETWORK BY REBUILDING TRUE WILDERNESS WITH BROUGHT-BACK POPULATIONS OF NATIVE WILD- LIFE, FOREMOST BIG CARNIVORES, IS SUCH A VISION OF HOPE

Since 1992, The Wildlands Project (TWP) has worked to put together a vision for conservation on a continental scale. Beginning with the Sky Islands Wildlands Network in 2000, a few other land-scape visions—grounded in linked networks of Wilderness Areas and other wild havens, and regained populations of wild hunters and other keystone wildlife—have been published for the greater southwestern United States by TWP and cooperating regional groups.[47] In 2004, Is-land Press brought out my book, *Rewilding North America,* in which I set out a vision for a North American Wildlands Network along Four Continental Wildways (formerly called MegaLinkages). Many local and regional conservation clubs are working to bring this vision into being on the ground, foremost those in the Rocky Mountains Spine under the leadership of Wildlands Network (the new name for The Wildlands Project).[48] Conservationists outside the Wildways need to put together sweeping protected-area and species-recovery visions for their landscapes, too.

In 1954, Supreme Court Justice William O. Douglas led folks out of Washington, DC, on a 189-mile walk along the C & O Canal Towpath next to the Potomac River to boost the fight against paving the towpath

---

47 Dave Foreman, Kathy Daly, Barbara Dugelby, Roseann Hanson, Robert E. Howard, Jack Humphrey, Leanne Klyza Linck, Rurik List, and Kim Vacariu, *Sky Islands Wildlands Network Conservation Plan* (The Wild-lands Project, Tucson, Arizona, 2000). See www.rewilding.org for more wildlands network visions.

48 Foreman, *Rewilding North America.* The Rewilding Institute website www.rewilding.org.

for a highway and to make it a National Historical Park, which it became in 1971 after President Eisenhower had made it a National Monument in 1960.[49] Such news-friendly hikes have long been a good boost
for conservation visions. In 2011, John Davis of the Wildlands Network
and The Rewilding Institute walked, canoed, and bicycled thousands
of miles from Everglades National Park in southern Florida to the end
of the Gaspe Peninsula in Quebec as "TrekEast" to make folks aware
of the need for a rewilding vision all along the Appalachian Mountains and Atlantic Seaboard. Throughout his way he met with conservationists, agency managers, schoolchildren, and newspapers to learn
from them and to gain backing for a Wildway for wildlife wandering
along his trail. In 2013, he will take on an even bigger trek—TrekWest,
from a private jaguar reserve in northern Mexico to Canada's Rocky
Mountains National Parks.[50]

I think the key rewilding vision now is the recovery of a healthy,
linked cougar (mountain lion) population in the eastern United States
and Canada. Carefully thought-out reintroductions of genetically diverse North America cougars should be made in key landscapes along
the Appalachian Mountains from northern Alabama and Georgia to the
Gaspe Peninsula in Quebec and on into New Brunswick, Canada. The
goal should be for these populations to link together as an ecologically
effective population along the mountains and spilling out into wilder
country east and west. Likewise thoughtful reintroductions or augmen-
tation of existing populations should be made in the wilder spots east of
the Rocky Mountains—for one, from Michigan's Upper Peninsula and
the Boundary Waters south to the Ozarks of Missouri and Arkansas.
For rewilding North America no other single project is as important

49 Stephen Fox, *The American Conservation Movement: John Muir and His Legacy* (University of Wisconsin Press, Madison, 1985), 241-242.

50 http://www.wildlandsnetwork.org

as bringing back America's big cat to its homeland in the East so that it can take on the heavy job of rewilding suitable lands there and bringing the booming populations of white-tailed deer and feral pigs into balance with what the land can keep. I'm so hot on this plan that I hope to spend more of my own work boosting it. A good network of cougar lovers is already on the ground in the East, led by the Cougar Rewilding Foundation.[51]

Tackling the crash of the Tree of Life, wild-loving conservationists are putting into words and deeds a new dream for North America, one in which true wilderness and the wildeor can live with a healthy human civilization. This vision is bold, scientifically believable, workable, and *hopeful*. I emphasize hopefulness because I have found that all kinds of folks in the United States and Canada answer wholeheartedly to the hope underlying the North American Wildlands Network. I believe that this vision, as the heart of a conservation strategy for North America, tied to the other steps in this and the chapter before, can take back and breathe new life into the wilderness and wildlife network. And it can wake up North Americans to come together as good, thoughtful, caring citizens of the land community and work to do things right. Rewilding a North American Wildlands Network is the soul of true citizenship for the Twenty-first Century. It won't work, however, if we water it down by leaving out wolves and big cats so as not to frighten the wealthy and mighty, the dullards and the quaking-hearted.

Once again, I find myself at the end of a book, where I should start singing "Zippity doo dah, zippity ay, my oh my what a wonderful day!" And, once again, I can't do it. We face deep, dark days ahead. There are

---

51   Cougar Rewilding Foundation www.cougarrewilding.org

no wizards with drylic answers.[52] No Mount Dooms in which to throw the evil ring of Sauron.[53] No otherworldly park rangers in flying saucers are going to come zooming in to hand out citations to Mankind and make us follow the rules for a healthy Earth Galactic Park, much as I may daydream.

But I can say this: Shielders and keepers of wild things and wild Earth can stand up, take back the conservation network, step up to the looming dread forthrightly, bring population stabilization to the fore once again, and work like hell for a *hopeful* vision of wildeors and true wilderness side by side with a caring civilization. We cannot fail to stand up in this do-or-die, eleventh hour for the thriving, thronging, and manyfold dazzle of all life and the unfathomable evolutionary tomorrow.

Will the defenders of Nature please rise?

---

52 Magical.

53 *Searu* meant machine in Old English. J.R.R. Tolkien, author of the
    Lord of the Rings, was an outstanding Old English scholar at Oxford and
    sprinkled many meaningful OE words through his works.

GLOSSARY

<hr />

THIS GLOSSARY GIVES THE MEANINGS for those words and phrases
that might be little known to the reader of any of the five books in the
For the Wild Things series.[1] They are of two kinds. First are those of a
set, technical meaning; glossaries are most often for such words and
phrases.

The second kind is for some archaic English words with which I
write. Today's English is an odd and tangled tongue. Although English is within the Germanic (Deutsch) Family of Indo-European Lan-
guages, and has evolved from an unwritten Proto-Germanic, most of
the words in it now are from the Romance Language Family, mostly
French and Latin, also in the bigger family of Indo-European.

With the Norman Conquest of Great Britain one thousand years
ago, French became widely spoken, as it was the tongue of the new
overlords and landowners. Many French words made their way into
English over the next few hundred years thereby shoving aside wide-

<hr />

1   A version of this glossary will be in each book.

ly spoken and written English words meaning the same thing. Latin words, first through the Roman (Catholic) Church and later as the way for European intellectuals to write and talk amongst themselves, seeped into everyday speech and writing in English, and shoved out yet more good English words. Although some linguists say that one cannot write anything but doltish English without using mostly French and Latin-rooted words, I do my best to show them wrong—though I have to sling about a few Romance words on every leaf if I don't want my writing overtangled or even daft. There are also technical terms in conservation that are Latin-English. Some of my good Anglo-Saxon (A-S) or Old English (OE) words are still widely spoken; others are yet in the dictionary but tagged as "archaic." I am also working to bring back some even older A-S words no longer found in dictionaries—*wildeor*, for one. Such words are given meaning in this glossary. If there are other words you don't know, look in a dictionary—that's what such wonderful books are for.

Now—you may ask—why am I so queer for Anglo-Saxon English? In some odd way, I'm drawn to Old English by mood quirks that also draw me to wilderness, though I do not want to muddle language and wild things. I guess my love for Old English comes somewhat from my antimodernist bent. I'm a stodgy, mossback, old conservative in mood (but not in the ideology of today's phony "conservatives"). When we get down to it, I like the way A-S words sound and feel in my mouth and look on the leaf. Indeed, Strunk & White and other word-crafters of their ilk tell us to write with true English words instead of French and Latin gatecrashers for a stronger, pithier style. Nonetheless, sometimes I have no choice but to write with Latin-rooted words—such as "style"—since there is no good Deutsch-rooted word with that meaning left in our tongue. So, to get down to it, I write and speak as much as I can with Anglo-Saxon words on the grounds that I like to do so.

For each of the words or phrases in this glossary, I give which books in the *For the Wild Things* series they are mostly to be found.

AMATEUR TRADITION: In his insightful book *The American Conservation Movement: John Muir and His Legacy*, historian Stephen Fox clove the conservation of the late 19th and early 20th centuries into *amateurs* and *professionals*. Fox sees citizen conservation clubs as within the Amateur Tradition (to wit: John Muir and the Sierra Club) and government agencies and professional societies (Gifford Pinchot and the U.S. Forest Service) as within the Professional Tradition. One needs to understand that amateur and professional in this meaning are not about whether one has a job or is paid for conservation work, but *why* one does conservation work: out of love for wild things (amateur) or owing to a career in resource management (professionals). Moreover, some professionals working for the Forest Service and other government agencies are themselves within the Amateur Tradition and some who work for nongovernmental conservation groups may be very much in the Professional Tradition. *Take Back Conservation* and *Conservation vs. Conservation* both look at the amateur and professional traditions.

CANNOT: Aldo Leopold wrote, "There are some who can live without wild things, and some who cannot." Those who need and love wild things, then, might be called *Cannots*. Such Nature lovers or Cannots are the conservationists who work to keep and rebuild wilderness and wildlife. Therefore, I sometimes toss about *Cannot* as a name for believers in the good of wild things for their own sakes. John Davis warns me, though, that *Cannot* is too negative a name for wildlovers. On the other hand, that jarring may be what grabs one's heed.

CARRYING CAPACITY: A key yardstick in ecology is the carrying capacity of the ecosystem (neighborhood) for each species. How many mule deer can the Kaibab Plateau in Arizona "carry" without harm to the ecosystem or starvation of the deer? Today, population writers look at carrying capacity for Man, too, either for standalone islands or neighborhoods or for the whole Earth. There are bumps here, though. For one, most Men, whether thoughtful or not, bristle at biology having anything to do with ourselves. This dislike is toasted in all cultural, political, economic, and religious clubhouses. Two, those who weigh carrying capacity for Man mostly do so in a narrow way, overlooking the needs of all other Earthlings. Man's carrying capacity too often means only whether Earth can give Mankind what it needs; wild things do not play in this reckoning. It is past time for Man's carrying capacity to be reckoned by its impact on wild things and on evolutionary processes, not only on the flow of raw goods into our industrial web. I look at carrying capacity in *Man Swarm* and in my earlier book, *Rewilding North America.*

C.E.: *C.E.* means *Current Era*, and is written instead of *A.D.;* likewise *B.C.E.* means *Before Current Era,* and is written instead of *B.C.* So, 1800 C.E is the same year as 1800 A.D. Other abbreviations are *B.P.* for *Before Present* and *mya* for *million years ago* (*kya* for *thousand years ago*). So, five mya or 5 mya means "five million years ago" and 10 kya means "ten thousand years ago" or 8,000 B.C.E.

CLUB (CANNOT CLUB): A threat undercutting the work of those who need wild things is the shove toward corporatization, institutionalization, and professionalization in nongovernmental conservation outfits. Wilderness and wildlife keeping should be a grassroots, folk undertaking of kith and kin instead of nine-to-five work in posh offices where there are sharper eyes for institutional growth than for the hallowed call to keep wild things wild. Words such as *corporation, organization,* and *group* bring with them the whiff of institutionalization. I would rather think of the Sierra Club, Great Old Broads for Wilderness, and others as *clubs* instead of *organizations* so as to underline the high worth of putting the Amateur Tradition at the fore. We can see each conservation organization, then, as a Cannot Club, and the conservation movement as a kinship of such Cannot Clubs. What of conservation outfits such as The Rewilding Institute and Center for Biological Diversity? They may or may not have dues-paying members but do not have volunteer activists. Instead of club, then, I call them *teams*.

Likewise, I think the words *network* and *web* are better for the overall gathering than is *movement*. *Kith, kinship,* and *family* may be even better for their homey feeling and for how they make the whole web of conservation outfits and loners higher than any club or team (even your own). I have always felt that I was in the conservation or Cannot family much more than I was in The Wildlands Project or Earth First!. I go into some of these cares in *Take Back Conservation*. (I know, I know that some will see me as an overfussy schoolmarm, but I make up for it by being loose in other ways.) Also see *Team*.

CONSERVATION: Since their beginnings in the late 19th century, there have truly been two conservation movements or networks—Nature conservation, caring about keeping wild things wild, and resource conservation, given to taming and squeezing wild things for the short-time good of Man. I rather call resource conservation *resourcism* and keeping and bringing back wild things *conservation* (although lately I've had a growing dislike for the word *conservation*, therefore you'll see other words for our bunch, such as *wilderness and wildlife network*). Moreover, the wild kind of conservation is not the same as *environmentalism*, which is not about wild things at all but about the health, safety, and quality of life of children, women, and men, nor is it the same as *animal rights* or *animal welfare*, both of which care more for the well-being of *individual* animals than about species or wild things. Therefore, I put resourcism, conservation, environmentalism, and animal rights/welfare in their own camps and not in one big-tent network. However, there are not high, hard walls between these, and one can have leanings for more than one of them. It is good when they can work together, but there will always be times when one network wrangles with another.

CORNUCOPIAN: The *cornucopia* from classical Greek mythology is a ram's horn overflowing with fruit, grain, vegetables, and other good things, which never run out. Those who do not believe that Earth has limits, then, are widely known as *cornucopians* and are the foes of those worried about overpopulation and overconsumption. Cornucopians are always uber-optimistic, so they can also be called *Eco-Pollyannas*. *Man Swarm* and *The Nature Haters* look at cornucopians.

DEOR: The Anglo-Saxon word for animal was *deor,* which now is given to only one bunch—*deer* (of which there are some 38 to 43 kinds in the Cervidae Family). The Normans switched deor to *beast,* which was later switched to the Latin *animal.* Other Deustcher (Germanic) tongues, however, kept their early words, so Deutsch (German) has *tier* for animal and Swedish has *djur.* I'd like to bring back deor in English as the everyday word for animal and *wildeor* for wild, untamed animals, and so I often write or speak deor and wildeor for animal and wild animal.

EARTHLING: One of Charles Darwin's great breakthroughs was to understand that all Earthly life kinds are kindred, that we all come down from one forebear (the Last Common Ancestor or LCA, biologists say now). Thus, all living things from microbes to fungi to plants to animals are Earthlings as much as we (Men) are, and we should see all of them as kin.

ECOLOGICAL WOUNDS: Aldo Leopold wrote, "One of the penalties of an ecological education is that one lives alone in a world of wounds." In our wildlands network plans for the Southwest U.S., Dr. Bob Howard, who had been a pathologist, and I, both then with The Wildlands Project, took Leopold's thought to deal out the kinds of harm Man has done to wild things. We finally settled on Seven Ecological Wounds, which I then fleshed out in *Rewilding North America. Man Swarm* also delves into the Seven Ecological Wounds.

Environmentalism: Environmentalism and conservation are not the same thing. Environmentalists and conservationists have their own drives, folk heroes, goods, and lore, although there is overlap: most conservationists are also environmentalists and many (but not all) environmentalists are conservationists, too. *Take Back Conservation* looks at how conservation and environmentalism are not the same.

"The Environmental Movement": I put "The Environmental Movement" in quotation marks to show that there is truly no such thing, but that conservation (wild things) and environmentalism (human health) are each their own network, though they sometimes overlap and are akin. This is a key thrust in *Take Back Conservation*.

Environmentalist Stereotype: The "Environmentalist Stereotype" is wielded by foes of conservation and environmentalism to make a leftist caricature of "environmentalists" out of step with "real people." The Environmentalist Stereotype, which some environmentalists and conservationists fit and a few even boost, is that pollution fighters and wilderness shielders are leftists or progressives within the Democratic Party, and that they are therefore anti-gun-ownership, antihunting, vegetarian, urban, intellectual, politically correct elitists. *Take Back Conservation* and *The Nature Haters* deal with the Environmentalist Stereotype hurdle.

Enviro-resourcism: *Enviro-resourcism* is my rather clumsy word for the foundation staffers, media and other consultants, board members, political operatives, executive directors and other staffers of conservation clubs who likely can live without wild things, and who are slowly taking over our clubs and the whole conservation network. They undercut tough stands and weaken or shove aside the lore, grassroots/amateur tradition, and outspoken belief in wild things for their own sake, and bring in their stead such Man-saked mush as "ecosystem services," economic worth, political pragmatism, anthropocentric values, organizational might, and leadership by paid "expert" staff and outside consultants. Enviro-resourcists are a blend of environmentalists and resourcists, not lovers of wild things foremost. Enviro-resourcist is a broad sweep and some may not fit the whole bill but only in one or two ways. *Take Back Conservation* is a call to take back wilderness and wildlife clubs and their network from the enviro-resourcists. *True Wilderness* will also look at enviro-resourcism.

FOLK CONSERVATION: Clif Merritt, the great field director of The Wilderness Society after the 1964 Wilderness Act, called the unpaid grassroots wilderness lovers fighting agency logging, road building, and other land-taming *citizen conservationists*. I call them *folk conservationists* or *grassroots conservationists*.

FOOTPRINT: The "Ecological Footprint" is a new, helpful yardstick for the population and consumption impact on the world for each of us, for chosen bands, and for nations. It is weak in that it mostly looks at impact on raw goods and "ecological services" for Man's good instead of our impact on wild things. Cannots need to craft a "Wilderness Footprint" to weigh the impact of population growth and consumption on wild things. I deal with footprints in *Man Swarm*.

GLOBAL WEIRDING: Pollution by carbon dioxide and other "greenhouse gases" is leading to much more than overall warming. The upshot is tangled beyond anyone's ken, hence the need to use "global weirding" instead of "global warming."

GOOD(s): *Good* in early English is a noun meaning that which is good. I often write *good* or *goods* instead of *value* or *values*.

GOOD: In Ethics, that which is good is good-in-itself. In other words it has intrinsic value. It may also have instrumental value (good because it is good for something else), too, but it always has intrinsic value. I believe that acknowledging all other Earthlings as good-in-themselves or good for their own sakes is the bedrock of wilderness and wildlife conservation values. Belief that wild things are good-in-themselves is also called Deep Ecology, biocentrism, and ecocentrism, though each of these has tweaks to their meanings.

GRASSROOTS: Those for whom conservation is a calling; not only a job for hire. See also Amateur Tradition and Folk Conservation.

GRASSROOTS CONSERVATION: Nonprofit conservation clubs and teams; not government agencies or professional groups.

GROWTH: "Growth for the sake of growth is the ideology of the cancer cell," wrote Edward Abbey. Since at least Gilgamesh's great-great-great granddaddies, population, economic, and infrastructure growth have also been the ideology of Mankind, which is why we cannot deal meaningfully with global weirding, extinction, rainforest scalping, and manifold other ills. Founders of the Wilderness Area Idea were driven by fear over growth in the United States after World War I; conservationists and environmentalists today should likewise see growth as the big, bad foe of true "sustainability."

INBORN: Inherent, intrinsic, as in inborn value or inborn good.

KIND: *Kind* is an Anglo-Saxon word for *species* in long use, even by Charles Darwin.

LAND (AND/OR SEA): Aldo Leopold wrote, "The land ethic simply enlarges the boundaries of the community to include soils, waters, plants, and animals, or collectively: the land." *Land*, then, is a much better word than the dreadful *environment*. I rail about this in *Take Back Conservation*.

MAN, MEN, MANKIND: I use *Man* or *Men* capitalized as the overall ungendered word for the species *Homo sapiens*, *woman* for the female of the species, and *man* uncapitalized for the male. This is more in keeping with Anglo-Saxon English, which had another word for male *Homo sapiens*: *wer*, which lives on today as werewolf. *Wiv* or *cwen* was the word for a female *Homo sapiens*. Today's English is odd for not having a straightforward word for our kind that is also not the gendered word for the male. Deutsch and other Germanic tongues still have an ungendered old word for the species that is not the same as the gendered word for the male. Later English tangled things by doing away with a standalone word for males and using man for both male humans and humans of both genders. To have to call ourselves by a Latin word, *human*, is cumbersome and abstract. I do not write Man in a sexist way but for the goodness of the English tongue.

NEIGHBORHOOD: The science of ecology often writes *community* to mean *ecosystem*. Aldo Leopold wisely wrote that Man had to stop being the conqueror of the land community and become a plain citizen and member of it. I like the Anglo-Saxon word *neighborhood* better for its cozier feeling than community. Wild neighborhoods, then, are ecosystems, and their members—whether plants, animals, fungi, or microbes—are our neighbors when we stop by or wander through. The goal of natural history is to meet and know your wild neighbors.

NETWORK OR WEB: A political, activist, etc. movement.

NOBLE SAVAGE MYTH: Jean Jacques Rousseau is the best-known flag-waver for the Myth of the Noble Savage, which holds that Man in a natural state was noble, egalitarian, peaceful, and ecologically sweet be-fore being besmirched by civilization. Anthropology, archaeology, pa-leontology, history, field biology, conservation biology, and so on have shown this belief to have no ground on which to stand. It in no way puts down living tribal folks to acknowledge that Man has long been anything but peaceful or that Man is not an inborn conservationist nor ecologically minded. In *True Wilderness,* I show that the Myth of the Noble or Ecological Savage is mistaken, unfair to tribal folks, and some-times gets in the way of keeping wild things.

RAW GOODS: *Raw goods* are natural resources such as metal ores, coal, tar sands, petroleum, timber, grass and other forage, groundwater, stream water, and such that are still in the ground, not yet exploited and refined for use by Man.

RESOURCISM: Beginning with Paul Shepard, academic conservation-ists have called resource conservation *resourcism* instead of *conservation,* so as to underline the overweening drive of wildland and wildlife man-aging agencies worldwide to tame wild things, to lift resource extrac-tion above other "multiple-uses," and to wink at whatever wounds such "management" brings on. I delve into resourcism and what is wrong with it in *Take Back Conservation, True Wilderness,* and *Conservation vs. Conservation.*

SHELTER, SHIELD(v): To shelter and to shield come from Old English and mean to protect, save, or defend, all of which are used so much they are rather worn-out.

STEWARDSHIP (ALSO CARETAKING, KEEPING, WARDING): *Manage-ment* is what resourcism does and it carries within it the meaning of stamping Man's will over self-willed things, be they forests, rivers, or wildlife. Conservationists have long been unhappy with management as the word for what we do with wild things. Instead, many of us write and say *stewardship* or *caretaking*. *Keep* and *ward* are other verbs that can work instead of manage. *Steward*, however, comes from *sty-ward*, or the one who takes care of the pigpen. Still, stewardship is a better word than management.

TEAM: A conservation outfit that is all staff without active members. See Club.

THEY, THEIR, THEM: Today's overseers of the English tongue have worked to hack out so-called "sexist language." Among their key targets is how the male-gender, third-person, singular pronoun (*he, him, his*) has been used when the sex of the person is unknown. Some rather cumbersome wording has been offered instead of *he, him, his*—such as *his/her*—or even, good heavens, *hiser* or *shhe*. We've shut our eyes to the good pronoun *it,* which is used for a gender-neutral, third-person, singular pronoun for everything but Man. *It* and *its* would be my choice instead of *he, his, him,* but most English speakers would gag on it. Even when I call a baby *Homo sapiens* "it," I'm browbeaten. It's quite funny that we are so unsure about our proud "human exceptionalism" that we can't take the most likely and wieldy choice for a gender-neutral, singular, third-person pronoun. It.

The next best choice is for the plural third-person pronoun *they, them, their* to become the gender-neutral singular third-person also. We are told this is bad grammar even though many of us unthinkingly say or write it in this way. In sooth, I was wrong to use "become" at the beginning of this paragraph since *they, them, their* was the run-of-the-mill genderless, single, third-person pronoun from Chaucer and likely earlier, until Anne Fisher wrote *A New Grammar* in 1745 (the first English grammar, by the way). Fisher, though an early feminist, was the school mistress "first to say that the pronoun he should apply to both sexes," wrote Patricia O'Connor and Stewart Kellerman in the *New*

York Times Sunday Magazine column "On Language" (July 26, 2009). Therefore, I write *they, them, their* instead of the clumsy *he/she, his/her, her/him.* And, should you wish to wield good grammar in your writing and speaking, I would coax you to go forth and do likewise.

TREE OF LIFE: As has been written by others (beginning at least with Darwin), I write or say Tree of Life instead of biodiversity or Nature. Tree of Life paints a much better picture of the whole of life than do biodiversity and Nature, both of which are abstract and rather worn-out.

WARD (v): To ward something is to guard or defend it.

WIGHT: In Old English and as an "archaic" word in today's English, *wight* means "creature" or "living being." In Old English, a wight could be a deor or a Man. I sometimes write it for either.

WILDEOR: In Old English, *wildeor* or *wildedeor* meant wild animal, or more literally a self-willed animal instead of a tamed or domesticated animal. *Deor* meant animal. *Deor* is in today's English as *deer.* I write *wildeor* widely in its early meaning as an undomesticated animal, one who is not under the will of Man. *Wildlife* means the same, though it can mean plants and other kinds of life, too. I write wildeor only for animals.

WILDERFOLK: Grassroots wilderness lovers and backers.

WILDERNESS: Self-willed land and sea, where Man "is a visitor who does not remain." Mostly self-willed lands with year-around settlements are better called *Wildlands.*

WILDERNESS DECONSTRUCTION: Some humanities and social science academics within the cult of postmodern deconstructionism have questioned how biologists, naturalists, and conservationists see "Nature," some going so far as to say we create Nature in our minds. Some postmodern deconstructionists have gotten their bowels in an uproar about ideas of wilderness and have even questioned whether Wilderness Areas should be set aside. Some link themselves to those calling for so-called "sustainable development" instead of protected areas (wild havens), and with followers of the Noble Savage Myth in its put-down of Western science. I call this intellectual giddy-gilding *wilderness deconstruction* and such naysayers of wildlife and wilderness conservation *wilderness deconstructionists*. Now, The Nature Conservancy has jumped over to wilderness deconstruction with their celebration of the Anthropocene, Man's full takeover of Earth. In *True Wilderness*, I deconstruct wilderness deconstructionism, sustainable development, the Myth of the Ecological Savage, and Anthropocene enviro-resourcism.

WILD HAVENS: Throughout the world and Man-time there have been and are many kinds of protected areas set aside and stewarded for wildlife, wilderness, natural scenery, sacredness, nonmotorized outdoor recreation, and biodiversity. National Parks and Wilderness Areas are among such lands. *Protected areas* is the catchall term for such set-asides; I like *wild havens* instead.

WILDLAND: The word *wildland* is slung about in many clumsy and tangled ways. Some think it means the same as *wilderness*. But wildland has a wider meaning than wilderness. In other words, all wilderness is wildland, but not all wildland is wilderness. Wildland is pretty much land that is not cropped or urbanized. It has native vegetation although sometimes in a beat-up state. A National Forest clearcut still is wildland, but I would not call a tree plantation wildland. Wildlands may have scattered settlements as well, whereas wilderness should be kept as the name for lands without year-around dwelling by Men.

WILDLIFE: Not until the 1870s in the United States did hunters and conservationists come up with *wild life,* then *wild-life,* and at last *wildlife* for wild animals. I call all wild beings, whether animals, plants, fungi, or microorganisms *wildlife.*

WILDLOVERS: Wilderness and wildlife conservationists.

WILD THING: Living beings that are not under the will of Man are wild things. Geological processes (earthquakes), weather (hurricanes), atmospheric phenomena (sunsets, rainbows), landforms (mountains, oceans), and so on are also wild things if they are not made by or under the will of Man.

WILD THINGS: I often write wild things to mean Nature or biodiversity. See Tree of Life.

WORT: In Old English *wort* was a plant or vegetable. It is still in play for the names of plants such lousewort, St. Johns wort, and so on. I sometimes write *wort* instead of *plant.*

ABOUT THE
REWILDING INSTITUTE

The Rewilding Institute is a small nonprofit working for the network of those who love wild things. We offer guidance on how to stay true to the wild by means of the "Five Feathers": grassroots leadership, far-reaching vision, toughness on policy, doggedness over the long haul, and a straightforward biocentric ethic (wild things for their own sake). We do this by means of:

- A meaty, thoughtful website (www.rewilding.org) with a blog;
- An Internet conservation column on policy, ethics, and lore—*Around the Campfire* by Dave Foreman (to subscribe—free—contact Susan Morgan: rewilding@earthlink.net);
- An in-the-works series of five books *For the Wild Things* by Dave Foreman with help from Institute Fellows;
- Public lectures and seminars by Dave Foreman for colleges, nonprofit groups, conservation conferences, zoos and museums, and such (to set up a talk, contact Christianne Hinks: christianne@rewilding.org);

- A series of widely distributed "Wildeor" brochures offering visionary protection and recovery plans for key wildlife in North America; and
- Working through sundry means for a meaningful, sound, and strong North American Wildlands Network with at least four Continental Wildways to bring back native wildlife to suitable habitat.

The bedrock work of The Rewilding Institute is to fight the extinction crisis. The 6th Great Extinction now ongoing and driven wholly by one species—*Homo sapiens*—comes from what TRI calls the "Seven Ecological Wounds": Overkill, Habitat Destruction, Habitat Fragmentation, Loss and Upsetting of Evolutionary and Ecological Processes, Invasion of Harmful Exotic Species, Biocide Pollution, and Greenhouse Gas Pollution. The underlying drivers are the human population explosion and our overblown and wasteful consumption.

FOR THE WILD THINGS

A series of five books from

The Rewilding Institute and Raven's Eye Press

By Dave Foreman

There are some who can live without wild things,
and some who cannot.

—Aldo Leopold

For the Wild Things is a much-needed gathering of five new books from one of Earth's leading wilderness thinkers and shielders. The five books are thoughtful, hard-hitting, and targeted.

MAN SWARM and the Killing of Wildlife $20—published May 2011
The population blowup thunders through the world and the United States. It is the underlying driver of how Man wounds Earth and wild things by killing wildlife, taming and scalping wildlands, and belching out greenhouse gases. Here are the hard truths about population growth and how our growth is the overwhelming threat to wild things and a healthy Earth. A wide sweep of answers to the plight of too many is offered.

TAKE BACK CONSERVATION—published November 2012

The grassroots conservation network, made up of defenders of wild things and of conservation biologists, has been undercut and taken over. Instead of tough grassroots clubs that fight for wild things for their own sake; bureaucrats, environmental careerists, funding professionals, consultants, political party operatives, and others want to make over grassroots wilderness and wildlife clubs and the scientific fellowship of conservation biology into middle-of-the-road, compromising, resource management institutions that talk about "ecosystem services" and other goods wild things give Mankind. True conservationists— those who love wild things for their own sake—need to take their clubs and their science back. Foreman lays out the whole threat to hamstring the holy work to keep wild things wild and offers tough, yet sound and fair-minded, steps to take back the conservation network by wildlovers.

TRUE WILDERNESS: Why Wilderness Areas and other Strong Protected Areas Are Still the Best Tool for Keeping Wild Things*

Wilderness Areas, National Parks, and other strongly held and policed wildlife havens have long been the backbone of wildland and wildlife protection in North America and worldwide, and they have been acknowledged as the best tool conservation has. For twenty-five years, though, such wild havens and traditional conservation have been under fire from postmodern deconstructionist academics; the sustainable-development scam of international financial institutions, consultants, and anticolonialist ideologues; and the well-meaning but fuzzy belief in the "Myth of the Ecological Savage." Lately, The Nature Conservancy (TNC) has been taken over by its board of international businessmen and now turns its back on protected areas. TNC's head scientists are biological postmodern deconstructionists celebrating Man's full takeover of Earth—the Anthropocene. Foreman deconstructs all of these "wilderness deconstructionists" and shows that strongly enforced protected areas for wildlife must always be the heart of the work to stop mass extinction and the scalping of Earth's last wild havens.

CONSERVATION VS. CONSERVATION: The 20th Century Fight Between Wilderness Lovers and Land Managing Agencies Over America's Last Wilderness*

Here is the lore and understanding every wilderness keeper needs. The first half of the book looks at how European settlers killed wildlife and scalped wilderness, and then at how public lands came to be in the United States. The last half goes into depth on the 20th Century fight over America's last wilderness and wildlife, highlighting the struggle between Resourcism (the Forest Service, Park Service, and state wildlife agencies) and Wild Things Conservation (the Sierra Club, Wilderness Society, and many other citizen clubs).

THE NATURE HATERS: And How To Stop Them*

While conservationists love wild things, there are those who hate wild things out of fear, selfishness, narrow-minded but tightly held beliefs, and greed. Who are they, what are their backgrounds, what are their arguments against keeping wild things, and how do wildlovers answer them? Foreman has a matchless background for understanding and thwarting the Nature Haters.

Titles may change.

These books, written by Dave Foreman in the *For the Wild Things* series, will be published by The Rewilding Institute and Raven's Eye Press from 2011 to 2013. Fliers will go out as each is released. Series Editors are John Davis and Susan Morgan, with Christianne "Hawkeye" Hinks as research assistant, proofreader, and last copy editor. Foreman has a matchless 40-year background of fighting for wild things and of thorough scholarship and research in the history of both grassroots and organizational conservation.

To order books, get further information, and to learn when titles are printed, go to The Rewilding Institute www.rewilding.org or POB

13768, Albuquerque, NM 87192. Discounts are available for bulk purchase by wilderness and wildlife clubs for fundraising.

INDEX

Dasmann, Ray, 152
Davis, John, 40, 106, 212, 287-88, 324
Davis, Jeff, 30f
DDT, 51, 56, 195, 219
Dean, John, 165
Death Valley National Park, CA, 251
Declaration of Independence, 209
Deep Ecology, 75, 166, 303, 335
Deer, 181
Deer, white-tailed, 238, 325
Defenders of Wildlife (DoW), 47, 56,
 162, 241f, 246-47, 266
Democratic Leadership Council, 270
Democratic Party, 9, 99, 114, 116, 157-
 62, 171, 265, 313
Denali (Mt. McKinley) National Park,
 AK, 129
Department of Energy, U.S., 223
Desolation-Gray Canyons, UT, 239
Dewald, Scott, 228
Diamond, Jared, 84-85, 225
Dickens, Charles, 48, 50
Dilg, Will, 13, 74, 118, 193
Dinerstein, Eric, 292
Discovery Institute, The, 286
Disney, Walt, 27
Dodson, Tim, 65
Dold, Robert, 192
Domenici, Pete, 205
"Domesticated Nature", 140
Donahue, Debra, 248f
Douglas, Justice William O., 323
Dowie, Mark, 167, 170
Driven Wild, 202, 291
Dugout Ranch, UT, 136
Duke University, NC, 2
Durango, CO, 108
Durnil, Gordon, 161

Early conservation reformers, 69-72
Earth Day 1970, 15, 17, 20, 22, 41, 52,
 166, 321
Earth First!, 58, 114, 148, 159, 167, 174,
 177, 182, 304
Earth First! Journal, 114,148f, 183, 284
Earth Liberation Front (ELF), 176, 181

Earthlings (other species), 2, 12, 16,
 17f, 25, 33-34, 37, 45-46, 53, 58, 67,
 74, 86, 94-95, 140-41, 176, 183, 215,
 298f, 299-301, 304, 309-10, 321, 330,
 332, 335
Eastern Wilderness Areas Act of 1975,
 93, 195
East St. Louis, IL, 224, 253
Ebonics, 208
Eco-cons (Canada), 259
Ecological restoration, 34, 79, 83, 130,
 132, 149, 232, 235, 239-40, 246-47,
 292-93
Ecological Society of America (ESA),
 128-29, 150, 154, 244-45
Ecologists Union, 129
Economics, problems with as grounds
 for conservation, 91-92, 201, 234,
 299, 308, 310
Economics, push to make it key value of
 conservation, 8, 32, 37, 82, 84-85, 90-
 92, 145, 210, 244, 246, 300, 333-34
Economics America, 160
Economist, The, 226
Ecosystem Services, 32, 37, 82, 85-86,
 90-92, 108, 121, 145, 210, 247, 334
Edge, Rosalie, 13, 70-71, 73f
Egan, Ronni (Veronica), 119f, 290
Ehrenfeld, David, 13, 75, 88, 94, 142,
 153, 298
Ehrlich, Anne, 13, 56, 89, 319f
Ehrlich, Paul, 13, 56, 89, 181, 245, 319f,
 320f
Eisenhower, Dwight D., 192, 324
El Coronado Ranch, AZ, 235
Eliot, T. S., 207
Elitism of conservationists, alleged, 15,
 17, 20, 38, 151-52, 254, 333
Emergency Conservation Committee, 70
Endangered Ecosystems, 128f
Endangered Species Act 1973, 16f, 152,
 195, 205-6, 212, 242, 244-45
Endangered Species Act reforms to be
 landowner-friendly, 244-46
Endangered Species Sales Tax proposal,
 240, 245

[354]

ABOUT THE AUTHOR

For forty years, **DAVE FOREMAN** has been one of North America's leading conservationists, working to shield and rebuild wilderness and wildlife. He is acknowledged for having a matchless depth and breadth for fighting for wild things, and for bringing together traditional conservation lore, the science of conservation biology, and wild-things-for-their-own-sake ethics into a mighty vision for the future—The North American Wildlands Network. In his last book, *Man Swarm*, he showed his bold leadership on the knotty plight of overpopulation. He is also the author of *Rewilding North America, Confessions of an Eco-Warrior, The Big Outside* (with Howie Wolke), the novel *The Lobo Outback Funeral Home*, and other books. He was the lead author and designer for the Sky Islands Wildlands Network Vision and the New Mexico Highlands Wildlands Network Vision. Among the wilderness outfits with which he has worked as a staffer or volunteer leader are Black Mesa Defense, River Defense, University of New Mexico Students for Environmental Action, *Albuquerque Environmental Center, Gila Wilderness

Committee, The Wilderness Society, New Mexico Wilderness Study Committee, *Southwest Rivers Study Committee, *American Rivers, The Nature Conservancy, *Earth First!, *Wild Earth Journal, *The Wildlands Project, *New Mexico Wilderness Alliance, Sierra Club, and now *The Rewilding Institute (* cofounder of these clubs). *Audubon magazine* picked him as one of its "100 Conservation Champions" of the last 100 years. Foreman is a sought-after speaker on rewilding and other wilderness and wildlife issues. He has canoed and rafted some of the wildest rivers in North America, and is a hiker, birder, and photographer. He lives in his hometown of Albuquerque, New Mexico, with his wife, Nancy Morton, who is a nurse, and a cat named Blue (after the Blue Range Primitive Area in Arizona).

photo by Nancy Morgan, Noatak River

ABOUT THE EDITORS

JOHN DAVIS is a wildways scout, editor, and writer, working part-time for Wildlands Network and full-time for wild Nature. Along with Dave Foreman and a dozen other prominent conservationists, John was a co-founder of Wildlands Network twenty years ago and has served on its board of directors most of the time since. He serves now on boards of The Rewilding Institute, RESTORE: The North Woods, Wild Farm Alliance, Champlain Area Trails, and Cougar Re-

photo by Nancy Morgan,
Noatak River

wilding Foundation. John was also co-founder of *Wild Earth* journal (with Dave Foreman, Reed Noss, Mary Byrd Davis, and David Johns) and served as its editor from 1991-96, when he turned editorship over to his long-time friend Tom Butler and went to work for the Foundation for Deep Ecology. John oversaw FDE's Biodiversity and Wildness program from 1997-2002. He then joined the Eddy Foundation as a board member and continues to serve as volunteer land steward for that foundation in its work to conserve lands in Split Rock Wildway. This wildlife corridor links New York's Champlain Valley with the Adirondack High Peaks via the West Champlain Hills. For the last few years, John worked as conservation director for the Adirondack Council. He left that job in 2011 to begin TrekEast.

In 2011, John completed TrekEast, a 7500-mile muscle-powered exploration of wilder parts of the eastern United States and southeastern Canada (following lines suggested in Dave Foreman's book Rewilding North America), to promote restoration and protection of an Eastern Wildway. This year, John is writing a book about that adventure, catching up on Split Rock Wildway land-keeping tasks, and preparing for TrekWest. John will set out from Sonora, Mexico, in early 2013 to traverse the Rockies as far north as southern British Columbia, Canada, before winter sets in, again promoting habitat connections, big wild cores, and wide ranging species, including top predators – all of which would be well served by fuller protection of the Western Wildway he'll be exploring.

SUSAN MORGAN, PhD, just retired after six years with the Northfork Library in the Whatcom County Washington Library System and is an editor and conservation advocate. In 1968 she began her conservation career as outings coordinator for The Wilderness Society, then became Director of Education, and has subsequently worked on wilderness, wildlands, and public lands conserva-

photo by John Miles

tion for over forty years. Susan was a founding board member of Great Old Broads for Wilderness. She served as staff with LightHawk, the New Mexico Environmental Law Center, the Washington Wilderness Coalition, The Wildlands Project (now Network), and was communications director for Forest Guardians (now WildEarth Guardians) in New Mexico. Susan volunteers for the Alaska Coalition of Washington, is on the board of Wilderness Watch, and is President of the Board of Directors of The Rewilding Institute.

DESIGNER

elle jay design

Lindsay J. Nyquist
www.ellejaydesign.com
lindsay@ellejaydesign.com

PRESS

Raven's Eye Press

Rediscovering the West
www.ravenseyepress.com

Try our other Raven's Eye Press titles:

Why I'm Against it All
Ken Wright

The Monkey Wrench Dad
Ken Wright

Livin' the Dream
B. Frank

Ghost Grizzlies, 3rd edition
David Petersen

Racks
David Petersen